JAMES MONTGOMERY FLAGG

Dear To→ Mr Shaw

LONDON
OR - WHERE - EVER - HE - HAPPENS -
TO - BE - AT - THE - MOMENT!

Selections from
Bernard Shaw's postbag

Compiled and Edited by Vivian Elliot

With an Introduction by Michael Holroyd

BLOOMSBURY

First published 1987
Linking text copyright © 1987 by Vivian Elliot
Shaw letters copyright © the Bernard Shaw Estate
Introduction copyright © 1987 by Michael Holroyd

Bloomsbury Publishing Ltd, 2 Soho Square, London W1F 5DE

British Library Cataloguing in Publication Data
Dear Mr. Shaw
1. Shaw, Bernard – Biography   2. Dramatists,
English – 20th century – Biography
I. Elliot, Vivian
822'.912   PR5366

ISBN 0-7475-0095-9

Designed by Mekon, London
Phototypeset by Rowland Phototypesetting Ltd
Bury St Edmunds, Suffolk
Printed and bound in Great Britain by
Butler & Tanner Ltd, Frome and London

Bernard Shaw calculated that he could have written about twenty more plays in the time expended on the quarter of a million letters and cards he sent in reply to those who wrote to him. The embodiment of many things to many people, he was baffled and amused (and frequently irritated) by what was expected of him – from literary patronage to a new pair of boots.

After he was awarded the Nobel Prize for Literature, Shaw said 'some 50,000 people wrote to me to say that as the greatest of men I must see that the best thing I could do with the prize was give it to them.' Instead, he returned the money to the inventors of dynamite. 'Then they all wrote again to say that if I could afford to do that, I could afford to lend them £1,500 for three years.'

Many women adored Shaw and at one point he was receiving up to three proposals of marriage a week. Included here are mutual declarations of love exchanged with Virginia Woolf and a final letter to one long-standing correspondent: 'Dear Elise, Seek younger friends; I am extinct. G. B. Shaw.'

'I have become the father confessor to the world,' he declared, and might have added: marriage counsellor, banker, psychiatrist and dietitian. But no one could ever predict his replies. For W. H. Davies he ensured the immediate success of *Autobiography of a Supertramp*. To another aspirant he responded, 'Who would want to read your rubbish after my preface?'

Vivian Elliot has put together a divertingly varied collection of 'Dear Mr Shaw' letters from around the globe, demanding attention to troubles great and small, serious and ridiculous. In the replies, Shavian wit, obstinacy, didacticism and generosity abound unpredictably from the plea for a new doggie – agreed – to the offer of lunch at Chequers and a knighthood – declined.

In memory of my dear father – who thought coming to England would do me good.

Acknowledgments

I would like to thank the Shaw Estate and The Society of Authors for their approbation and encouragement and The Phoenix Trust for its financial support. My thanks also to Vanessa Whitburn of the BBC who directed and produced my Radio 4 programme, *Dear Mr Shaw*, in which a number of the letters in this book were first given 'an airing'.

I am also grateful to the following institutions for their assistance: Bernard F. Burgunder Collection, Cornell University Library; The British Library of Political and Economic Science; The British Library (Reference Division and Newspaper Library at Colindale); Dartmouth College Library; Ellen Clarke Bertrand Library, Bucknell University; Henry W. and Albert A. Berg Collection, New York Public Library; Humanities Research Center at the University of Texas; Mugar Memorial Library, Boston University; The National Trust; Astor, Lenox and Tilden Foundations, The New York Public Library; Pattee Library, The Pennsylvania State University; Polish Cultural Institute; *Punch*; RADA; University of Saskatchewan Archives.

While much of the material in this book has been drawn from newspaper and manuscript sources, some published works have also been useful. These include: Allan Chappelow, *Shaw 'The Villager and Human Being'* (1961) and *Shaw 'The Chucker-Out'* (1969); Archibald Henderson: *Bernard Shaw: Playboy and Prophet* (1932) and *George Bernard Shaw: Man of the Century* (1956); Dan H. Laurence, *Bernard Shaw: A Bibliography* (1983) and *Bernard Shaw: Collected Letters*, Vols. I–III (1965, 1972, 1985); Blanche Patch, *Thirty Years With G.B.S.* (1951); and Stephen Winsten's *Days with Bernard Shaw* (1951), *Shaw's Corner* (1952) and *Jesting Apostle* (1956).

Among others who have assisted with this book are: Richard Atkins, Alan Barnett, A. Cole, Vivien Devlin, Richard Evans, Fraser Gallie, Jenny de Gex, Jean Hundleby, Timothy Hurley, John Lucas, Alex MacCormick, Fraser McDermott, David McGrath, Caradoc King, Dr Joan Margaret MacKinnon, David Manderson, George Meredith, Ewen Montagu CBE, Jonathan Morris-Ebbs, David S. Nicholl, A. J. Perfect, Eden Potter, Ivy Rae, Kathleen Doreen Rogers, Dr Julian Salomon, G. Bernard Shaw, James Tyler, Sue Walliker, Rodelle Weintraub, Prof. Stanley Weintraub, John Westmancoat, Margaret Wheeler, John Wilde and Roma Woodnutt.

I am grateful to Miren Lopategui and Jane Carr of Bloomsbury for their editorial skills and patience. I would particularly like to thank Dan H. Laurence for his support and for making a number of letters available to me, and Michael Holroyd, for his great generosity of time, material, and above all, encouragement.

I have tried wherever possible to trace the copyright holders of the items in this book and can only apologize sincerely if anyone has been omitted.

Picture Credits

Despite diligent enquiries, it has not been possible to trace the photographers and artists of some of the illustrations in this book. Our apologies are due to those copyright holders who can substantiate their claims. Upon application to the publishers they will receive the usual fee for reproduction.

We are grateful to the following for permission to reproduce material:

Contents

Introduction

In a letter to Ellen Terry, Bernard Shaw described his childhood as being 'rich only in dreams, frightful & loveless in realities'. He was not physically ill-treated: he was ignored. If he had failed to come home from school one day, he later remarked, he did not think his parents would have noticed. His mother, Lucinda Elizabeth Shaw, was a ladylike lapsed Protestant, and his father, George Carr Shaw, an alcoholic ex-civil servant. They were an unattractive couple and between them they achieved a miserable marriage in an 'awful little kennel' in Synge Street, Dublin.

'Sonny', as he was called, loved his mother, but she did not love him. She despised her husband and felt that their son was contaminated with the same male ineffectualness. It was obvious to her that he would come to nothing. In fact she was contemptuous of all men – all except one. This was a musician originally called George Lee who, in the days of his vanity, blossomed into George John Vandeleur Lee and became a model for du Maurier's Svengali. Lee, who was a Catholic, invited the Shaws to share his much smarter house in Dublin and so it was a highly irregular *ménage à trois* in which the boy grew up. Here Lee gave singing lessons to Lucinda, who had a good mezzo-soprano voice and became the right-hand woman of his prosperous amateur musical society, while George Carr Shaw was reduced to nullity in the home.

Partly because of his unorthodox success, Lee decided somewhat hurriedly to leave Ireland in 1873. There was a rumour of scandal which increased when Lucinda Shaw followed him a fortnight later on her twenty-first wedding anniversary. She was to take her two daughters with her to London, but left her son – the youngest of her children – with his redundant father.

The effect of this on the seventeen-year-old Shaw was crucial. He questioned his own legitimacy and to quell these doubts he later eliminated the Christian name he shared with both men in the house from the title pages of his books. 'Don't George me,' he would instruct people. He took George Carr Shaw as a model father in the paradoxical sense that he offered the perfect example of how not to do everything. He took Lee – whom he resented for having appropriated all his mother's attention – as an early prototype of the Shavian Superman, and was to model his own creation 'G.B.S.' on the hypnotic 'Vandeleur Lee'.

'Everything in real life is based on *need*,' he told Ellen Terry. His own need as an adult was for attention to compensate for the love he lacked as a child. He orphaned himself from his parents and grew into the famous and fêted personality who took the place of the socially insecure and neglected adolescent whom his mother had abandoned.

I

These are some of the origins of the besieged public figure who so entertainingly fills the pages of Vivian Elliot's *Dear Mr Shaw*. He was reborn in the twentieth century as the child of his writings and as a parent to his readers: someone who had converted the dreams of his childhood into operatic fantasies for the stage, and who laboured to reduce the frightful realities of economic injustice by a Fabian redistribution of wealth. His complex personality and multifarious talents answered many needs and provoked many misunderstandings which were responsible for the almost supernatural status G.B.S. achieved in the public imagination.

One of the features of his worldwide fame has been the extraordinary number of books published about him in many languages – well over three hundred by the 1980s. *Dear Mr Shaw* is unique among this vast library and has the special advantage of handing him back to the general reading public for whom he primarily wrote. It exhibits him as a man of unexampled patience and concealed generosity, as humorous-natured and kind-hearted in his fashion as his compatriot Oscar Wilde, who perfected the technique of demolishing an opponent's opinions without dismantling his self-esteem.

Besides being a treasury of wit and amusing anecdotes, *Dear Mr Shaw* gives a revealing insight into our need for mythological figures. For in making him its universal uncle, the public was responding as much to what was suppressed as to what was so brilliantly expressed by G.B.S. For nearly half a century he was consulted as guru, joker, genius, eccentric and adviser on all subjects. Yet on this crowded stage he remains a lonely figure who felt himself to be a stranger on this planet. He had needed attention and he had tried to use this need for honourable political purposes. But:

> The gods are just, and of our pleasant vices
> Make instruments to plague us.

Dear Mr Shaw is the perfect complement to Dan H. Laurence's four comprehensively edited volumes of Shaw's *Collected Letters*. As a Canadian who lives and works in London, Vivian Elliot combines the industry of New World scholarship with the more peculiar distinction of being a genuine Shavian – one of a select band that includes Brigid Brophy, Benny Green and Colin Wilson. The result of her mixture of perspiration and inspiration is a book that will delight and endear itself to many readers as well as providing a stimulating corrective to some popular misconceptions about the fabulous 'pantomine ostrich' known as G.B.S.

Michael Holroyd

A Great Man's Postbag

Mr. Bernard Shaw's readers and the spectators at performances of his plays number many thousands. The little time remaining to him at his age is fully occupied with his literary work and the business it involves; and war taxation has set narrow limits to his financial resources. He has therefore to print the following intimations.

He cannot deal with individual grievances and requests for money, nor for autographs and photographs. He cannot finance schools and churches. His donations go to undenominational public bodies, and his charities to the Royal Society of Literature.

He cannot engage in private correspondence, nor read long letters.

He cannot advise literary beginners nor read their unpublished works. They had better study The Writers' Year Book (or other books of reference), and join the Society of Authors as associates.

He cannot discuss his published views in private letters.

He cannot receive visitors at his private residence except from his intimate friends.

He will not send Messages.

He begs to be excused accordingly.

Ayot Saint Lawrence,
 Welwyn, Herts.

Troubles great and small, serious and ridiculous, were brought to Bernard Shaw and he was faced daily with a multitude of professional and personal requests: for money – to finance medical studies, to buy a wheelchair, for concentration camp victims, Spanish refugees, and ambulances in Ethiopia ... requests for £2 for a few shirts, socks and a pair of shoes, £20,000 to purchase land for intensive food production, and £5,000 to marry off an Indian gentleman's six daughters and thereby help him to 'regain a footing in the world'; for help with a walking stick exhibition, getting radio apparatus for a whaling expedition to the Antarctic, introducing the Russian frost-resistant potato into England; what to call the new baby – or new pig – or what to do about child slavery in China; requests for his opinion on Chastity and Intellectual Development, and the definition of a gentleman.

There were letters from Martha Gotch regarding 'the forceps inside her', from Philip Keen on headlights, Lawson Dodd on Ethel Dair's teeth, from 'The Telephoning Schoolboy', the Cyclists' Touring Club, the London Vegetarian Society, a cloud disperser, and the West Texas Gas Company (regarding cattle brands); as well as 'A Conscientious Objector', 'Two Bathing Enthusiasts', and a number of would-be suicides.

There were letters with questions: 'Will you invest in a magazine, lend an old hat for an exhibition, buy a barometer, mind being mentioned in a song?' And there were those letters which made no request at all, but gave something instead: socks, songs about himself, poems, seaweed and other nutritional items. There were offers to sharpen his scissors or knives and replate his silver teapots, dishes, spoons and forks. One American man passed on a fantastic plan for the marriage of Mrs Simpson to Edward VIII on the deck of the U.S. battle-cruiser, *Indianapolis*, attended by two other cruisers and a division of destroyers at anchor off Southampton. 'If,' he added graciously, 'the Archbishop of Canterbury were present, he could perform the ceremony.' And there was the ham sent in lieu of royalty by the Baxter Theatre, Virginia, who were using farm produce as money. Shaw returned the offering with a 'Don't you know I am a vegetarian?'

Dear Mr Shaw is a compilation of what G.B.S. referred to as letters from worldly people 'howling to be answered'; individuals who for one reason or another wanted to write to the 'great man' (whose name one correspondent would insist was 'magic'). Many hundreds of these letters still exist as Shaw often preserved the most inconsequential items of correspondence, despite claims that he tore such letters up on the spot or when answered, unless there was some special reason for keeping them: 'I never keep copies of my letters and I regard the keeping of letters as, on the whole, a mischievous habit. Dickens did so for some time, and then burnt the lot at Gadshill.' And, again, to fellow Fabian Hubert Bland: 'I have destroyed your letter: it is my general rule. Never keep a letter, and never write one that is fit for publication.' However, in his lifetime Shaw did both and did so frequently.

Some of these 'Dear Mr Shaw' letters are charming, some pathetic, some presumptuous; others endearing in their very ordinariness and appeal to common humanity; some are laboured scrawls and others laborious epistles. Even the most sketchily addressed letters eventually arrived at their destination, which for many years was 'Shaw's Corner, Ayot St. Lawrence, Hertfordshire'. According to G.B.S:

> I often get letters addressed to the Reverend George B. Shaw. You can deceive people some of the time, but they ultimately discover your true vocation. As a Quaker I would make an excellent Archbishop.

SHAW WITH HIS LOYAL SECRETARY BLANCHE PATCH

Although Shaw might repeatedly complain of having to deal with his correspondence himself, he was in fact ably assisted in this activity by his secretary of long standing, Miss Blanche Patch, who came to work for him in 1920 after being summoned by the dramatist with the words: 'Will you come and be my secretary? My own has gone and got married on me.' She was to remain with G.B.S. for thirty years until his death in 1950 and during this time was to handle many thousands of 'Dear Mr Shaw' letters from all over the world. Later, she would recall:

> The foreign stamps from this correspondence of thirty years make a brave collection: for there were not many corners of the earth from which some inquirer had not something to ask. It might be how to find a wife; or would he permit a caricature of himself on the stage; or was Shakespeare a homosexual.

Shaw's postman, Mr Harry Rayner, would later recall:

> I remember once when I was working at Welwyn Garden City Sorting Office an envelope came into my section with an excellent sketch on it in lieu of Bernard Shaw's name and address, and just the words, '*To whom it may concern.* ENGLAND.' Then a few days later I saw the same envelope passing through the sorting again. Shaw had crossed right through the sketch in red ink and put an arrow to the top corner where he had written the address of the sender. 'You can have it back' was evidently his attitude in that instance.

One envelope from America had a postage stamp photograph of Shaw in the bottom left-hand corner of the envelope; above it, a postage stamp cancelled 'George' (in Texas) on New Year's Day; in the next corner one cancelled 'Bernard' (Iowa) on May 24th (Empire Day); below it, a third cancelled 'Shaw' (Virginia) on July 26th, his birthday. As the United States apparently has four towns named George, two Bernards, and four Shaws, another admirer went to the trouble of repeating the tribute, this time from Iowa and Mississippi.

While a number of Shaw visitors were rather suspect (such as the American who resembled Shaw and carried a singing kettle around with him!), his mail was even stranger at times. According to his secretary:

> The oddest missives which the postman left for us were a series of badly written letters that did not make much sense, with dirty little packets addressed in the same hand and containing bits of coal and sprigs of ivy. I got in touch with the Chief Constable of the neighbourhood indicated by the postmarks and he traced the packages back to a poor woman who was rather feeble-minded. She intended the coal to mean coals of fire and the ivy friendship.

Only one letter addressed to G.B.S. and not intended for him slipped through the postal net. And this, Shaw's secretary insisted, was not the sorter's fault! 'I opened the envelope automatically and could make nothing of the letter. Then I saw that this time "G.B.S." stood not for George Bernard Shaw but for "Greyhound Breeding Society"; and that the writer was a man who wanted his dog entered in the stud-book.'

Over the years, the 'Dear Mr Shaw' letters presented the British Post Office with many challenges. From Karachi (in an envelope 'On Divine Service Only'), 'George Bernard Shaw Esquire, Philosopher and Writer, London (England)'; from Vienna, 'Mr. Bernard G. Shaw, Man of Letters, Writer, Statesman, Politician, etc., London'; from Dr Karl Goldmann, 'To: G. B. Shaw, Esq., Playwright Author of *Man and Superman* etc. England'.

According to Miss Patch, many correspondents paid homage on their envelopes: 'Grand old Author Playwright' (Denmark); 'Greatest English Comedy Writer' (Buenos Aires); 'Wit of the World' (The Gag Writers' Protective Association, New York); 'Irishman, Care Anybody, Anywhere' (Michigan); 'The One and Only: Please Find Him Mr Postman' (New York); 'Author (of all he surveys)' (Beverley Hills); 'Critic of Things As They Are' (California). They came from China, Denmark, Germany, Austria, South Africa, Moscow, Brazil, Colombia, addressed to His Excellency Mr Bernard Shaw, Dr Bernard Shaw, Hon. Bernard Shaw, or Sir Bernard Schaw, at 'Where-ever He Lives'; 'c/o the great newspaper *Times* (if you please)'; 'c/o Hon. Mayor of London'; or 'c/o Buckingham Palace'.

And then, there were of course the salutations on the letters themselves: 'Cher et vénéré maître' from Paris; 'Monsieur le Grand ecrívain Shaw' from another; and 'Monsieur et cher confrère'; 'Hochgeehrter Herr Meister!' from Prague. 'Very honoured Master!' from Lányi Andorné of Budapest who later in her letter referred to G.B.S. as 'the king of writing'; and an unadorned 'Master' from Glyn Thomas of Saltaire, Yorkshire who closed his letter of request with 'Your servant'. From Martin Witt of Hamburg who had sent Shaw a manuscript to consider came, 'Are you the very gentleman Bernard Shaw known as a playwright?' A publishing request began 'Revered Sir' and another Dear Mr 'Bernard Shaw the novelist'. From Kurhaus Hoven a letter to Dear 'Great One' and from Battersea to G.B. SHAW 'PHILOSOPHER'-FRIEND. And from Olivotti of Italy, 'Dear and great maestro – Why do I write to you – I wonder . . ?'

From one correspondent came 'Dear famous gentleman', and from another 'My dear Saint Bernard', from concert singer Dame Clara Butt 'Dear Wonderful', actress Winifred Emery 'You most kind "Man of Genius!"', and from another female acquaintance, 'Delightful Wind bag of a genius'. However, for floweriness few could surpass the letter from '"The World's Greatest Spritiual Healer" (cures all kinds of aches and pains on the spot)' who wrote to his 'Respected Dear Precious Holy Soul' to say that 'a foreign visitor passing by the land of pride you dwell upon has for a long time carried with him a keen desire to meet you personally before leaving your shores; provided the so-established desire be not considered out of the reach of possibility.' On the whole, strangers were usually more diffident and polite than many of Shaw's friends, for example, from theatrical colleague Arnold Daly on 11 January 1906 came 'Senile One'... whereas a stranger would write 'G. Bernard Shaw (Esq if it does not offend you!)'.

A Czech, writing to 'His Majesty, Author King, George Bernard Shaw, London, Anglie', and 'bowing to kiss his noble hand', remarked, 'I to be poor eighteen year old, alone learn your language in order i to be Sir Author to write', and requested him to sign 'two smal picture'.

Many gambits were tried to secure the great man's attention:

If this poorly written letter has in some way managed to reach your hands sir, you are probably wondering 'this one

must want advice on how to reach the age of ninety or how
to practise polygamy without a guilty conscience.'

> (Luis C. Galaviz, Houston, Texas)

I am very much interested in what you eat every day . . .

> (Martha Mahler, Staten Island, New York)

I have waited till the Captains and the Kings depart to offer
to you the homage and prayers of a very obscure
Irishwoman . . .

> (Mary MacCarvill, Dundalk, Ireland)

In the year 1888, two remarkable things were happening in
London. You were writing dramatic criticisms for the 'Star',
and Jack the Ripper was murdering ladies of easy virtue in
the East End of London . . .

> (Norman Edwards, Amalgamated Press, London)

. . . as a last word I would ask you, if ever I do meet you, not
to be surprised by my lack of stature. I in no way regret this
particular failing.

> (a young man from Hertfordshire)

There were also the interrogative closings:

Wondering whether one can afford a bus fare is rather a
handicap to ambition. I don't know if there is a male
equivalent to a Fairy God-Mother, and if so whether the
role would appeal to you at all? If not – then forgive me and
forget this letter.

> (an actress in New End Hospital, London)

And the strange, such as '*Not your enemy*' from Jimmie Durkin of Spokane,
Washington.

A number of friends and business contacts had unusual ways of catching
Shaw's attention, as in the following, from the playwright James Bridie:

In my bath this morning I had a fancy which may cause you
some fleeting amusement . . .

And, from childhood friend Edward McNulty:

One night when I was about to fall peacefully asleep I was
suddenly roused by seeing you as vivid as lightning with a
singularly new expression – upper teeth exposed and right
end of upper lip curled up: you glared in a concentrated
manner for some minutes. Then you faded away . . .

Finally, from P. Herbert Jones, General Secretary of the Cremation
Society, May 25th, 1943, in response to Shaw's request for information on
the possible mixing together of his and his wife Charlotte's ashes . . .

I thank you for your letter of May 24th from which I am
sorry to note that you contemplate the possibility of your
own cremation.

Shaw kept correspondence lists on which letter contents were described
daily in a capsular fashion. Although these were generally compiled by his
secretaries, he occasionally added to the lists in his own handwriting. A
quick glance through surviving lists, while showing that the notations given
were, more often than not, more than a little tongue-in-cheek, reveals the
wide-ranging subject matter of the 'Dear Mr Shaw' letters.

Trevelyan, Prof.	*What to do with your money*
Strasser, D. J.	*Will you answer 3 questions?*
Woolf, Eric	*A schoolboy*
McDonagh, T. W. M.	*A second letter begging you to go &* *speak to the Savings Bank Dept of* *Civil Servants*
Tweedie, Mrs Alec	*Is giving an Empire Pageant*
Ripley, Joseph (Singer)	*Can you help him to get a pension?*
Allen, Constance	*Re Homeless Men*
Mitchell, Ethel	*Are Americans barbarious?*
Meller, Claude	*Would you like to buy a barometer?*
Spiers, Mrs	*Widow of the Wandsworth prisoner*
Holland, Clive	*Will you help Ealing girl guides?*
Evans, Frank	*Re: Dumping*
Jagger, H.	*Out of work Accountant*
West Texas Gas Co.	*Re: Cattle Brands*
Sons of Temperance	*wants a message*
Closset, P.	*Wants your autograph*
Yeats Brown, J.	*Letter to relieve his mind*

Davies, E. M.	*Tells you what he thinks of you*
Writers International	*want a message from you on the last destructiveness which militarists are preparing*
Hall of Fame Club	*Wants suggestions on how to succeed*
Hodge, Gerald	*Wants to work for you*
Liswell, Sylvia	*Where to sell a Caruso caricature*
Barker, E.	*Why did Major Barber (?) allow herself to stray?*
Sandwith, M. E.	*Invitation to Fruitarian Lunch*
Davies, Bob	*May he come & have a shot at you?*
Copo Ltd. (Certificates)	*Re Apple planting*
Roberts, L. E.	*An embittered artist*
Stone, Harvey	*Will you tell him how to write fiction?*
Newman, C. R.	*Ambulances in Ethiopia*
Rowell, Miss	*Do you think there is a Creator?*
Hatters' Assoc	*Will you lend an old hat for exhibition?*
Wells, John C.	*Wants to buy a wheel-chair*
Harvey, Mrs Miriam	*wants advice for daughter*
Neil, Judge	*Birthday Greetings & wants £100*
Sarkar, M.	*wants to translate St. Joan into Bengali*
Nagai, Rai	*sends you his 'Great Thoughts'*
Muller, Werner	*Defence of Hitler*
Dakers, Andrew	*Will you write a book on World Peace?*
Mockridge, W.	*sends a song for your opinion*
Smith, Miss Gudrum	*Wants to see you about raw food eating*
London Vegetarian Soc.	*Re: public ox roasting at a school*
J. H.	*asks Why are you silent on public affairs?*
Shriver, Donald	*Re. Christ's birth*
Spencer, John	*Re. Leap year calculations*
Bruid, Miss	*Will you help her to marry?*
Herben, Hubert	*Wants to be in one of your films*
Walshe, Christina	*wants money for Concentration camps*
Sister Therese	*wants help for aged poor*

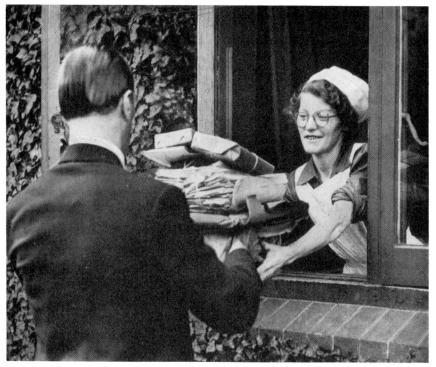

THE ARRIVAL OF THE POST AT SHAW'S CORNER

Shaw spent two or three hours over his sparse midday meal, and while he ate, read through his letters, deciding which ones to reply to before leaving the table. He told a newly married friend that his letters automatically went into two classes: the 'ordinary ones', to be answered by his secretary, and the special ones reserved for his own hand, 'in the next moment of intimate leisure and friendship'. While in theory an excellent plan, it had a serious drawback as he never had a moment of leisure, 'only an occasional pause from exhaustion'. 'This,' according to his secretary, 'meant that the ordinary correspondents got efficiently answered and the friends never got answered at all, even when they made such violent gestures to attract attention as getting married.' However, to one soon-to-be-married acquaintance, he wrote, 'It's not me you want, but the wedding gift – here's £15!'

Certain types of 'Dear Mr Shaw' letters were more likely to be answered than others, or answered quickly: those which were particularly novel, audacious, or amusing, or those relating to such specific Shavian themes as vegetarianism, the alphabet, women's suffrage, compulsory vaccination, capital punishment or teetotalism.

It has been estimated that in his lifetime Shaw wrote at least a quarter of a million letters and postcards, squeezing as many as two hundred words on a single card. He calculated that he could have written about 20 additional plays in the time he had spent writing to correspondents, insisting that a large office and about thirty clerks would be required to handle all his post, and an income of £30,000,000 to satisfy the never-ending requests for money he received.

Shaw implored theatre impresario Laurence Langer not to describe him as an 'adorable human being'; 'but rather present me as detestable, avaricious, merciless, contemptuous, and everything odious enough to

discourage people from writing to me. Otherwise you may hasten my already imminent death.' He told Ayot neighbour Stephen Winsten that in the good old illiterate days he might well have become the village letter writer. 'Who listens to the village idiot?' he is reported to have said to Winsten. 'I'm just the fellow who lives at Shaw's Corner and cultivates corns on my hindquarters. The only thing they know about me is that I buy more stamps than the rest of the village put together. They no doubt conclude that I must be always writing letters to myself . . .'

Along with picture postcards of the village and its famous tombstone tribute to longevity – 'Jane Eversley. Born 1815. Died 1895. Her time was short.' – the Ayot St Lawrence post office-cum-general store, which finally closed in 1978, used to offer the tourist photographs of its resident 'genus loci', Bernard Shaw, and his home, Shaw's Corner. Shaw's very considerable mail was delivered along with the rest of the village letters direct from the central sorting office at Welwyn Garden City in a van which cleared the letter box. Out of kindness he made a point of buying his stamps in £5 lots every six weeks from the widowed village post-mistress Mrs Jisbella Lyth, thereby assuring her a small but much needed source of income, as a local postmaster/mistress was permitted to make a profit on stamp sales.

'Even when he was away,' she later recalled, 'he would send me his stamp order. I kept all his letters. I had several hundred, but I sold nearly all of them at an average of £5 each. I used to joke with him that I would sell his letters, and he would reply: "They will only be worth 2½d." Tuppence ha' penny each, indeed, I told him. Why, I sell them for 10/6d. and you're still alive!'

When Mr Clark, owner of a taxi-cab at Harmer's Green, heard about the good prices Mrs Lyth was getting for Shaw's signatures he was furious with himself as he had destroyed the hundreds of notes Shaw had regularly sent him securing his services. 'Ugh,' he said, 'autographs! Bah! Hundreds of them – all thrown on the fire . . . Every one of them worth pounds to the tourists who come here now, and I threw them away, because in those days they were not worth anything.'

As Shaw advanced in age there was no recession in his status as a public personality, and he had to develop new letter-substitutes to handle the influx of mail. These postcards were printed off by the hundreds. The 1940s – as G.B.S. aged into his nineties – occasioned a whole new batch of cards. One general-purpose brown postcard with an Ayot St Lawrence address satisfied most needs:

> Mr. Bernard Shaw, though he is always glad to receive interesting letters or books, seldom has time to acknowledge them; for his correspondence has increased to such an extent that he must either give up writing private letters or give up writing anything else. Under the circumstances he hopes that writers of unanswered letters and unthanked friendly donors of books and other presents will forgive him.

Over the years there were thirty-odd G.B.S. postcards and stereotyped letters, stock answers to particularly frequent requests. Although many of the postcards said NO to the correspondents' requests, not everyone received a refusal. In fact, as his housekeeper and others testified, he sent gifts and donations to many private individuals and a number of institutions, and frequently responded favourably to a wide variety of approaches.

He is reputed to have read every communication, acknowledging those he felt merited an answer, sometimes by complying with requests – with a lengthy reply in his own hand or typed and corrected by himself – but more often by using one of his famous printed replies. However, even when a printed postcard was dispatched, Shaw – like Freud, apparently – would often get perverse satisfaction from penning the address himself, a fact unrealized by most recipients. He often added a personal message in the neat handwriting he learned as an office-boy to a private banker in Dublin. A space was left at the bottom of the printed cards on which he could add more personal remarks – either friendly or biting, as the mood took him.

He was so inundated with sympathy letters on Mrs Shaw's death in 1943 that he issued a general 'thank you' via the Personal column of *The Times*.

> MR BERNARD SHAW has received such a prodigious mass of letters on the occasion of his wife's death that, though he has read and values them all, any attempt to acknowledge them individually is beyond his powers. He therefore begs his friends and hers to be content with this omnibus reply, and to assure them that a very happy ending to a very long life has left him awaiting his own turn in perfect serenity.

Focusing on Bernard Shaw and his public correspondence, *Dear Mr Shaw* is for the most part a book about little people who for one reason or another wrote to the 'great man'. 'And come and close my eyes too, when I die,' he asked the Hon. Mrs Alfred Lyttelton, the day her husband died, 'and see me with my mask off as I really was.'

As part of his self-protective measures Shaw created the celebrated 'G.B.S.' monomark which as early as 1901 he described as one of his most successful fictions.

Of the people who wrote to G.B.S, that fantastic public personality, many knew very little about the man behind the mask. Some had perhaps read or seen one or two of the plays, if any, or had heard that he was kind or nice; had noticed his picture on the cover of *Time* or *Life* magazines or perhaps seen a Movietone interview. One wrote because 'You are a great writer, at least they say you are . . .', and another admitted that, as for his 'being a great writer, I learned in school that it was so.' Many wrote to a Shaw of their own imagining, each having as the object of his or her attention a highly personalized Shaw answering some individual need. Perhaps more than anyone else, Shaw was himself aware of this phenomenon, commenting: 'People accept all that a successful person does for them as a matter of right. If I swerve an inch from the Shaw of their own making they say "Give us the money back. We've been had."'

He held that a reputation was a mask which a man had to wear, just as he had to wear a coat and trousers, a disguise insisted upon as a point of decency. Questioned about his own reputation, he replied in mock indignation, 'Which one? I have at least fifteen different reputations.' These he once enumerated for a biographer: a critic of art, music, literature and drama; a novelist; a dramatist; an economist; a funny man; a streetcorner agitator; a Shelleyan atheist; a Fabian socialist; a vegetarian; a humanitarian; a preacher; and a philosopher. His activities were as varied as his interests. During the same period he would take part in meetings in support of a Disarmament Conference, lecture on socialism, join a play-reading society, follow such scientific interests as meteorology (in quest of a sunshine recorder and anemometer for measuring wind velocity), and assist in the founding of a model public house.

J·H·DOWD·28

THE NEW STAR IN THE FILM FIRMAMENT.
Suggested typical *rôles* for Mr. George Bernard Shaw, who, in the Movietone at the New Gallery, gives an impersonation of Signor Mussolini.

During the course of his long life Shaw at one time or another spoke and wrote on every subject under the sun, delivering opinions and messages on such varied subjects as: vegetarianism, sweated industries, war, flogging, revolution, unemployment, Poland's right to independence, forcible feeding, evening dress at theatres, marriage and love, vaccination, vivisection, sex, religion, nudity, sanitation, the naming of children, censorship . . . He relinquished the platform at age 67, his chairmanships at 80, and on his 86th birthday resigned from his many committees. However, like many a great primadonna, he gave repeated farewell platform performances, continuing to speak until his death.

He was constitutionally miscast for the role of Sphinx. However, having become an international barometer, he sought to fill the post of contemporary Delphic Oracle, going one step further than those traditional oracles, explaining as well as delivering utterances. In doing so, Shaw became the closest thing England has had to a popular philosopher on unpopular and often controversial issues.

'Who wouldn't care,' asked one correspondent, to overlook our so moved time with your spectacles?'

From time to time an effort would be made to consult the oracle in person, as in 1940 when an Ayot St Lawrence farm labourer found him hedge-clipping.

'Will 'Itler get 'ere?' he asked.

'Napoleon, you know,' replied G.B.S, 'tried it and couldn't.'

Clip, clip . . .

After an initial period in which he found his often unsolicited opinions treated with contempt, this self-made sage became many things to many people. His extensive political, polemical and dramatic writings made 'G.B.S.' the best known initials in Great Britain, if not the world. His comments on an issue would ensure press coverage and readership; his name on the list of speakers would fill a hall otherwise embarrassingly empty, and the gift of an interview could guarantee an unknown journalist a publication.

'Should you answer my questions,' wrote one supplicant, 'I will be in a position to storm the most obdurate editor. Whereas if I went empty-handed I should be flung out. I have but to mention your name and the entrance doors will be flung open wide and there will be much bowing and scraping.'

Similarly, as each caricaturist created a Bernard Shaw of his own, each country had its own image of Shaw. Biographer Archibald Henderson put this succinctly when he said that the 'Russians interpreted G.B.S. as Great British Satyr, the French as Genre Britannique Saltimbanque, the Germans as Great British Sophist, the Chinese as Genus Britannicus Sapiens, the Latins as Gay Bantering Satirist, the British as Gaelic Brandy and Soda, and the Americans as Genu-īne Ballyhooist Supreme.'

Towards the end of his life he would warn would-be visitors wishing to meet the 'great man' to stay away for their own good, if they wanted to protect their illusions. He advised one such individual not to meet his favourite author face to face if he wished to preserve his ideals as the poor old gentleman could not possibly live up to his expectations. Again and again the telephone rang but nothing could induce him to answer it. 'Tell them I am dead,' Shaw once ordered. 'That will keep them going for a few years.'

A twentieth-century Delphic Oracle-cum-Sage, both articulate and informed, he was one of those rare outside observers to whom – because of the magic of the name and the kindness of his face – people would write, hoping for a word of advice, comfort, hope, or, more tangibly, money. Many *Dear Mr Shaw* letters were received when Shaw was over 90 and had suffered several accidents and injuries. Even so, people writing him long and often complicated letters expected a personal reply. He was not expected to become frail and die but to remain a comforting presence, as confirmed time and time again by the manifold nature of the *Dear Mr Shaw* letters.

Texts are reproduced as far as possible from the original corres-pondence, retaining original spelling and punctuation, whether Shaw's (which was on occasion idiosyncratic) or his correspondent's. In the case of the latter, the original layout of a letter has often been preserved, where it serves to reflect the personality of the writer. Deletions are shown by ellipsis marks (. . .). A number of facsimile letters have been included to illustrate, for instance, Shaw's periodic habit of noting his response – particularly if short – on a correspondent's letter before returning it.

The idea for *Dear Mr Shaw* arose by default. Researching a dissertation on Shaw's 1884 lecture on Shakespeare's *Troilus and Cressida*, housed in the Manuscript Room of the British Library, I became hopelessly engrossed in its many volumes of general correspondence to Shaw: letters of great charm, audacity, pathos, delight and – on more than one occasion – downright rudeness. After laboriously transcribing many hundreds of these holograph letters, many little more than mere scrawls ('Dear Sir, Your name is either illegible or incredible,' Shaw informed one correspondent) approaches were made to Shaw archives in America, and letters requesting public help placed in newspapers, in Britain and abroad. Many weeks were spent at the British Library's newspaper collection at Colindale sifting thousands of clippings hunting for anecdotal instances of Shaw's associations with the public and reported exchanges between himself and ordinary individuals whose paths – for one reason or another – had crossed with 'the great man'. An attempt was made wherever possible to trace the whereabouts of the correspondents. Many could not be found and a number had died – in some cases decades before. Many a letter of enquiry was returned, 'Addressee Unknown'. Often the house or even street in question no longer existed. In a number of cases, however, the quest was successful and contact established with the original correspondent, who, more often than not, was surprised and delighted that his letter – penned at least forty years earlier – should have come to light. While a very few couldn't recall having written to Shaw, let alone why they had written, for most the memory remained vivid, as they had written to Shaw when the need was great, often at a turning point or formative period in their lives. Several of Shaw's old correspondents are now writing to me in a similar vein to that in which they wrote to him four decades ago.

In the case of one young man who had written from South Africa asking Shaw for personal advice, the letter sent to his 1946 address was forwarded to his solicitors who replied with their client's current British address. And one would-be writer was traced to Dublin . . .

In 1946, three months after receiving it, Shaw returned Dubliner Timothy Hurley's three-act play *Are the Sane Mad?* with an autograph on the flyleaf. He soundly criticised the play, correcting the text in a few places, particularly spelling errors. However, his response was not totally damning. He would not be surprised, he assured the would be writer, if the author were to succeed as a playwright within the next six years or so. Despite Shaw's mild encouragement, Hurley gave up the profession, settling for 'a secure, pensionable occupation.' Forty years later, in 1986, he recalled the incident with gratitude: '. . . of all the professional people, Bernard Shaw was the only one who treated me with dignity and respect.' A very fine tribute indeed.

Autographs
&
Autograph Hunters

How to get an autograph from a famous person:

- *insult him or make an audacious request*
- *write on a subject of interest to him*
- *threaten to name something after him*
- *offer money*
- *flatter*
- *trick him out of it*
- *list names of other illustrious people already collected*
- *just ask for it!*

To a young admirer:

> *Don't waste your time in collecting other people's autographs, my boy. Devote it to making your O W N autograph worth collecting!!*

and to another:

> *Your business in life is to make your signature valuable, even if it is only at the bottom of a cheque . . .*

There was a pink card (latterly it turned blue-green) for the autograph-hunters, in numbers Shaw's greatest pest. Usually, the postcard carried a rebuke to the effect that:

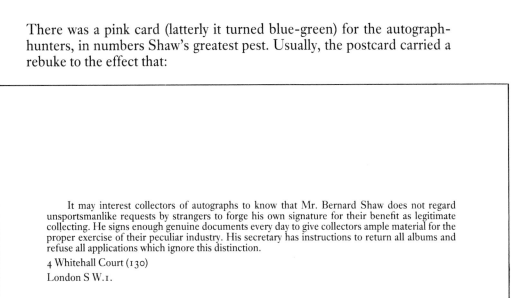

It may interest collectors of autographs to know that Mr. Bernard Shaw does not regard unsportsmanlike requests by strangers to forge his own signature for their benefit as legitimate collecting. He signs enough genuine documents every day to give collectors ample material for the proper exercise of their peculiar industry. His secretary has instructions to return all albums and refuse all applications which ignore this distinction.

4 Whitehall Court (130)
London S W.1.

According to his secretary, Blanche Patch:

> 'Unsportsmanlike' aroused the ire of schoolboys, many of whom protested; so, on my own authority, I altered the reproof to 'requests by strangers for his signature'. All was peace. Upon occasion, too, if the approach were especially skilful, I might add after 'his secretary has instructions to return . . .' and so on, 'but she sometimes obliges if she happens to have a spare signature by her', gumming on an autograph clipped from a returned cheque . . . if one of his household monthly bills was under £1, he would instruct whoever was paying it to get a postal order . . . mainly because he reckoned that, if a cheque was for more than £1, nobody would think it worth selling for the signature, as some sold cheques for lesser sums . . .

He paid American debts with British cheques instead of bank drafts on New York. When asked for an explanation, he replied that his autograph was so treasured by Americans that instead of cashing his cheques, they framed them and hung them up, an excellent arrangement for all concerned.

According to a July 1936 newspaper report:

> These Names
> Make – Money
>   What's in a name, in cash? It
> depends on whose it is.
>   Here is what American auto-
> graph hunters pay for signatures
> of the great:–
>   King Edward, £3 to £5; Musso-
> lini, £6 to £8.
>   Ex-Kaiser Wilhelm, £1; Presi-
> dent Roosevelt, £1 to £4.
>   Mr. G. B. Shaw, £2; Mr. Lloyd
> George, 5s.
>   Shirley Temple, 1s.

As in his later years Shaw continually protested that his finances were dwindling – going to the state in the form of taxes – it was highly fitting that the last time he wrote his signature before he died was on an income tax return.

One young woman staying at Peebles Hydro (about 20 miles south of Edinburgh) in 1921 with her family was delighted by the presence of Shaw and his wife Charlotte. At mealtimes he would prop his book up on a book-rest and read during the entire meal, which, although his common practice at home, surprised many of the other guests. At eighty-five, this woman recalled what was one of the highlights of her young life:

> I met him one day in the main corridor of Peebles Hydro
> and asked him if he would sign my album. He looked down
> at me and replied 'no', but immediately said 'Yes I will, but
> if you tell anyone in this hotel by God I'll strangle you!'
> Shortly after this I went home and my sister went to Shaw's
> suite to collect my album and on giving it to my sister Mr
> Shaw said 'Tell your sister she should sell this now.' I only
> wish I had taken his advice as my album which had many
> interesting signatures was stolen from me . . .

'YOU CANNOT AFFORD IT'

Others, however, were not as fortunate:

> Dear Mr. Shaw
> I was ill advised
> enough to ask you for your autograph
> in Jermyn Street last night, a request
> which you refused me on the grounds
> that in making a verbal and not a
> written application I had approached you
> in an improper manner . . .
> I feel assured now, both
> by my behaviour of last night and by my
> attitude today I have most successfully

burned my boats in obtaining the autograph
of the author of St Joan which I badly
wanted, but at least I have spent what
seemed at the time an eternal two minutes
being roundly rebuked by the Great
Man for my impertinence, which in
retrospect anyhow affords me no little
satisfaction.

According to Blanche Patch, his eyebrows would seem to shoot up at the
autograph-hunters who lay in wait for him in person.

I remember one of a party of schoolgirls struggling towards
us across the stalls as we left a play at the New Theatre.
'Please may I have your autograph?' said she, opening her
album. 'Certainly not!' snapped G.B.S, 'and if you are going
to collect autographs you will come to a bad end.' 'What a
frightful nuisance,' sighed the child, turning away.

However, when he was ninety-two he did give in to a Cheshire
woman to whom eleven years earlier he had answered, 'No; I don't ask for
yours.' He now gave her both an autograph and a birthday photograph of
himself taken in his Ayot St Lawrence garden.

According to his neighbour, Stephen Winsten, Shaw was once asked to talk to the girls working at a local aeroplane factory. G.B.S. had been called in to help when there had been some trouble at the factory, with the draughtsmen refusing to mix with the mechanics. As he recalled later, Shaw's reception was decidedly frigid. 'I don't think,' he told Winsten:

> I increased the sale of my books by one. To
> see if I could write, two or three girls very
> politely asked me for my autograph, but I
> warned them that the most intelligent men
> I know cannot even count the number of noughts
> on their cheques and always sign their names
> with a cross. These are the men you should
> be after; they are worth getting, conquering
> and putting in their place.

A little cheek or audacity could cause Shaw to change his mind, as shown by his encounter with ace autograph-hunter Frederick T. Bason. Bason, who, in his prime, had collected more than ten thousand autographs, was in his earlier days refused by Shaw. Not to be put off, he tried again. 'You may be famous, one day,' said Mr Bason. Shaw, delighted, signed.

On another occasion he would freely offer autograph-hunting advice to Miss Margaret Bee of Edinburgh, who claimed her only two failures were Paderewski and Lord Baden-Powell. Her greatest victory was securing a Shaw signature after her fourth attempt. 'Never tell one author that you have obtained another author's signature,' was Mr Shaw's advice when she told him that she had already persuaded J. M. Barrie to sign her album. Shaw's advice was based on personal experience as many tried to entice him into giving them an autograph by listing the illustrious company his name would share. Whereas one American claimed to have a collection of presidents, princes, great musicians and others of less fame, and another claimed to collect only the signatures of 'top notchers'; a third, William E. Tolbert of Maryland, sent him a press clipping describing his collection and a letter listing his conquests.

Fairchild Aircraft
Maryland U.S.A.

Dear Sir:
    You will see by this clipping just what I do for a hobby and
famous people like yourself who I cannot meet right away
why I just sit down and write to them hoping that they will
be kind enough to grant me my request. I will appreciate it
more than you will ever know Sir: if you will let me have one

of your pictures and Autograph it to me personally for my
Collection in my Album. In my book I have such famous
people like Mrs Franklin D. Roosevelt, Secretary of State,
J. F. Brynes, J. Edgar Hoover, F.B.I., His Royal Highness
'Duke of Windsor', Post Master General Robert Hannegan,
Governor Thomas E. Dewey New York City, Governor
Herbert R. O'Conor Maryland, Governor Edward Martin
Pennsylvania, Mayor Laguardia N.Y.C., Mr. James F.
Farley N.Y.C., Vincent Lopez, General Pershing, General
Eisenhower, General MacArthur, General George S.
Patton, General Wainwright, General Arnold, General
Spaatz, Adm. Halsey, and a score of others so you can see
why Sir, I would be honored in having your picture and
Autograph in my Album with the rest of the famous people
who was kind enough to grant me my request. With my
kindest regards to you. I am

Sincerely
Your American Autograph Friend,
William E. Tolbert.

From Atiya Begum of Bombay:

16 December 1944

To 'George Bernard Shaw'
  (World Famous playwright)
  Whitehall Court
  London S.W.1

'Seasons Greetings'
May it bring you Health & Peace.
Respected Friend – I am presuming
that you have not forgotten us.
India too celebrated your Birthday.
    I have a request to make
& I am sanguine you will graciously
grant it – I am creating a
'*distinguished Personalities Museum*'
devoted to world famous friends

whom I have the honor of knowing
& keeping their letters & photographs
for the future generation as rare
ties – May I request you to
send me a letter as your
message to be preserved
(informal & friendly) for
all generations to come?
We are still hoping to
meet you before we step
into Eternal Regions!

INDIANS GREET 'G.B.S.'
'INDIANS WELCOME MR GEORGE BERNARD SHAW ON HIS ARRIVAL IN INDIA. ONE OF
THEM IS GOING TO ASK MR SHAW FOR HIS AUTOGRAPH!'

Daily Express, *Manchester (January 30th, 1933)*

One juvenile American novelist was far from willing to accept Shaw's
refusal with good grace. When in 1920 eleven-year-old Horace Wade's
first work, *In the Shadow of Great Peril* – a novel of romance and adventure –
was published in Chicago, he sent a gift copy to Bernard Shaw. According
to Horace:

Before my book was published I thought it would be fine to

get Mr. Shaw's opinion of its merit. So without consulting a soul I wrote Mr. Shaw addressing him in London. After a few weeks I got a slip of paper on which this unsigned sentiment appeared:

> You are not a little boy – you are a big liar; you are only fishing for my autograph, but you must use a more plausible fly if you would catch me.

HORACE
WADE

When I got this I was aflame with indignation. I felt that I had been unjustly dealt with and that the gruff old literary ogre across the pond owed me an apology. So I wrote him a letter to this effect:

> Mr. George Bernard Shaw,
> London, England.
>
> Do you think it was nice of you to call me a "big liar"? I am a little boy eleven years old, while you are a big man. Don't play the school bully. I simply asked you to criticize my book. It was good enough for the Chicago papers to want it and I thought you would like to encourage a boy

who wanted to go ahead. Some day, if you live long
enough, MY autograph will be worth more than YOURS. I
didn't want your NAME. I asked for your OPINION. I read
the 'Young Visitors' and you have in Sir James Barrie a
liar big enough without coming to America to abuse a boy
of eleven years. I am sending you my picture, and if you
doubt that I wrote my book, write the book reviewer of
the Chicago 'Post' and then you'll find out and quickly
apologize for calling me a liar.

And on the back of the snapshot Horace sent Shaw he wrote: 'FROM THE
BIGGEST LIAR IN AMERICA TO THE BIGGEST CRANK IN ENGLAND'.
However, the young man's prophecy that his autograph would one day
prove of far greater worth than Shaw's never came true, as the several works
of his which followed his much celebrated juvenile work, *In the Shadow of
Great Peril – Great Scott* (1932), *To Hell with Hollywood* (1931) and *Tales of
the Turf* (1956) – never received the jubilant reception accorded his first
literary effort.

Many ruses were tried to provoke a Shavian response. He quite
innocently walked into a trap set by one American autograph-collector who
had asked whether he might name a new pill 'the G.B.S. Pill'. Shaw's reply
was immediate: 'If you dare to do it, I shall sue you.' The man later
confessed to Shaw that he had never manufactured a pill in his life, and had
no wish to do so, but that he had made a bet with a friend that he could get
Shaw's autograph, and thanked him for letting him win.

While certain requests were ignored, like that of the American
woman who, most inappropriately, wished to name a new soap after him –
as Shaw never used soap, washing in oatmeal – he sent a most scorching
reply to a request by Mr Kenneth MacDonald of Detroit to use his name to
advertise a new vegetable cure for digestive troubles.

In the first instance, having heard a rumour that Shaw charged $1
per letter, MacDonald – wishing, perhaps, to preserve his 'amateur status'
as an autograph-collector – worded his request in polite terms and asked
for the autograph free of charge. Shaw did not reply. Politeness having
failed, MacDonald tried guile instead, sending a most businesslike letter in
which he declared that Mr Kenneth G. MacDonald had organized a
company to sell a new vegetable compound, a cure for digestive troubles,
and asked Mr Shaw's permission to use his name to market this wonderful
preparation. Mr MacDonald added a postscript (and this is where his guile
came in). It declared that Shaw's failure to reply would be interpreted as
assent. To this second letter, G.B.S. replied most promptly, and in his own
handwriting:

If you attempt to use my name in the manner proposed, I

shall certainly take every legal step in my power to restrain you and to warn the public that I know nothing of your remedy.

And, he added – most important of all – the magic signature:

G. Bernard Shaw

Shaw later paid homage to this trickster. 'I was tricked by an elaborate advertisement of a patent medicine to which my name was attached. I threatened legal proceedings (not unkindly), and the forger wrote that I need not worry, as the advertisement was a fake to get my autograph. He deserved it for his pains. It took me in completely.' However, such threats of legal proceedings didn't stop one German from naming a cigar after the confirmed anti-tobacconist!

Shaw did respond favourably to a young girl's wish to name the new pig after him. 'I have no objection,' he responded graciously, 'but I suggest that you ask the pig first.'

However, he refused a similar request from the Montagu children, Ivor and Ewen. Over seventy years later, in February 1985, Ewen Montagu, C.B.E., Q.C., D.L., would recall the incident:

> . . . My younger brother Ivor (age 7–9) and I (age 10–12) started to collect autographs and wrote letters asking for them – with very little success. We (I can't remember which started the idea) thought of a scheme. We were, at the time, feeding a wild hedgehog (*not* a guinea pig) with saucers of bread and milk. We linked the idea with my small sister as a more potent lure and wrote, in an artificially childish handwriting, to many people saying, 'Dear So and So. Please may we call our little sister's pet hedgehog after you?' (In fact we called it 'Prickles').
>
> We had a very considerable success – looking back, most were unctuously flattered.
>
> But the real success was Bernard Shaw. He sent (in an envelope) a post-card-photo of himself, autographed across the bottom right hand corner, '*G. Bernard Shaw*'. On the back was written 'Certainly NOT – how do you know that the hedgehog's political opinions are the same as mine? G.B.S.'

Shaw was dismayed when parents wished to name their children after him, as Mr and Mrs R. T. Shaw of Selby were to find in 1928 when, after deciding to call their son Bernard, they accepted the challenge of their friends to prefix George to his name. The original 'G.B.S.' was notified of his new responsibilities, and was apparently impressed with their weight, for he at once returned one of his well-known postcard photographs with this message on the back:

> Shocking outrage on a defenceless infant. How do you know that I will not be hanged, or that he will share my notions? If you had read my play 'Getting Married' you would not have done it. – G. Bernard Shaw.

And when in May 1957 George Bernard Shaw II got married, his father gave him the photograph with the G.B.S. inscription as a wedding present. 'I have been teased no end about my name all through my life and still am,' he wrote in January 1985. 'I am married and have a son whose name is *Charles Bernard Shaw*.'

GEORGE BERNARD SHAW (of Selby), with a photograph of George Bernard Shaw (the playwright).

G.B.S. AND HIS NAMESAKE

"SHOCKING OUTRAGE ON A DEFENCELESS INFANT"

Daily Express, *Manchester (March 9th, 1932)*

Shaw to the noted socialist and formidable Edwardian hostess, Lady Warwick:

2nd March 1927

My dear Lady Warwick,

My letters have gone astray; but I gather from my secretary by telephone that you want me to godfather your grandson. I am tempted to make the disgraceful reply that I had much rather father your son; but that excuse, however true, is superfluous, because I am eternally disqualified from sponsorship by the fact that I do not believe either the Apostles Creed or the Church Catechism; and as for the doctrine of original sin I abhor it, and would do anything in my power to turn the infant against it. I should simply register him, taking care not to give him any names that would tar him with doctrines that he might grow up to detest, or that might raise expectations that he might not be able to fulfil. It is bad enough to have a famous grandmother (a thing that can't be helped) without having a famous godfather as well. He might want to write plays. Mozart's unfortunate son wanted to be a musician, and would have been thought a very good one had his name been Muggins.

Call him Kingmaker Raggedstaff: then they will expect something from him; but they won't know what.

According to theatre producer Basil Dean, Lady Warwick's son-in-law and the baby's father, the sex of the child had been changed in the telephone call from Shaw's secretary. However, at the end of the day, Dean's old friend Roger Ould became his daughter Tessa's godfather.

Over the years 'Bernard Shaws' would appear in many different contexts. There was the Coffin Maker down the Walworth Road towards Camberwell in 1923, and later the conscientious objecting chemistry student and, more humorously, the 44-year-old street trader who in July 1941 was fined 20s at South Western Police Court for being drunk in charge of a horse and van. When the magistrate, Mr Claud Mellor, asked the gaoler: 'Is he known?', the gaoler replied: 'Not this one.' The defendant told the magistrate that although Bernard Shaw was his real name, 'it has not brought me any luck'.

Periodically a 'Bernard Shaw' would appear at Bernard Shaw's door, hoping for a word with the great man, as was the case in July 1948; on which occasion, the other G.B.S. was a short, thick-set, dark-haired fellow of forty, an ex-RAF Kentish Town packer. Looking for a lock-up to rent for a café, he turned up at Shaw's Ayot St Lawrence retreat 'for fun'. It was only after he sent in his RAF release papers as evidence of his right to the

'Bernard Shaw' name that the 92-year-old G.B.S. agreed to see him.

Oxford undergraduate Gerald Shaw was not so successful, when in September 1936 he tried to make contact with Shaw. Having had returned from the laundry three collars and a shirt not belonging to him, and each bearing a neat tab with the name 'G. B. Shaw', Mr Shaw, then holidaying at Ayot St Lawrence, wrote to G.B.S. stating that he believed he had some of his laundry, which he would be delighted to forward on payment of 1s 4d. To his disappointment, by return of post came a typed disclaimer:

'Mr. Shaw does not send his washing to a laundry.'

Later, after returning the washing to the laundry, Mr Gerald Shaw sighed, 'Mr. Shaw might have added his autograph!'

There are also those who played Shaw the highly dubious tribute of imitation, as in the case of American Mr L. Gaylor, a New York broker. Bearing a striking resemblance to Shaw, he would, when holidaying at Southend, don a Shaw beard and happily sign autograph books, something the real Shaw would never have done. G.B.S, however, was delighted when he was sent a picture of himself clipped from a Copenhagen newspaper, beneath which appeared the caption: *Rita Hayworth.*

Many other attempts were made to trick an autograph from Shaw. The following artifice was perpetrated by a young would-be music critic, who in May 1932 decided that as an enthusiastic Shavian he should secure his hero's autograph.

> But it also occurred to me that if I wrote in the ordinary way requesting one, I should receive only the customary curt reply, not from G.B.S. himself, but from his secretary, saying, either, that the great man does not give his admirers autographs, or else that he only sells them at exorbitant prices. As I did not wish to be disappointed in this way I decided to write an inarticulate letter, pretend that I was a poor workman, enclose a two shilling postal order (the money for which, I explained, had to be saved up from my limited earnings), and give a working man's address in the suburbs. Having scrawled all this on a cheap piece of paper, I signed myself not with my real name (which he may have read somewhere) but with *S. B. Gordon.* In the letter I purposely made mistakes of spelling, grammar, and syntax. Also, I made a point of enclosing a small piece of white paper, on which I asked for the autograph to be written, and enclosed, in addition, a stamped and addressed envelope for the reply.
>
> Imagine my surprise and joy when, after thirty-six hours of curious suspense, I received not only the autograph but also

a photograph and the returned two shilling postal order! On the back of the post-card size photograph was this:

Ayot St Lawrence, Welwyn. Herts. 11/5/32
Who told you that I sell autographs? It is just what I never
do. All the same, buying them is much honester than
begging them, as most people do; so I will present you
with one, and return your generous bid with many thanks.

G. Bernard Shaw

And, on the flap of the envelope Shaw had written, 'By the way, it's a trick, isn't it? If so, it is clever enough to deserve success. G.B.S.'

The correspondent, a Mr Henry Welsh of 5 Jermyn Street, London, SW1, then wrote to Shaw in his real name, confessing his subterfuge and asking for forgiveness. He told Shaw that he was a young freelance music critic on the threshold of his career, and that he had been reading a number of his plays and his criticisms in the *Star*. Two days later, he received one of G.B.S.'s celebrated postcards!

Dont apologize: I smelt the rat, and notified my suspicion on
the envelope.
    The misspelling was too consistent; and the construction
not quite idiomatic proletarian, only good literary
pastiche . . .

A woman from Arlington, Massachusetts, admitted that after considering the ruse of insult, she had dismissed the idea.

August 7, 1946

Dear Mr Shaw:
    I know it must seem bold of
me writing you – especially since I
am not a famous person – but I
am going to be honest with you. You
see, Mr Shaw, I would like a great
deal to have an autographed picture
of you for my hobby picture-collection
of famous people.
    A friend of mine told me to write
to you and say that I didn't like
your work, that you were a poor
writer, etc., and you would surely
enjoy it and send me your autographed

picture. But I guess I really can't
say that. I liked reading your
play 'Major Barbara' and seeing it,
too, and hope to see 'St. Joan' when
it comes to New York if they will
let me take time off from work to
go down to see it. And as for
being a great writer, I learned
in school that it was so . . .

One correspondent, hoping to receive a witty postcard from Shaw in
1947, wrote in response to his statement that 'Manchester would be vastly
improved by an atom bomb,' asking, 'Is it correct that you were christened
by Canon Spooner, and your real name is *George Shernard Baw*?' Forty years
later, she is still waiting for a reply!

Over the years Shaw became very suspicious of correspondents'
intentions. In response to one particular request for literary assistance he
wrote these instructions to his bibliographic assistant F. E. Loewenstein:

Obviously I cannot connect myself in any way with a work or
an author of whom I know nothing . . .
Write to him to the above effect. I suspect him of
autograph collecting. His foolishness is overdone.

He certainly could be forgiven for being suspicious of a number of
correspondents. The following 1936 letter from a New York doctor was at
best a waste of Shaw's time. It could have been a ruse to get Shaw into
correspondence, a trick to get him to read something, or else yet one more
effort from the autograph-hunters brigade!

. . . I am writing to you because you are the only man in the
world to whom I can write about it. For you are the only one
who can decide a wager between me and a friend of mine.
Recently this old friend came to see me and read the
enclosed article during his visit. He is a great student and
admirer of George Bernard Shaw. When he finished the
article he made the following statement. 'If Mr. Shaw read
this article of yours and knew that the author of it was a Jew
I know exactly the thought it would evoke in his mind and
what he would say.'
I most naturally denied that he could know any such thing
and so we made a wager and we beg you to decide it for us.
It is only a pleasantry and at the same time an interesting
experiment in psychology. It can do no harm and no one

needs to know a thing about it as far as we are concerned.

　　We beg you, therefore, to grant us fifteen minutes of your valuable time, read the article bearing in mind that the author is of the Jewish persuasion, note the mental reaction it creates in your mind and compare it with that in the enclosed envelope which according to my friend is the thought it will create in your mind. You will then be good enough to let us know whether my friend is right or wrong . . .

Shaw's temperance foiled one shipboard scheme to sell autographs. When he boarded the *Empress of Britain* for a world cruise in 1932 he insisted he would not comply with a single request for an autograph. The liner's smoking-room stewards thought they would be able to get around this refusal easily, as the policy on board ship was for guests to sign a stub for drinks. The stewards therefore figured they would save the stubs and cash in on them with autograph hunters. However, by the time the ship reached Suez they had learned something about Shaw they did not know before – that he was a teetotaller. Hence no signed stubs and no profits!

　　To an unidentified correspondent:

> It is against my rule to give my autograph to collectors who misspell the word presumptuous and make it sound prezumpchis.
>
> G. B. S.
> 19/2/1947.

And then there was John Carveth Wells, who reversed the situation, offering Shaw *his* autograph – an incident recorded later in his autobiography, *My Candle at Both Ends*.

> One day I heard that Bernard Shaw was in Cairo, and was refusing to see any reporters. In fact, the editor of the *Mail*, then a woman, said that 'G.B.S.' had been quite rude to her, and she was in a state of great indignation. It seemed that here was an opportunity for me to get a feather in my cap if I could obtain an interview with Shaw. The main thing was

the approach; it would have to be something out of the ordinary to get by the great man's guard. I went to Shaw's hotel, and made sure that he was in the building; then, autographing one of my souvenir cards, I sent it in to Shaw with a note. This read:

Dear Mr. Shaw,
    You get so many requests for your autograph, that I feel sure that, for a change, you would like to have mine. It may be valuable some day!

This piece of impertinence achieved the desired result and Wells was sent for. A long conversation ensued, during the course of which Shaw characteristically advised the young would-be writer never to write for fun or on speculation, but *'be sure you are going to get paid before you write a word'*. Before the young man left, Shaw handed him a pound note, saying that he would pay for the autograph, an action which would lead Wells in the future to claim that he was the only person who had ever sold Bernard Shaw his autograph! After a most adventurous active life, Wells in 1935 became a victim of infantile paralysis. The following year Shaw responded favourably to his request for money to buy a folding wheelchair, renewing the gift in 1939.

Shaw's autograph would appear in the oddest places; even at Gallipoli, after the first Dardanelles landing. A postcard from Shaw to Private T. Eardley of 'A' Company, 7th Manchesters, was published on August 18th, 1915 in the *Yorkshire Post*. Found in a trench after a charge, the postcard had been forwarded by a British soldier to a contemporary in England.

> A man who goes on calmly hunting autographs with all civilisation crumbling around him, and the Turkish enemy not far below the horizon, really deserves to succeed. So here goes.
>
> G. Bernard Shaw

Private Eardley of Greenheys, Manchester, having enlisted in 1904, was mobilized when war broke out in August 1914, and was sent to Egypt the following month. He was later transferred to Gallipoli, where, after taking part in the landing at Cape Helles, he fought in the Battles of Krithia. Reported missing, and presumed to have been killed in action on June 4th, 1915, he was entitled to the 1914–15 Star, and the General Service and Victory medals.

Twenty-four years and another war later, Sgt E. F. McCarthy would also be awarded a much coveted Shaw signature. In 1939, before Sgt

McCarthy embarked for service in Hong Kong, Shaw sent him a signed photograph, which he kept during capture by the Japanese, and during the torpedoing, and bombing of his prison camp in Kobe by the Americans. On his return to England in November 1945 he sent the photograph to Shaw 'to look at and see where you have been and what you have been through.' Shaw returned the photograph, after scribbling on the back his comment: 'Don't risk it again. I'm ninety.'

Shaw tended to respond favourably to unusual requests. He would often in the process rebuke the writer, as in the case of a young woman student of Western Reserve University in America who sent a blank postcard, requesting that he write the main facts of his life on the card and return it to her! To her astonishment, he did this, adding the postscript:

> I note your striking address, Western Reserve. In view of
> your preposterous request to write the story of my life on
> a postcard, may I inquire: What about western cheek?

Mr Cyrus Andrews, editor of *Radio Who's Who*, was less fortunate when he requested Shaw's 'life story in brief'.

> Life story not brief. I am in my 94th year and too
> well-known. People curious about it can read my 'Self
> Sketches', 1949.

Despite repeated approaches by Mr Marion Peters of the West Texas Gas Company, Shaw's 'brand' would never adorn Texas cattle. Mr Peters, a collector of cattle brands drawn by famous persons, had asked Shaw to reproduce a brand for his assortment. 'Why?' the playwright wanted to know. 'There is evidently some catch in this. Explain!' An explanation was attempted, but it was not to Shaw's satisfaction. Again he wrote: 'I am more in the dark than ever and can only say that I regard the branding of cattle as a horrible and hellish practice.' Unwilling to admit defeat, Peters tried again:

> In your last note you indicated your personal contempt for
> branding cattle with hot irons; now, in the same spirit of
> interest may I ask how you would place this cabalistic mark ℔
> if it were yours, upon a cow so that it would not come off but
> remain for the life time of the cow as a positive mark of
> identification?

Shaw's handwritten reply penned on the bottom of Peters' letter was somewhat less than gracious:

<u>Paint</u> it on them, you idiot.
You can put your name on your handkerchief
without using a red hot poker, can't you?

G. Bernard Shaw
16th Oct. 1934

American requests for autographs tended to be more ebullient than British. From Chester McDonald of Boston, Massachusetts:

August 5th, 1946

Dear Sir:–

It seems strange, even fantastic, that I, a mere person of no significance should dare write so great a person as you.

I know you are a very busy person and have no time for such things as this, but please forgive this freakish letter and read it through.

I am one of your many million admirers.

I think you are one of the greatest, most humane persons I have ever heard of or read about. I am sure I have read every article written about you (that I could get my hands on) and all your published works.

It would do my mind, soul, and heart untold pleasure and happiness if I could but have a momento of you. Even if just a letter or name.

I read an article about you one time, of the time you gave an autographed picture of yourself to the person guessing nearest your weight. The person that won it sold it for $4 to the mistress of Ayot's pub, 'The Brocket Arms.'

How thrilled I should be to have that picture autographed by you.

Maybe some day you may find time to make me happy beyond my fondest wishes.

During his 1933 visit to Hollywood Shaw refused John Barrymore's request for an autograph for his little son.

'How old is he?' asked Mr. Shaw.
'One year,' replied Mr. Barrymore proudly.
'Too young,' replied the great man. 'If it was

41

your grandfather and he had only a couple of
years to live, I'd give it to him.'

On this occasion, however, Shaw apparently relented ... for he was
subsequently to receive the following 'thank you'!

> Beverly Hills
> California
> May 24, 1933

> My dear Mr Shaw
>   Thank you so much
> for your autograph. May
> I come and see you to
> thank you for it when I
> grow up?
>   John Barrymore Junior

Requests from the young were particularly appealing:

> Farmington, Mich
> July 29 1946
> United States Amer.

> Dear Mr Shaw
>   I saw your picture
> in the paper and I wanted
> to cut it out but couldn't.
> You see my sister delivers
> papers and it was in one
> of her papers. Would you
> please send me your picture
> Because I admire you very
> much. I am 9 and Irish
> and you are 90 and Irish
> and neither one of us live
> in Ireland.

And, from one ten-year-old who *did* live in Ireland, came the following:

Coalisland
Tyrone
Ireland
26-7-46.

Dear Mr Shaw
    Please will you
give me your autograph. I am ten
years old and I would like
a real Photo-graph of
you.
    I congratulate
you on your 90th Birthday
You are a very wonderful
man.
    Every morning at class
when I remember I shall
say a little PRAYER for you
that God will take care of you . . .

There were those who wanted to have their Shaw first editions signed. Some sent bookplates to be signed or just pieces of paper as, in the following request:

May 24–44

Dear Mr Shaw – For many years I have wanted to
send you my first edition of St. Joan to ask you to
kindly autograph it for me – but I will not trust
it to – even the registered post. – Will you for a
country woman of your own, just write your name
on a bit of paper & send it to me for the precious
book? Not that I agree with more than half
your opinions – ?? I expect you like 'taking in'
the English & that's why you tell them things which
you sometimes only half believe yourself –.
But t-is the grandman you are & I often do –
shall – say a prayer for you. Blessings on you &
thanks.

The economics of signing books were expounded upon on another printed postcard:

Mr. Bernard Shaw is often requested by correspondents not personally known to him to inscribe his name in copies of his books which they offer to send for that purpose. No doubt many of the requests are made in good faith and appreciated by him as such. But if he were to comply he would be immediately overwhelmed by applications from speculators anxious to get rich quickly by purchasing his books at shop prices and selling them at the fancy prices which autographed copies command. He is therefore obliged to reserve his autograph for volumes which are his spontaneous personal gift, and begs you to excuse him accordingly.

However, to O. D. Peterson of Stafford, Iowa, who had sent him a first edition of *Cashel Byron's Profession* to be signed:

> This authentic copy of the first edition . . . I dedicate to Mr.
> O. D. Peterson . . . who has sent me a dollar bill. If every
> collector of autographs in the United States would do the
> same at the present rate of exchange I should be a
> millionaire . . . G. Bernard Shaw, London, 15th Oct. 1915.

On one occasion he did take five shillings from sixteen-year-old Sheila Sleigh of Aldridge, Staffordshire, who had forwarded her autograph album, together with a postal order for any charity he was willing to support. When the book was returned, she found that he had written:

> To Sheila Sleigh, who has sent me five shillings.
> – G. Bernard Shaw, Ayot St Lawrence.

However, another time Shaw returned to New Zealand an autograph request together with the five shillings the petitioner had included for his favourite charity. In doing so, he advised the autograph-hunter to spend the money sensibly, that anyone who furnished his autograph forged his own name, and that he should burn his autograph collection and find some way instead of giving value to his own name.

As the following postcard to Mrs Colhurst of Edstaston, Shropshire, makes clear, Shaw claimed he *never* provided presentation copies for sale.

16th July 1929

Autographing a book for sale at a bazaar or the like is utterly, totally, completely, inexorably and violently out of the question.

I will autograph a book for *you*. You can then present it to whom you please; and the recipient can gratify charitable impulses in any desired direction. But nothing must be done to shake the conviction of the charities, established by long and laboriously maintained tradition, that it is no use asking me to send them autographed books for sale at their shows.

If you only knew what a bother they are!

G.B.S.

'I'm damned if I will,' said Shaw, when asked to add his autograph to a book being prepared to help newspaper charities. 'Why should I sell my autograph to relieve the country of its responsibilities?'

While Shaw might not have inscribed books for sale directly, however, he often suspected they would be sold, and occasionally even advised recipients as to their possible commercial value. A rehearsal copy of *The Millionairess* in which Shaw had written, 'When you are done with this it will fetch enough to buy a utility hat,' was sold at Sotheby's for £22 in 1952. However, he more than once overestimated the value his signature would put on a book. A woman with whom he had a long correspondence was rewarded with a copy of his *The Simpleton of the Unexpected Isles*, one of twenty-five privately printed proofs. 'Dear Baby Bainbridge,' Shaw wrote in the book, 'Dont bother me for more letters: read this "mockery of religion"; and then sell it as an autographed and very scarce unpublished rehearsal copy. It will keep you in pocket money for a month. But mind you read it first.' When Miss Bainbridge sold the book at Sotheby's in 1949 she had hoped to buy a new easy chair with the proceeds, but the sale fetched only £10.

As an act of kindness he would occasionally inscribe books to people in financial need. When an old trade unionist died, Shaw, knowing that the family had many copies of his works – including first editions – and that the widow would be too proud to accept money, volunteered to autograph all the books, thereby greatly enhancing their value. As a friend wrote to G.B.S. in 1949 about the Sotheby's sale of Shaw-owned books: '*The Seven*

Pillars fetched £180 last week: your inscription put it up to £460. Would T E[Lawrence] be pleased? I think he would laugh . . .'

He would not only autograph books but write messages in them and tell the owners to run round to Mr Gabriel Wells, the book-collector specializing in Shaw first editions and manuscripts, and demand £50 or £100 for each! According to Shaw's secretary:

> A pious journalist in the Bahamas once called him an old goat who was 'bound to catch hell' for selling a copy of the Breeches Bible. G.B.S. had found it lying about and thought it an unattractive piece of book production. Some pages were missing and it would not have fetched much had not Shaw scribbled on the flyleaf, 'I can't bear to have this ugly old thing in the house,' which put the price up to £40.

When, in 1918, Lady Mary Murray wrote to Shaw requesting an autographed book for a wartime charity, he quite characteristically refused. However, in doing so he wrote a most saleable letter! When her husband, Gilbert Murray, asked Shaw if the letter could be sold instead, Shaw refused, afraid that he had made a libellous remark about a commercial product which had upset his digestion. Instead, he rewrote his letter to Lady Mary, who then decided not to sell it!

> My dear Lady Mary
>
> I call this an abuse of my confidence . . .
>
> Every promising young man I know has been blown to bits lately; and I have had to write to his mother . . . When I open your eyes to the fact that this bazaarbarism has been overworked to such an extent that the public loathes the sight of an autographed book and the best tempered authors burst into torrents of imprecation when they are mentioned, you revile me, call me unkind and unreasonable (which I am not), rude (which I am: what is a friend if you may not be rude to her?), accuse me of having blacked your eye, and ask me generally do I know whom I am addressing. Well, I dont care: it is a naughty world and I may as well be in the fashion. Those Scottish ladies never took any notice of me when I offered them unlimited opportunities for heroism before the war. They waited for the stimulus of statuesque heroes with their limbs blown off, bathed in liquid fire, suffocated with poison gas; and now they are nerved to ask me for an autographed copy of Arms & The Man. Oh, these heroes and heroines! When will the Coward come to his own? . . .

GEORGE BERNARD SHAW 1922 BY NERMAN

One day, while browsing in a secondhand bookshop, Shaw ran across one of his own books, on the flyleaf of which was written: 'To . . . with the author's compliments. G. Bernard Shaw.' After buying the book, Shaw added under the inscription: 'With the author's renewed compliments. *G.B.S.*' and posted it to the original recipient!

Occasionally, a Shaw refusal could have quite humorous consequences. There was the instance, for example, when he received a letter from a woman asking for a free copy of his book, *The Intelligent Woman's Guide to Socialism and Capitalism,* for a society of ladies she had just inaugurated. Shaw wrote across the bottom of the letter, 'No, damn it, a women's society that cannot afford to pay 15s. for a copy of my book has no right to exist.' He signed his note and returned the letter. The woman soon wrote again, saying that she had taken the letter to a bookseller, who had exchanged it for a copy of his book. Shaw then wrote across the bottom of *that* letter, 'What fools women are; if you had taken it to the right place you would have got £50 for it.' He signed that and sent the letter back.

Some correspondents were advised to make as much as they could out of G.B.S.'s letters by selling them on the open market. When Shaw manuscripts and letters began to command huge prices, Shaw, according to actress Mrs Patrick Campbell, wrote advising her in the following manner:

> DEAR STELLA
> While the prices for my manuscripts are so altitudinous, I suggest that you establish a pension for yourself. Sell immediately my love-letters to you. But for God's sake, keep copies.
>
> Yours ever,
> JOEY

And 'Why not sell the letters you have of mine,' he asked his old friend the Humanitarian Henry Salt, 'and live in comfort for the rest of your life?' Salt wisely took the tip and passed his remaining years comfortably at 'Shaw Lodge', Brighton. Similarly . . . 'Don't hesitate to sell any letters of mine you may find,' he told drama critic Arthur Bingham Walkley's widow. However, while advising owners of Shaw letters to sell while the market was good, he warned purchasers that legal proceedings would inevitably follow unauthorized publication!

'I shall always disparage relics because I am Irish Protestant to the marrow of my bones,' Shaw wrote to Gabriel Wells, who had cornered the market in Shaw first editions and manuscripts. 'I tear up manuscripts with savage glee.' Although he might claim with great pride that he had never sold a manuscript in his life, he derived perverse satisfaction from the successès of those doing so – particularly bogus transactions! Journalist Lewis Wynne passed off a number of forged Shaw manuscripts and letters to dealers between 1929 and 1931, which, according to Dan H. Laurence, found their way over the years into most major American Shaw collections. Shaw's attention was drawn early on to the forgeries and he was informed of the forger's identity. His contempt, however, for autograph-collecting and collectors was such that he made no public or private attempt to stop Wynne's activities, which only ended in 1931 when he was imprisoned on unrelated charges of theft.

Occasionally, Shaw would help bring a miscreant to justice. In 1937 Foyle's bookshop sold a batch of 'Shaw' letters to an autograph-dealer for £15. The dealer brought them back, claiming they were fakes. Foyle's then sent the letters to Shaw, who confirmed the dealer's suspicions. Foyle's returned the dealer's £15, but the fake letters, together with Shaw's note describing how he helped catch the forger, were later sold as an autograph curiosity for £25.

As well as autographs, Shaw received requests for other collectable items, often personal ones – an old hat or a walking stick, and, most pathetically, a handkerchief from a woman from Pittsburgh, Pennsylvania, who had been confined to her home for fifteen years with arthritis. She signed her August 1946 letter, 'Your new little Shut In friend Clara Ernst'.

> After spending six months in the hospital I am told I may
> never walk again for my condition what is known as
> deformity Arthrithis which effects the joints leaving one
> crippled, it now has affected my arms and hands preventing
> my lifting my arms my fingers bent but through perservering
> I manage to hold a pen to write which means so much to me
> . . . so many wonderful friends have so generously sent me
> hankies some also autographed. Gen. Dwight Eisenhower
> and Gen. Wainwright have sent me one of their own
> personal hankies enclosed a letter from them Ill prize as
> long as I live. also many of our Ambassadors and Consulars
> have been so many expressions of friendly interest which I
> am deeply grateful. Ive made scrap books of my hankies
> which are covered with celephane labeled with the
> wonderful friends name, and from where it was sent also
> letters, so dear friend Mr George Bernard Shaw, words
> cannot express my sincere appreciation to you if you would
> be so very kind in also helping add to my hankies collection
> which has brought me so much happiness . . .

Begging

'The philanthropist is a parasite on misery.'
Man and Superman

Please do not ask Mr. Bernard Shaw for money. He has not enough to help the large number of his readers who are in urgent need of it. He can write for you: he cannot finance you.

Shaw postcard reply to many a supplicant

From very early days, Bernard Shaw was generous to people, from sweepers to poets, giving sometimes a penny, a shilling or hundreds of pounds, until he became so inundated with requests that it was impossible to handle them. Advertising himself as a skinflint, he warned those to whom he gave annuities that if they mentioned his gifts publicly, they would come to an end. 'As to my uncharitableness,' he wrote actor William Faversham in 1917, 'I hope you will do everything in your power to confirm any notion of the sort that may prevail: a bad reputation in that respect is my only defence against begging letters.'

Shaw's obsession with the tax collector grew through two world wars. He seemed convinced he was being taxed into poverty. He would ask:

> Why come to me of all people, a man who pays 24 shillings
> in the pound income tax? I have refused within the last few
> days to prevent destitution in India, to help desperate
> refugees in Timbuctoo, and 15 repertory theatres from
> going under . . . You see, I do my good deeds in private
> because once I get a reputation for generosity, I'll have to
> employ a dozen secretaries to answer the begging letters;
> and a couple of psychologists . . .

Shaw's charitable habits were notoriously 'idiosyncratic', as a correspondent from the House of Commons informed one supplicant:

> Dear Mrs Soermus,
>   I do not know how an application for assistance to G.B.
> Shaw such as you suggest would be received. He is a curious
> devil and no-one knows how he would re-act. He might
> send you £100, or he might send you to hell . . .

Or to the workhouse:

> 24th February 1919
>
> Dear Mr. Cragg,
>   What is the use of coming to me with all this? It is a case
> for a philanthropist; and I am not one. If you can't find work,
> there is nothing for it but to have one wild spree with
> enclosed couple of pounds, and then go into the workhouse.

It's not difficult to guess the reply one Indian supplicant would have received when he asked Shaw for £5,000 to marry off half a dozen daughters and 'regain a footing in the world', begging to bring to Shaw's kind notice 'that a daughter's marriage at the age of 12 or 13 is compulsory upon a father or guardian and it costs about £200 to £250 per marriage and I have to perform 2 or 3 marriages this year.' 'And there is,' Shaw recalled, 'one letter I received from a girl who is asking me to support her and her illegitimate child or some such request . . .'

'I am the sort of man who devotes his life to the salvation of humanity in the abstract, and can't bear to give a penny to a starving widow,' Shaw wrote to the Reverend Mother of a Catholic college in Dublin, who had unwisely attempted to sell him a raffle ticket. And yet his deeds would repeatedly belie such a claim, as in the case of one Jamaican who wrote telling him that he had been unhappy in England for some years, and how, as he rested his foot on a newspaper while blacking his boot, he had seen Shaw's picture and thought he had a kind face. So would Mr Shaw pay his passage back home? After thinking the matter over for a day or two, Shaw sent the money.

Then there was, according to his secretary, Blanche Patch:

> . . . our friend the sailor. Every six months, for the first three or four years I was with Shaw, a letter would arrive from him, always starting off 'Able-bodied Seaman . . .' and always alleging that he had the chance of quite a good job which he could not take because his jacket and vest or his medals were in pawn. With the letter he would enclose the pawn tickets, amounting to a little under ten shillings, for these items, together with a photograph of himself, taken, I imagine, many years earlier. It became a regular routine to post back to him his photograph, pawn tickets, and a ten shilling note.

Shaw claimed that he often received as many as twenty begging letters a day, and that every time he hardened his heart, his wife, Charlotte, opened her purse. She used her own discretion in the matter, and in her will left £100,000 in trust for a foundation 'to teach the Irish manners and how not to be shy.' And although one American G.B.S. met was interested in transporting his Ayot St Lawrence home, Shaw's Corner, brick by brick across the Atlantic, most were far more interested in his money than his residence. A flood of begging letters followed his refusal to accept the award money which accompanied his 1925 Nobel Prize for Literature. As Shaw said later in mournful retrospection:

> After the executors of the inventors of dynamite awarded me the Nobel Prize, some 50,000 people wrote to me to say that as the greatest of men I must see that the best thing I could do with the prize was to give it to them. Instead, I gave it back. Then they all wrote again to say that if I could afford

to do that, I could afford to lend them 1,500 pounds for
three years . . . I am now practising a complicated facial
expression which combines universal benevolence with a
savage determination not to save any American from ruin by
a remittance of 500 dollars . . . I can forgive Alfred Nobel
for having invented dynamite. But only a fiend in human
form could have invented the Nobel Prize.

As *Major Barbara* made clear, Shaw's antipathy to institutionalized
charities was that they attacked (with small success) the symptoms, rather
than the causes, of poverty.

On one occasion, however, he was 'caught' for £100 at a Hammersmith meeting where he and Gerald du Maurier and others were appealing
on behalf of Mrs Cecil Chesterton's Cecil Houses for homeless women.
According to his secretary, when Shaw heard that Mrs Chesterton had
gone on the streets to discover for herself the problems of a homeless
woman, he commented that if she had only stayed there a little longer 'she
would not have gone back home, having found what a pleasant life it was.'
Having first declared from the Hammersmith platform, 'Not a penny do I
give,' he announced that if a hundred pounds were collected, he would add
a second. The inevitable happened. The money was raised and Shaw had
to send his cheque along. Shaw's generosity on this occasion was not
surprising for he made it a personal rule not to ask others to give financial
support to a cause unless he did so himself.

However, even a Shaw refusal was of considerable financial benefit
to a supplicant; and in many instances his rejection postcards (with
signature) could be sold to dealers for sums amounting to a most generous
subscription to the charity in question. Shaw found it necessary to explain
that his apparent callousness sprang from the fact that relieving people
financially always resulted in mutual hate: '. . . Giving curses him that gives
and him that takes. And when you give anything you make an enemy for life.
Perhaps that is why God refused to give Jesus Christ anything, and made
him buy what he wanted with his blood.'

I am neither a philanthropist nor a cadger by temperament. I
don't want to be kind to the poor: I hate the poor, and am
doing all I can to exterminate them . . . Of course you can't
be a complete Gradgrind. Hard-up people who can't help
themselves must have a lift occasionally. But it is better not
to meet or know the lifted.

As an ardent socialist Shaw believed that it was up to the Mother
Country and not private charity to support those in need. Applications for
financial assistance, great and small, left him publicly unmoved, although

he was immensely benevolent to both relatives and strangers in quiet, private – and usually unsolicited – ways. Newspaper accounts after his death of Shaw's reputed meanness angered his housekeeper, Alice Laden, who remembered him as a very generous man who did his good deeds by stealth. 'He often gave away considerable sums to deserving causes without anybody knowing about it except Maggie [the parlourmaid] and myself; we used to see him putting the notes in his letters sometimes before they were posted.' Over the years Shaw assisted a number of impoverished individuals by completing their questionnaires in his own handwriting, which they could then sell.

> 'My letters are often sold,' he wrote. 'So are other
> manuscripts which have passed out of my hands. But they
> are sold, not as literature, but as material relics of a modern
> saint. I have never protested. Often when some impecunious
> journalist asks me to give him £500 worth of copy to sell for
> thirty shillings, he implores me to at least refuse on an
> insulting postcard, so that he can dispose of it to a collector
> for the price of a meal. In weak moments I have complied.'

Other charitable acts included allowing a performance of his *Augustus Does His Bit* for the benefit of Belgian refugees, and the writing of *Passion, Poison and Petrifaction, or The Fatal Gazogene: A Brief Tragedy for Barns and Booths* for the annual Theatrical Garden Party benefiting the Actors' Orphanage.

To one relative, Georgina Rogers, he gave an allowance for thirty years, until her death, having promised his mother on her deathbed that he would look after her sisters, and then provided an annuity of £52 a year in his will for each of the two children. When actor Robert Loraine sailed to Buenos Aires to recover from his World War I lung injuries, Shaw inquired, 'Have you any money? If not, can I be of any use? . . . I always make it a rule to inquire into a man's private affairs with extreme delicacy; but I think my meaning is clear.' He also gave financial advice – whether requested or not. As he wrote to actress Janet Achurch in April 1905, 'And if I do have to pay £100, I shall be moral and sarcastic to its full value.' Perhaps fortunately for her, Shaw on this occasion deemed her a lost cause. It is obvious that the following correspondent, in need of financial help while holidaying in Austria, must have at one time or another fallen victim to the Shavian 'wit'.

> My dear GBS, An SOS from Le Diable au Corps!
> Please don't be horribly squashing this time. I know you
> will be scornfully inclined at yet another female failure – it's
> really bad enough to have to own up to oneself & worse still
> to you but here goes, an earful of grist for your kindly but

terribly wear-spotting sarcasm! . . .

   Don't hammer me to bits for ineptitude, I cdn't bear it –
really, from you however justifiable, & don't relegate me to
the scrap-heap, I've <u>not</u> been used up yet to the
uttermost . . .

He was careful with his royalties and author's fees in London, but that
reputation was belied in Radnorshire, where on one occasion in paying a
tailor for repairs he put down twice the sum he had been asked for. When
the tailor pointed out the error Shaw told him, 'I earn my money more easily
than you.'

   When struggling to find a niche in his early London days, Shaw
categorically refused all offers of financial help from others, including his
closest friends. The embodiment of the self-help doctrine, Shaw would
only accept aid to self-help. Paradoxically, that very financial assistance he
would frequently offer others, he would never accept himself. Anyone who
knew Shaw, knew his generosity. When one of his former fellow St Pancras
Councillors went bankrupt, G.B.S, who had ceased to be a member of the
Vestry Council, sent £10, wondering what the devil —— had been up to! In
1914, when Hubert Bland was dying and felt troubled as to whether there
would be enough money for the education of one of his sons, he told his
daughter: 'If there is not enough, ask Shaw.'

In Shaw's early days as a music critic, he was walking along the street with some friends when an organ grinder solicited him for money. With a bored air, Shaw said 'Press' – and nonchalantly walked on, leaving his companions convulsed with merriment. This entirely untrue story was invented by the late Arthur Bingham Walkley, theatre critic to *The Times*, and dedicatee of *Man and Superman*, as a retort to Shaw's pretence that the word 'Press', on the bell button beside Walkley's hall door, was an announcement of his profession.

Over the years Shaw wrote in support of many causes including the Medical (VD) Home for Children at Waddon.

8th December 1922

Dear Mr Tomalin

I hope you will succeed in getting a substantial endowment for your hospital . . .

It is quite horrible to think of the years during which children suffering from the consequences of other people's vices have been abandoned either to no treatment at all, or to treatment along with the very persons whose contamination is the beginning of the trouble – persons of whose existence no child should be aware. If a child steals a penny it is now taken to a special children's court instead of, as it used to be, sent to herd with professional thieves and started by them on the road to ruin. But if a perfectly innocent child falls a victim to the most virulent of poisons, it is still sent to get cured as best it can with professional prostitutes. There is, as far as I know, nothing but your Hospital between it and that fate . . .

Shaw sent a 20 guinea donation to the Lord Mayor of London's United Nations Appeal for Children with the comment 'No acknowledgment necessary'.

Shaw prided himself on never being sentimental. 'I have always disliked your poetry,' he wrote to one major literary figure who had fallen upon hard times; 'I enclose my cheque for £400.'

A Russian, who had killed several of his enemies, fled to London. Wishing soon afterwards to go elsewhere in Europe, he interested his friends in raising money for the move. Although suggested as an improbable contributor, Shaw, when importuned, responded with a handsome donation, accompanied by a note:

Dear X—,
    Why should I be called upon to export this interesting young murderer? Is there no scope for his particular talent in this country?

G.B.S.

War charities were a Shavian bête noire.

April 1918

My dear Dorothy Robson,
    I will do anything for you except autograph a book for a war charity.
    I believe it is the general opinion of the French, British, and American nations that wars are fought by soldiers, and financed by singers, actors, and authors, all singing and acting and autographing as hard as they can for ten hours a day and never asking for any payment.
    I consider this view, widespread as it is, to be economically unsound. It encourages Governments to throw the victims of the war on private charity; and it destroys the livelihood – precarious at the best of times – of the unfortunate artists.
    I refuse your request, but give you this priceless advice to guide you through the war. 1. Double your fees as a singer to enable yourself to survive amid the doubled prices of provisions and clothing. 2. Pay your taxes punctually. 3. Buy War Bonds if you can afford it. 4. Do no professional work without being fully and honestly paid for it. 5. When people beg from you under cover of the war, send for the police.

To dramatist Charles McEvoy:

> ... But whenever I see your handwriting, I say 'How much
> does he want now?' and I am quite pleased when you only
> want me to read a book or see a film. I rather despise your
> want of thrift though. You see, when you borrow money, you
> sell a friend. To sell him for two pounds or the like is
> ridiculous. If you made a rule not to dispose of a friend for
> less than, say, £2,500, there would be something in the
> business ... I never lost sight of the fact that it would give a
> supreme charm to my conversation if it never led up to a
> request for the loan of five shillings. On the whole, I have
> never regretted this policy ... I do not suggest that you
> should reform. If you are that sort of man you will not
> succeed. It may be your destiny – probably something wrong
> with your medulla or your adrenal capsule ...'

Over the years the Ayot St Lawrence village church received a measure of
Shavian support.

17th January 1942

My dear Churchwarden
    I used to pay £2-2-0 pew rent whenever your
predecessors dunned me for it. They stopped doing this for
some reason: perhaps because I had to pay £20 to keep the
tower of the old abbey church from falling, and later on
£100 to preserve the Lyle tombs and colonnade of the newer
church.
    Now that I have succeeded our late neighbor Archer as
the Village Atheist and the late gravedigger Richards as the
Oldest Inhabitant the occasion seems a fit one for resuming
the two guinea arrangement ...
    I renew my offer to defray the cost of removing the trees
which now hide and disfigure the classic front of the church
as soon as labor can be found to do it.

The parishioners will not consider this generous on my part, as they believe me to be a millionaire. You, being a banker, know better. A windfall of £29,000 (estimated in the newspapers as £55,000) has cost me £50,000 in taxes. I shall live this year on overdraft, and may yet die not only in this parish but on it.

Shaw to the Rev. George H. McNeal of Wesley's Chapel:

... I am happy to send a stray pound towards the £800 you need to meet the expenses of the death watch beetle trouble. It will kill a beetle and pay for the copy of the pamphlet which I have read with interest. Though an ancient alumnus of Wesley College, Dublin, I am not a Wesleyan, being more of a Quaker, though little better than an Atheist in the eyes of old-fashioned Wesleyans and Quakers. Hence the meanness of my donation.

'When I was a boy,' said Mr George Bernard Shaw, speaking on behalf of the 1935 Tewkesbury Abbey Tower Appeal Fund, 'I could get into beautiful buildings for sixpence. Now I have to have tea with the vicar and give him a banker's order.'

Asked to support the restoration of Sir Walter Raleigh's eleventh-century church, St Mary's in Youghal, Ireland, Shaw replied on the back of a postcard bearing his disgruntled photograph:

As you may see by my expression I do not care twopence about your church. You had better sell it to America, where Raleigh, Spenser, and Cromwell (including his curse) are more popular than they are ever likely to be in Cork.

G. BERNARD SHAW.

Shaw to suffragette Sylvia Pankhurst rejecting her appeal on behalf of her Princess Tshai Memorial Hospital Fund for Ethiopian women:

You are whitemailing me. I can't afford it. All my spare money is grabbed by the Exchequer. Hospital trained nurses kill most of their patients by untimely washing.

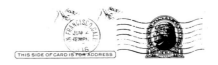

The 1906 case of 78-year-old socialist, Duncan C. Dallas, was a classic example of both Shavian tolerance and public abuse of his generosity. Throughout, he would repeatedly play upon the fraternal link, the 'fellow Socialist' connection, closing with 'Yours fraternally'.

Dallas's first letter, of March 10th, 1906, was surprisingly businesslike:

> . . . I feel that I am taking a great liberty in asking you to help me but I trust to your goodness of heart to help a comrade who is if possible more than ever an earnest Socialist & who for some 40 years past has been struggling to keep his head above water and avoid bankruptcy. Although now in my 79th year I am thankful to say that bodily I am hale & well & desirous to continue courageously working. Beyond a small amount of rent I owe my late landlords I owe very little and am not pressed except by the act of the new owner . . .

Dallas claims he has been forced to move quickly into new premises and asks Shaw for £50 to cover expenses, expressing his willingness to give him a first Debenture of his new Company at 6 per cent and redeemable in one year. Shaw sent the requested £50 unconditionally the very day he received Dallas's letter, penning on the Dallas I.O.U:

> In case I die before this is repaid my executors are not to attempt to recover this sum from Mr. Dallas as I lent the money on·the understanding that he was to choose his own time to repay.

Dallas's second £50 request came two months later. Again Shaw sent the money immediately. After offering to send Shaw one hundred £1 shares in his newly formed company, he adds that he would be pleased to give him fifty more shares as 'a grateful acknowledgment of your generous trust & timely help'.

With his second £50 I.O.U, Dallas thanked Shaw once again for his help, stressing their socialist link:

> I have once more to thank you for your great goodness in lending me another £50. I know you are not a millionaire. You are much better than such a social monstrosity. You are

a Brick! – a sterling gold Brick! Nay, better than all, you are
a true man & brother! Accept a brother's heart-felt thanks. I
shall do my best to repay you . . .

Less than two months later came a request for a further £35. Despite his obvious annoyance – 'Sent it – with a remonstrance (9/7/06)' – Shaw forwarded the money immediately. '. . . I will not come upon you again,' promised Dallas by return, '& I will do my best to repay you. I send on other leaf of this an I.O.U. for £35. My dear friend, the Workhouse must not be the lot of either of us.'

Dallas apologized in advance when 'begging' again a mere two months later: 'After writing you that my last application to you for a further loan which you so kindly responded to, was really the last, I am afraid you will think that I have no conscience in again asking your further help to the extent of £25 . . .'

A Shaw reply not forthcoming, Dallas wrote again five days later:

I wrote you on 6th inst: but as I have not heard from you I
am afraid I have offended you by again asking you for a
further loan to the extent of £25 after I had said so positively
that the £35 you sent me was the last. I sh'd be sorry indeed
to lose in any respect your esteem and I trust you will not
come to a hasty conclusion about me. I do not ask you for
this further proof to me of your kind consideration and
confidence without your having an opportunity of satisfying
yourself as fully as possible by your coming to see me here
that everything is fair and above board . . .

Two days later Dallas was penning a thank you letter for £6, which he assured Shaw would tide him over until the end of the month. Ten days later Shaw received yet another begging letter.

. . . The £6 you sent me will as I said enable me to tide over
till the end of this month but a quarter's rent becomes due
in a few days & that and current expenses for the next three
or four weeks will require about £20 to supplement what
comes in. If you can strain a point and lend me the £19
making up the £25 I asked you can really depend that that
will be and shall be the last.

Shaw not replying, Dallas repeated his £19 plea five days later, breaking the sum down.

I am afraid, dear Bernard Shaw, that you will have begun to

think me a very troublesome kind of a brother in asking your
further help as per my letter of 23rd inst . . . If it is any
convenience to you £10 wd be sufficient for the present and
the £9 in a fortnight afterwards . . .

Again, Dallas's efforts paid off as the extant letter bears Shaw's
holograph notation, 'Castle Haven sent £19 1/10/06'. Less than a month
later, Dallas was begging again:

I called to day at 10 Adelphi Terrace [Shaw's then London
flat] as I wished to see you & to show you an Agreement I
have just made with a manufacturer in Lancashire who has
appointed me his sole agent for London & *100 miles radius*
to promote the sale of a small machine of great domestic
utility and which has also a large sale in France, Austria &
other parts of the continent . . . I need about £3.10 per week
for a few weeks until the Cash which comes in becomes
greater as it will as the orders increase . . .

I shall not want more than £21 and I do not need to have
it all in one sum. If you will kindly let me have £7 now, £7 in
a fortnight and £7 in a further fortnight I shall be sufficiently
furnished and very grateful to you for I am in great anxiety. I
will report progress to you each fortnight and if I find I can
do with less than £7 I will honestly tell you.

I am giving the business every chance. I take out very little
for myself. I live on Minestrone, Spaghetti, Biscuits & a
couple of cups of cafe-au-lait. That is my daily portion
costing with sundry small expenses about 12/0 per week.

Two days later, in response to Shaw's kindly worded letter of
refusal, Dallas reduced his demand to £10: 'If you will let me have £10 now
I promise you most faithfully that I will not trouble you for anything
further.' No answer forthcoming, he tried again two days later. 'You may
think it strange that I shd not ask someone else,' he wrote to Shaw, 'but I
have no one I could ask who has means. All my friends are poor, and I have
not pushed myself among the rich.' After still no Shaw reply, Dallas wrote
yet again two days later what was his last begging letter to Shaw:

As you know 'it is the unexpected that happens' and 'you
never can tell'. Since I wrote to you a rift has opened in my
stormy sky and I have now the prospect of brighter weather.
I had a visit yesterday from a gentleman who has agreed to
come into the business to look after the outdoor work and
will bring a little capital at first & subsequently more. We

have agreed to terms and a draft agreement is to be put in hand at once. But he will not commence his duties till 1st Jan 1907 as he has to give a month's notice in respect of leaving his present employment but he will bring in some of the capital after the agreement is signed. I hope to get everything settled before 1st Decr so that from that date till Jan I trust to have the business in good swing for partner to commence his duties.

Now I shall be until the rest of this month somewhat crippled for want of ready cash. £6 will be sufficient. Will you lend me this? and as I shall be getting some salary from the business I promise faithfully to return the £6 to you by Xmas if not before. I trust you will do this and forgive but not forget your – I fear you must think – troublesome friend and brother worker

Duncan C. Dallas.

However, no further £6 was forthcoming. Having finally had enough, Shaw sent a card saying NO, noting for his records: '*Sent a card "I really mean it this time" 20/11/06.*'

On occasion, a begging letter could be audacious and charming at the same time, as this 1949 request for help setting up an acting company:

> . . . Before going any further I feel it is only fair to warn you that this is to be a cadging letter of the lowest order and I advise you to consign it to the waste-paper basket without further 'to-do'.
>
> However, since hope springs eternal even in the least sanguine of mortals and since it gives me no limited comfort and pleasure to write to you I will continue anyway . . .

As he often responded to the audacious approach, Shaw could on occasion be duped. A man once got a cheque from him on the pretext that he was leaving in such a hurry that there was no time to get a reference from his own bank to a London branch. In return, Shaw accepted a cheque on the fellow's bank. But, there was nothing there. To his secretary's surprise, he refused to prosecute. 'I certainly won't,' he told Miss Patch, 'I don't want everyone to know how easily I have been duped.'

65

From time to time Shaw had to contend with the accidents caused, not by himself, but by his chauffeur. One particular incident would belie the charge often laid at Shaw's doorstep of hardheartedness ... Shaw's chauffeur had accidentally killed the pet dog of an eight-year-old girl, Gladys Kershaw, while driving him through Accrington, Lancashire, on his way to a lecture meeting at Burnley on December 31st, 1909. This incident led to a revealing exchange of letters between father and play-wright, which began the day following the accident, when Mr Kershaw wrote to Shaw of his child's distress:

> Dear Sir
> On my arrival
> home last night
> I was told they had
> sad news for me –
> for a moment I thought
> our Daughter had got
> hurt   I was thankful
> I can assure you when
> I found such was not
> the case, yet very sorry to
> hear that our Pet Dog
> had got killed
> oh Sir if
> you only knew how bad
> our Daughter is
> you would
> I am sure or rather
> feel sure you would
> be sorry
> last night her
> Mother had to stay with
> her   it seemed to be
> her nerves,
> she kept repeat-
> ing Jess will never
> Bark again.
> one thing that
> hurt her Mother was
> the child saying that
> she did not want
> to say her Prayers
> because God had let her Jess
> get killed

she has just got of
to sleep for which we
are glad
    she is not like
the same Girl with
sobbing   her Eyes & Face
are quite swollen
she was to have gone
to her Auntys to day
but cannot unless
she changes   in fact
she does not want
to go now.
    A Manufacturer
called to see my
Wife who I suppose
spoke to you
he said you
was going to quick to
pull up for which
we were sorry
to hear
My Wife says he told
her that you said
you were sorry you
had not one[1] with
you we suppose you
meant a Dog
Now Sir I am sure
we shall be most
pleased if you have
one and would give
the same to our Daughter
& only Child to take
the Place of the one
Killed which was
so well known in
this district as a
Beauty not a Toy but
a Pet.
    It was like a
Large Size Brown Pom

1.   Shaw was trying to find his card, not another dog!

The man we bought
bought it from
called it a
Chinese Chew, Chew
Now Sir
      I hope you
can see your way
to send another
or P.O. towards
buying another
      If so
we shall I can
assure you be glad
especially our Daughter
Thanking you in
   Anticipation

            I remain
             Yours Truly
             A. B. Kershaw.

Shaw's reply was immediate:

Dear Sir

Your letter has only just overtaken me, as I have been on the road ever since the accident.

I am very sorry for the mishap to the poor doggie, and still more for the distress it caused your daughter. . .

She must not imagine that she was in any way to blame for the accident. Nothing, I am sorry to say, could have saved Jess. There were two other dogs in the road; and poor Jess was attending to them instead of the traffic. I was not driving myself at the time. We were passing another vehicle and just coming to a cross road, and were therefore pretty busy at the moment. My driver avoided two dogs, swerving a little to the left to do so. Suddenly a little brown dog, quite unconscious of us, and intent on the other dogs, stepped from the middle of the road right under us. It was so close that my driver did not see it. I warned him; but before he could get his clutch out we were over it. As it did not cry out, and we felt no shock or blow, we concluded that it had escaped either by crouching between the wheels or slipping out just in time; so we went on until I heard a shout, when I told my driver to stop, and looked back. The poor little creature died almost as I did so. It had been making a few convulsive movements, which must have been very heartbreaking to its young mistress; but it is very unlikely indeed that it suffered at all. My car weighs nearly two tons; and after the tremendous shock of being crushed by such a weight, it would be a long time before any living creature could feel anything. A hurt dog cries out piteously; but Jess only tried to get up; found that she could not; and died probably without feeling anything. I have had a violent accident myself, and can assure you that the pain does not begin until long after the smash.

Perhaps you had better not remind your daughter of the scene by repeating these details; but you may assure her that Jess never felt anything but a most bewildering shock, & died without knowing what was the matter; that she could have been protected only by keeping her on a string continually, which would have made her unhappy and unhealthy; and that I will buy another Jess for her if one can be found. By the way, what I was looking for and could not find was my card, and not, of course, another dog.

yours faithfully
G. Bernard Shaw

Before filing away Kershaw's letter, Shaw noted top left: 'Promised to buy the girl another dog if she can find one.' A cheque must have followed shortly afterwards, for on January 27th Mr Kershaw wrote again:

Dear Sir/
    Yours to hand last week
I now write to thank you for the letter
which will be prized very much not only
by Gladys but also her Father & Mother
We thank you also for the cheq, which we think
you have been most generous & takes away
any thought of hardheartedness & replaces it
with the thought not only of practical
sympathy but also of <u>Kind heartedness</u> & Love
Gladys Wishes me to send her love to such
a <u>Kind Gentleman</u>

PS
If you are not weary of hearing
from us
        we should like to write to

you again when met with a Dog
& should we meet with one & have
a balance left whatever it may be
our Daughter Gladys seems as though
she would like to purchase some
small article & Keep the Same as
having come from G. B. Shaw Esq.

PS
We are advertising this week for a Brown Pom.

On weddings and other occasions Shaw gave financial support to relatives and friends. In 1923 he provided a trousseau for his cousin Georgina, daughter of his mother's half-sister, Charlotte Rogers. (Three years earlier, buying Georgina at her request a violoncello, Shaw had written to her mother, 'I have bought a violoncello for your daughter. As she will have to take a cab when she wants to carry it anywhere it is the most expensive instrument she could possibly have chosen, except the double bass.')

To Georgina regarding her trousseau:

If you dont specify the sum you wont get anything. As it is, I will knock off £5 because you have put me to the trouble of writing a second letter.

How much will it cost you to go to your husband's house with a decent stock of clothes? Remember that underclothing is a safer investment than *much* overclothing, because it does not go out of fashion, and a change of figure does not affect it so much. What would your mother-in-law, for instance, consider a satisfactory and respectable trousseau for you? She must not be able to say that you came without a rag to your back. And your husband must not have to give you money for clothes until he is used to being a married man.

Now make a reasonable calculation; and I will see what I feel disposed to do.

I had no idea you were 21: I thought you were 16.

Mind: *dont* make me write one word more than you can possibly help: I have too much writing to do already.

And, finally:

23rd January 1923

My dear Georgina

That's better. Figures talk.

Very well. £65 for clothes, £5 for a trunk, £10 for odds and ends and pocket money. That makes £80. I shall have to give your mother £10 for the wedding breakfast. That makes £90. If you are very good, perhaps I shall give you the other £10 as a wedding present, but not until you are Mrs – by the way, did you mention the gentleman's name?

You certainly did not name the day – to *me*. When you do I will send the £10 to your mother. As she will spend it in about two hours I must not let her have it too long in advance, or there will be no breakfast.

You understand, dont you, that the £80 is to be spent on yourself, and not on paying debts or on other people?

In 1931 Shaw sat for a portrait sketch for an artist in Paris, after which the artist sent him his preliminary drawing. Deciding that he could do it better himself, the sitter then picked up a sheet of hotel notepaper and drew this picture which he afterwards sent to the artist with the comment: 'You have not drawn my legs on the caricature scale. This does them more justice.' After first checking that Shaw had no objection to the sale, the artist sold the sketch to an American collector for £150.

Over the years Shaw was frequently approached by impoverished artists wanting financial support. One – almost classic – exchange of letters took place in August 1906 between Shaw and the young artist Louis A. Sargent, and focused primarily on the subjects of money and genius. Sargent's lengthy letters detailed incidents of persecution, rejection and deprivation. He complained of having to prostitute his art by undertaking small commissions for money.

. . . I confess that I hate all this work, and only took it up to get money to paint; but while I had hopes in it, I put an immense amount of energy into the business.

Unfortunately, I never had any social connections. To this sketch I will add, that due to having been brought up on a diet of tea and white bread I have a very fickle digestion, and that my time has been, for the last 9 months, spent between more or less violent attacks of alternating appendicitis and pleurisy. I stop here to consider if I am piling it on thick. If it strikes you so, I beg to be excused. I wish to have my case entirely open before you . . . I hope you will see my work as soon as possible. Without my work, I am a begging-letter writer . . .

After telling Shaw that his avowed socialism and vegetarianism had led to his dismissal from the Royal Academy Schools ('Evidently I was not the right class – artistically, intellectually, or economically'), Sargent, very reminiscent of Shaw's own artist character Dubedat in *A Doctor's Dilemma* (begun in the same month), requested Shaw's help in getting his work exhibited.

> . . . So I am confronted with the extremely difficult task of convincing you that I am a genius. Should I not convince you entirely that I am a genius, I hope you will remember that all my painting has been done in wild spurts under unfavourable conditions, and that under reasonable conditions I should do much better. I do not intend this to be in the nature of special pleading, for if my work has not quality then I am very cheeky to write to you at all . . . Help me to get my work exhibited. Could you recommend me to anyone as a portrait painter, should I prove to you that I am competent as such? Do you know anyone who would like my work and buy it? And if my work appears to you to be sufficiently good, will you help me over my immediate difficulties by purchasing some. . . ?

Shaw, not normally one to buy works of art, did so occasionally to help particular artists. He took notice of Sargent's case, writing to the Secretary of the Royal Academy of Arts for information on the young man's student record. The Secretary replied immediately that as Sargent had not submitted the required work for the second term examination, he had ceased, *ipso facto*, to be an art student and that his political opinions would have been a matter of profound indifference. Then followed a further exchange of letters between Shaw and Sargent, G.B.S. passing on the information he had received from the Academy and Sargent countering the implied attacks at great length.

Eventually Sargent developed into a minor painter and sculptor, exhibiting in London and abroad between 1906 and 1927. Ironically, two years after his exchange of letters with Shaw, he would have a work exhibited at the Royal Academy itself! As with Sargent, Shaw checked up on the genuineness of a number of supplicants. One deserving case which came to light in the process was that of Clara Haines.

THE CLOVEN HOOF – AS G.B.S. DREW HIMSELF: 'MY AMBITION AS A BOY WAS TO BE A
GREAT ARTIST. I AM A WRITER ONLY BY FORCE OF CIRCUMSTANCES'

14th July 1907

Dear Sir
    The liberty I take in
writing to you is great,
but it is said of you that
you are 'a thorough going
humanitarian' which
emboldens me to write on
behalf of my son.
    He has gained a Scholarship
at Oxford with which, with
great care he can pay his
college expenses, but as
I am a Clergyman's widow
with other children to support,
I cannot meet the necessary
initial expenses at Oxford
for the elder boy.
    Can you help a woman

who tries to be independent
in this matter? If so,
you would be doing a really
good deed and gain the
gratitude as well as the
admiration (which you now
have) of us both:
The boy is thought to be
very clever, and a Candidate
for the Indian Civil Service:
He is looking forward to
being a member of the Fabian Society at Oxford.
With many apologies for addressing you

After receiving Mrs Haines's note of her son's initial £40 expenses, Shaw requested references. These quickly forthcoming, he sent the full sum. First commissioned April 1st, 1915, the young Haines (Maurice Arthur) joined the Indian Army three years later. He retired in 1947 to Canada with the rank of Lt Colonel.

A simple request from a childhood friend:

24th March 1910

Dear George Bernard
Will you lend me £400
for 15 years at 3p.c.?
Yours
E. McNulty

Shaw often gave more than was requested. When in April 1906 he was asked for a loan of £8.15.0 to publish three thousand copies of a socialist children's story, he sent £10 by return of post. Such requests would often lead to others, as in the case of one man, who, ready to repay the £10 he owed Shaw, enquired where he should send the money. He wrote of his growing photographic business and his desire to photograph prostitutes, adding:

> . . . But I badly need some money to keep me going until I get a living wage from my business. Do you feel sufficient interest & confidence in me to help me in this matter? I know of no adequate reason why you should . . .

And then, there was that proverbial ship coming in!

> Dr Sir,
>   If you are not too
> very much disgusted with
> me for not repaying the
> money you kindly lent me
> before I should like a
> <u>little</u> more till Monday
> morning when I will return
> both as the ship will
> arrive then.
>   Faithfully yours
>   Howard Williams.

In 1907 Shaw sent a young actor the necessary £10 to buy his way out of the army in which he had temporarily enlisted to escape what he fancied as 'the artificiality & emptiness of a stage career' . . . 'If,' the Lance Corporal wrote, 'you will do this for me, (my principal reason in writing to you is because you seem to be a Bohemian, a Free-thinker & certainly appear to have the courage of your opinions), I will promise to return the money in 8 weeks at the outside.'

While a variety of securities were offered for loans, many frankly admitted repayment was out of the question.

> Hammersmith, London
> 14th November 1937

> G. B. S. (Somewhere I hope)
>   Sir/(whether 'dear' is for later decision)
>   A begging letter but please don't go to Scotland
>   Yard about it . . .
>   . . . The wife and I (& a son) being perilously close to the
> very last ditch (& a dirty one at that), I am having a desperate
> shot at the most unlikely man I can think of. To quote a

certain playwright – 'Tis <u>not</u> b . . . dy likely' that anything will come of it.

I cannot try a preliminary swarm to get you into a receptive mood by stating I am an admirer of your various works. I have read but few of them & those don't stick. I prefer Edgar Wallace & even have the temerity to conclude you have not quite <u>yet</u> reached the standard of Bill of Stratford-on-Avon. Perhaps when you get old you may. But again 'not b - - - dy likely.'

I don't know you personally + that we may put down as mutually unfortunate . . .

I am perforce compelled to emulate the primrose by the river's brim. (This quotation is perhaps not altogether applicable to a fat old bloke of 15 stone) This obesity & rotundity, by the way, is not an asset to successful scrounging on (honestly) the very few occasions I try it. People won't believe that I can possibly be hungry with such a paunch. Yet I am too often empty bellied. Perhaps you will realise this when I tell you that the wife (an invalid terribly injured in a motor smash) & I have to exist somehow or other on 24/- per week from Public Assistance & that's all . . .

Will you lend me £50 which probably will <u>never</u> be returned? Any old sum would be a Godsend but I want permanent not temporary relief.

One ailing man of 42 wrote to the 87-year-old Shaw asking the latter to support him until the end of his days. 'I'm not whining,' he wrote, 'but I do want to live on, and I am getting weaker so noticeably now, for the want of so little – the right to live. I am 42, with my only relation a brother in Australia, I believe. I know you detest the poor, G.B.S. Does it go for the "maimed" too? . . . I am a fool to expect this will reach you. But I have written, I have tried.'

There were those, like the following Londoners, who gave Shaw accounts of their lives, a scenario of despair:

Leyton, London

Dear Mr Shaw,
. . . Here is a brief précis of my
decline to obscurity: – Met a girl
& fell in love. She was married but
as neither of us thought much of
the narrow minded dictatorship of

the law, we simply told her husband
& went our own way. Housing
shortage means we have to live
apart – so my expenses were doubled.
Superabundance of labour so
terrific that I was unemployed
for 3 months – result – got into
debt. Obtained job at £4 a week
– expenses £7 a week so am falling
further into debt. Baby is due 21st
August so hospital bills must be met.
– God knows how. Only hope is to
clear my debts & take 1 or 2 furnished
rooms together & fight it out till
divorce comes through about 2 years
time (can't afford to do it quickly
like the idle & intolerant rich).

So there you have the facts Mr Shaw
– my debts amount to £112.10s. – if
you could clear them for me, I will
pay back when possible, if you can't
help then I am, like most rebels – on
my own.

19th July 1945

Dear Mr Shaw.
    You perhaps never see begging
letters – I do hope you will see this one.
They say you are kind. I won't inflict
sheets of explanations on you nor try
to touch you by saying I'm Irish, hate
cruelty, and try to use my gifts.
I'll only say I am a woman in a
hole, a pretty deep one, and 'beg'
you for a hundred pounds. Please.
Please also, if you ever see this, forgive
me for bothering you.
<u>Please</u> help me.

Eighteen months before Shaw began *St Joan* he received from a young
Bulgarian woman, Franzi Trajanowa, a most pathetic letter, in which she
begged for money to restore the sight of her blind writer-husband. Joan's
dialogue, particularly that about the bells, is strikingly echoed by Mrs
Trajanowa's letter:

. . . I lifted up my work-worn hands to God, and begged the Almighty in my despair to save my husband's soul. Then my suffering ears heard the voice of an angel, that sounded like silver bells. The bells spoke the celebrated name of 'Bernard Shaw' and my eyes fell on your picture, showing you seated in your library, with your silver hair, and on your famous book 'The Devil's Disciple' of which we have a Russian translation. I remembered that when all the world was abusing poor, conquered Germany, you were the only one who lifted his voice in defence of them and spoke words of sympathy for a nation that had produced such great Masters, so that even non-Germans, such as we are, expressed their gratitude. How grateful I am to God for his message . . . I hope, honoured Master, that you will not resent this appeal, that you will understand the sufferings of my husband and myself and that you will stretch out a helping hand, a hand that has written so many celebrated works, to save us. Succour!! O heavenly word. My soul overflows in tears of gratitude – I can hardly contain myself – at the very thought . . .

Will you do this? Will you get us a piano, from the keys of which he can draw the wonderful music of the great composers, which will allow him for hours at a time to forget his hard fate and will carry his soul on angel's wings to the realms of melody and of greatest delight. Then you will have done the greatest deed in your famous career, my gratitude and later on that of the world will reward you. I am not appealing to you as an Englishman, but to you as a true artist and a noble being. Help me to lighten the darkness which surrounds my husband, to give him the moon which with her silver-blue light clothes everything in magic, can even turn the dull, grey village into a paradise, the dirtiest cow stable into a fairy hut, the rottenest bench into one of crystal, so that involuntarily one eagerly expects the arrival of the fairy prince and his suite . . . Trusting in God and in his guidance, in the hope that you, Master, will be prepared to help me, I close this long, badly written letter of my heart's sorrow, which will not permit good composition nor careful phraseology.

As did many of Shaw's correspondents, Mrs Trajanowa then apologized in a footnote/'P.S.' for the quality of her letter.

Honoured Mr Shaw,

I appreciate the unsuitability of the attached letter, but I can only ask you to forgive me. My brain has been much neglected lately, my hand is out of practice and the state of my nerves is likewise unfavourable for the penning of such a letter. I was awake all night and I was so agitated that I had to break off the letter frequently. Forgive me, Master, and listen to the woman who pleads with you from the bottom of her heart.

Soon followed another equally poetic letter in which Mrs Trajanowa described her husband's momentary return of sight.

Oh if you had seen his blind eyes weeping for one single moment of sight. It was indescribable what we experienced. I was petrified, I could not understand, I only saw his tears and his illuminated, godlike face, saw the pale, frightened child, that submitted silently to everything, as if he understood that this was the holiest moment in his and his parents' lives . . .

I plead with you oh Master, have pity on us, help us to go to Germany where they have had great success in restoring sight to the blind. I cannot bear it any longer, I am broken, my mind is confused and my nerves unstrung. I can hardly do my work in the house. . . . Oh Master, if you have ever had the desire to do good, then do it now and you will have done a noble deed for which God will reward you a thousandfold! If you know a true woman, who is a loving wife and mother, go to her and tell her of my trouble. She will understand me and will support me in our trouble and our effort to save my husband's one eye. . . . You as a true, famous author will help the artist and hero.

Forgive my insistence, my only hope lies in you. And ever and again the fear that the letters may not reach you, transfixes my heart with terror. My God, how shall I wait, how I shall tremble with the hope of good news which would give us relief. How sad and unhappy I am to be so utterly helpless. . . .

A 'P.S.' followed, more confident than the last:

I know you will help, I feel so comforted and strengthened. Please send to the Banque Nationale Sofia for credit of account in above name. Oh I beg of you, I beg of you. This is his 28th birthday, so young to have suffered so hard a blow.

Many of the most extreme letters – in language if not in need – came from Indians, as the following 1949 request from Cochin District, South India, addressed to *Mr. Bernad Shash*.

Respected Sir,
<u>Excuse me for my language which I am using here under.</u>
I, an Indian, beg to submit the following few lines for your kind consideration and favourable disposal.

I belong to a respectable family in this locality though very poor. I am surrounded by my close relations who are very rich, but insted of helping, they are troubling us especially on seeing my younger brother who is studying in a College. I have got my old father, my beloved mother, one elder brother with an unhealthy body and always sick, two sisters and one younger brother who is studying in the Maha Raja's College of this place. The above are depend upon me. I eagerly wish to give him education as possible as I can by begging with the Gretest men of the world. Thus I beg your help.

Also beg you to send me a copy of your Photo to place in my home to understand my present relations and my generations that there are human beings in the World who have got real education and who know the colour Black and white comes from the same.

Waiting the result of your Pen and Ink which are World renouned.

Yours faithfully,
M. Achutha Menon

On the very same day in 1949 the 90-year-old Shaw would receive two very different requests for loans:

McCauley's Hotel
Co. Donegal

Dear Sir,

I am seeking a loan of £20,000 for purchasing
land for intensive food production. I think that
in the present state of the world the greater the
food production, the better. More food and still
more food should be our aim. I shall be much obliged
if you would kindly say whether you will advance me the
amount mentioned (or part thereof). I should need
a period of ten years over which to repay the capital
sum together with interest. Repayment of £20,000
would be by ten annual instalments of £2,600 (other
sums pro rata). The rate of interest is *£5-1-6 per cent.*

There are some good estates on the market at the
moment. I shall be grateful, therefore, if you will
send me a reply stating the maximum amount which you
are prepared to advance.

John Coll

Dear Mr. Shaw

I am writing to ask you
if you could lend me the small sum
of twenty pounds for a few months
as I am terribly hard up which I
would pay back as soon as I could.
If however you did not survive
till then I would undertake to pay
to your estate the full £20 including
the death duties on the same. If I
did not survive (I am 60) I would
undertake to put in a good word for
you. I remain

Yours Hopefully
Robert S. Groves

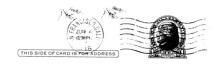

Periodically, correspondents, like the following unsuccessful writer from Swansea, offered to sell Shaw things:

> . . . Writing for nothing forces me to live on the winds, & unfortunately I haven't the ability to accomplish the feat. I am therefore forced to sell my typewriter, a £13.13.0 model Corona. I have had it for between three & four years, & used it very little. You can have it for £8 or £7, or you can lend me the money & I will send you the typewriter beforehand for inspection, & or security . . . I offer the typewriter to you because, being a socialist with plenty of money, you will be prepared to pay up to it's value . . .

But not everyone wanted money:

26 July 1946

Dear Sir,
    I read recently that you are very interested in photography and own two Leicas. To own a Leica is one of my lifes ambitions. I am employed on the Editorial Staff of one of the Irish Newspapers in a very junior position, and receive the sum of £1-17-7 per week, so you see I havent very much to spare. The purpose of this letter is to let you know that if by any chance, however remote that chance may be, you ever intend disposing of one of your Leicas please remember me . . .

Kevin Macmanus

On Books & Bookmen

Madam, no novelist whose mother goes bothering people to read her daughter's books has the smallest chance of success. The sooner Grace runs away from her home the better. Don't be a fussy maternal idiot.

Impolitely but sincerely,
G. Bernard Shaw.

– to a mother who wanted him to read her daughter's first novel

'I am not supposed to be an exceptionally modest man,' Shaw once commented, 'but I did not advance the fact that I have made more money by a single play than Shakespeare did by all his plays put together as a simple proof that I am enormously superior to Shakespeare as a playwright . . .'

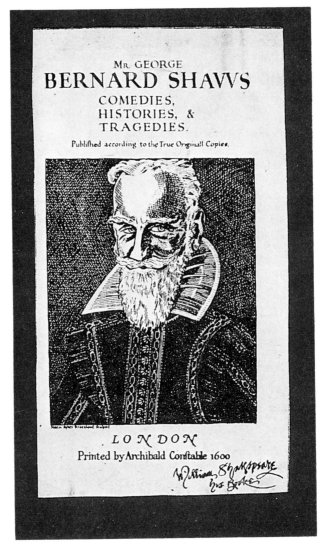

MR. GEORGE
BERNARD SHAVVS
COMEDIES,
HISTORIES, &
TRAGEDIES.

Published according to the True Originall Copies.

LONDON
Printed by Archibald Constable 1600

'WILL SHAKESPEARE'S OWN COPY OF G.B.S.'
A PICTORIAL JOKE PLAYED ON MR BERNARD SHAW BY MR
ALAN KEAN WHO DREW THIS TITLE PAGE OF THE SHAW FIRST
FOLIO, FAKED ON OLD PAPER TO RESEMBLE A LEAF FROM
THE TITLE PAGE OF THE FIRST FOLIO (1623) OF THE WORKS
OF SHAKESPEARE. MR SHAW RECORDED HIS VERDICT ON A
POSTCARD: 'AN EXCELLENT CONCEIT I'FAITH. I SHALL
STICK IT UP FOR MY FRIENDS TO LOOK AT'

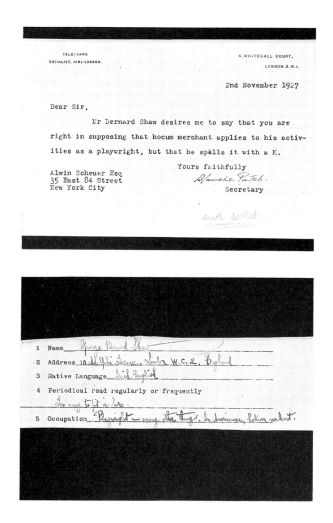

Over the years many different literary approaches were made to Shaw – for articles, copyright permission, and advice of all sorts. He was frequently asked to read both published and unpublished works and pass judgment on them. 'May the tiniest writer in the world write to the biggest one,' asked one supplicant. '. . . I shall not be able to eat, drink, or sleep, while hoping, and waiting, to hear from you.' He could be both encouraging and scathing in his responses, sometimes simultaneously.

> On the whole I found it a damned dismal book about people
> who ought not to exist . . . You make your people live all
> right enough. You would be much better employed in killing
> them . . . But you are probably worth insulting.

Works of varying degrees of competence were posted to him, dropped at his door, and in the case of the then unknown Lionel Britten, flung into his hands at a meeting of the Sexual Reform Congress. There were those who wanted professional advice on how to write, prepare a manuscript for submission, find a publisher or a career. 'There is nothing in literature for a man with seven children unless they are big enough to support him,' he told one would-be journalist. '. . . The circumstances point to your immediate retirement to the workhouse – all the nine of you. But somehow men like you don't do that. It is impossible for you to live; but the impossible will happen, somehow, though not until after a rough time perhaps, though I hope you will escape that . . .'

Many an author – both novice and experienced – tried to inveigle a Shavian preface, regarding such a contribution as a surefire guarantee of literary success. 'I never write prefaces less than 30,000 words long,' Shaw told one young man when turning down his request for a 200 to 300 word preface. 'My public expects to get its money's worth, and I give it. Besides, who would want to read your rubbish after my preface, I should like to know?'

Many a would-be poet or playwright, however, preferred money to advice, to be supported by Shaw whilst penning his own 'magnum opus'. One supplicant was engaged on a narrative written 'in the grand style', representing the 'passions and problems associated with the post-war phase in international relationships, viewed against a background of eternity.' Shaw, he hoped, would be disposed to support him for twelve or eighteen months, 'until the important work is finished' . . . One New York author felt his work to be 'infinitely more precious' than money. 'Here is a play,' he wrote Shaw, 'whose excellence astounded even me, its author. It is really, T H E play of the post-war era . . . whose vitality is so great that were it to be presented in a cow pasture, some sort of structure would have to grow up around it so as to house and shelter it fittingly . . .'

However, one sixteen-year-old 'poetess' from New York was far more diffident in her approach. 'I hesitate,' she wrote in October 1945, 'for two reasons, in writing to you. I feel that you perhaps will think my writing to you very strange and even a bit forward and secondly, I have read of your "terrible temper". The latter reason, however, I do not fear so greatly, since, with all due respect to the airplane, there is a great expanse of world between us.'

Some wanted Shaw to rework their efforts.

For the past 11 years I have carried in my head a plot for a novel, and (You will probably smile cynically at this) I have a queer idea that it could be fashioned into a best-seller . . .

   P.S. I hope you won't find any grammatical errors in this letter.

Still other correspondents wanted free copies of his 'best plaies', either for personal pleasure or, as one man put it, to judge for himself whether 'you are a great writer'.

And one group of performers, 'The Co-Optimists of 1930', wanted to include *The Apple Cart* in a performance of 'potted' plays at the London Hippodrome. Unamused by the suggestion that he should undertake the 'potting' job himself, Shaw sent his refusal via that convenient buffer, his secretary.

> Mr. Bernard Shaw desires me to say that his plays are useless for potting purposes. They are potted to the dispensable word before they go to rehearsal, and even in this condition they last three hours. And they cannot be burlesqued, because they are already as funny as they can be made.

An 'unsuccessful' New York writer wanted Shaw to pen his own life story.

> 'Once upon a time there was a man named Shaw. Shakespeare and Euripedes are jealous of his fame. Too busy living to write his life? Oh, pshaw! No one else can do his "Life" worthy of that name!'

> Uh – huh, I collect rejection slips when I can take time off from living and have money enough to waste postage! Only men of genius ought to set writing above living. I am neither man nor genius, except, perhaps, the latter as regards pie. Not genius? Humph! Any woman wants a man and mine, God and I love him even if he is a Scot, prefers pies to poems and dislikes jingles! So, I create pies. Proof? Eating! You're too far away to prove or disprove my contention. That's hard on you if you like pie. And the only time I ever got to Europe, you were away. Anyhow I was timid then!

> Couldn't you just announce in the newspapers that you were going to write your own life story? Then I would know you got this letter, and if you never got time to write it, people could say – 'Just another journalistic "filler"!'

I got a colossal nerve? Well, I have
seen several examples of that trait in
men like you whom I admire! The old
gag about irritation being a sincere form
of flattery is still good. All right – all right –
an irritation can be inferior in quality
and yet be made honestly! Enough.

As well as those who wanted a job, there were those who wanted professional advice on how to write fiction, drama, or poetry. Shaw told one writer
who requested a preface not to waste time on other authors but to badger
the publishers, and let his own light so shine before men that the publishers
would see his good works and put him among the best-sellers. In lieu of a
preface, he often read proofs, made amendments, and even added whole
passages to works. On the dozens of occasions when Shaw in fact wrote
prefaces to others' books, the result was a rush of letters asking for a similar
'send-off'. Most correspondents, however, had to be content with a
cream-coloured postcard.

Mr. Bernard Shaw is often asked to contribute prefaces to unpublished works. Sometimes the
applicants add that a few words will be sufficient. This obliges him to call attention to the fact that
his prefaces owe their value in the literary market to the established expectation of book purchasers
that they will prove substantial and important works in themselves. The disappointment of this
expectation in a single instance would destroy that value. A request for a preface by him is therefore
a request for a gift of some months of hard professional work. When this is appreciated it will be
seen that even with the best disposition towards his correspondents it is not possible for Mr. Shaw to
oblige them in this particular manner.

4 Whitehall Court (130)
  London, S.W.1.

Shaw refused to write a preface to either T. E. Lawrence's *Seven Pillars of Wisdom* or a new edition of one of Marie Stopes' books. He similarly rejected Dame Clara Butt's request for a foreword to give her biography a 'push off'. 'Good gracious,' he replied, 'I'd never dare . . .

> – You are a much bigger person than I. I should look like a
> ridiculous little busybody making a pretentious bow in your
> limelight . . . And, anyhow, what could I say? 'Witnessed her
> début as Orfeo. Loved her. Would have married her if she'd
> asked me. She didn't. Might actually have chosen Bernard
> Shaw and chose a Mr. Rumford instead! What a woman!'
> Don't you let anybody touch your book except yourself. If
> you find anyone impertinent enough to venture, burn his
> foreword and drop him into the dust bin – Ever and ever, G.
> Bernard Shaw.

Those fortunate enough to obtain a Shavian preface often got more than they bargained for, as in his preface to *The Poems of Mihail Eminescu*, where he described Sylvia Pankhurst's translation as 'astonishing and outrageous', continuing:

> Sylvia: you are the queerest idiot-genius of this age – the
> most ungovernable, self-intoxicated, blindly and deafly
> wilful little rapscallion that ever imposed itself on the
> infra-red end of the revolutionary spectrum as a leader; but
> that you had this specific literary talent for rhyming and
> riding our words at a gallop has hitherto been a secret.

The poet-tramp William H. Davies fared best of all, for his coveted Shaw preface ensured the immediate success of his book, *Autobiography of a Super-tramp*, now universally regarded as a classic. In his 1907 preface, Shaw described Davies' initial approach:

> . . . When Mr Davies' book came to hand my imagination
> failed me. I could not place him. There were no author's
> compliments, no publisher's compliments, indeed no
> publisher in the ordinary channel of the trade in minor
> poetry. The author, as far as I could guess, had walked into
> a printer's or stationer's shop; handed in his manuscript;
> and ordered his book as he might have ordered a pair of
> boots. It was marked 'price half a crown'. An accompanying
> letter asked me very civilly if I required a half-crown book of
> verses; and if so, would I please send the author the half
> crown: if not, would I return the book. This was attractively

simple and sensible . . . I opened the book, and was more puzzled than ever; for before I had read three lines I perceived that the author was a real poet . . . Here, I saw, was a genuine innocent, writing odds and ends of verse about odds and ends of things, living quite out of the world in which such things are usually done, and knowing no better (or rather no worse) than to get his book made by the appropriate craftsman and hawk it round like any other ware.

So instead of throwing the book away as I have thrown so many, I wrote him a letter telling him that he could not live by poetry. Also, I bought some spare copies, and told him to send them to such critics and verse fanciers as he knew of, wondering whether they would recognize a poet when they met one.

And they actually did . . . My purchase of eight copies of the book enabled him, I gathered, to discard all economy for about three months. It also moved him to offer me the privilege (for such I quite sincerely deem it) of reading his autobiography in manuscript . . .

Some were primarily interested in the mechanics of writing:

Dear Sir

Would you be good enough, before you leave this 'bank and shoal of time' – which I hope will not be for many years yet, to give a working man some practical advice as to the way to go about writing a book for publication; how to prepare the script; what size paper to use; what size margins to leave on the page; must there be one margin on the right – and one on the left of the paper?, how to put in corrections or alterations; must one's script be typewritten afterwards before a publisher will accept it; must one write in ink or will pencil do; is it best to write on loose pages or to use a special book of manuscript paper; etc. etc. etc . . .

Incidentally, who would be the best publisher to send one's script on Philosophy to?

I hope you won't think I am imposing upon you. I am a complete non-entity and I could think of no one better

qualified than yourself to ask advice on these matters and I
thought you would not mind setting one aspirant would be
Author on the right road to success before you quit us for a
higher sphere of usefulness.

There were, of course, those who wanted Shaw to read their manuscripts
or published books. In August 1937 a crowd in Whitehall Court, South
London, was surprised to see a policeman and a well-dressed, middle-aged
man kneeling together in the front hall of a service flat used by Shaw. The
constable had been called to remove the man, who had been asking for Mr
George Bernard Shaw. When told that Shaw was not in town, the man
remained kneeling in the hall for an hour, with a parcel of manuscripts by
his side, before being led away by the police.

The following is an extract from one of the most eccentric letters to come
Shaw's way. No signature or address were given, as the paranoiac correspondent feared someone trying to steal his cure-all for the world's ills: *room
ventilation*.

> Address & Signature to be
> forwarded later if req'd
> Writer
> anonymous.
> see text.

... to save millions from the dreaded cancer, lunacy,
suicide, domestic unhappiness; and the misery of
treatments for all these things and endless and useless
expense and degradation of it all, and colds, rotten
teeth, defective hearing, vision, and the senses of
thought, taste, and smell, and ruined and blasted and
made wretched carriers and shortened lives and
dreadful terminations from preventible disease,
can all be prevented and millions of the living and

countless ages of unborn posterity can all be saved
from these physical and mental and material
degradations due to ignorance of this simple
principle – any ordinary child can understand . . .

I should be glad of any title etc. That must be
of a striking and arresting character to compel
attention. I have concocted the following.

. . . This question is a fundamental; – above politics; above religion; – that it supplements and makes possible . . . My comment on this is; that bad air, I have proved in my own experience and Knowledge; causes all disease; lunacy, madness, hallucinations, suicide, and all the things put down to drug habits; inebrity, germs, colds, the climate, and cold and damp air – absence of sun – wearing too much clothing and the mosquitoes etc; that only transfer germs from diseased – to healthy subjects . . .

I am full of concern for the fact that rapidly increasing years are drawing shorter the time we shall have you with us – and have throughout, been using the utmost expedition within my power to complete the notes for your inspection whilst we have you still with us . . .

Yours very truly.
I nearly forgot.

And then there was the bizarre and convoluted eight-page letter in 1943 from a 73-year-old Wood Green gardener who sent an elaborate and confused film scenario for the 78-year-old Shaw to rework!

. . . / *Film* directed by Bernard Shaw and Dennis Warren *Charles Sills* / A Natural Play in Natural Surroundings. true in every detail. The characters are myself, the Village Folk. The scenery is the Beautiful Country.   The songs are already written, they suit the film in every way.   It would be the cheapest film ever produced.   The only outlay would be for the Photography.   Refreshments, Mr. Bernard Shaw & Mr Warren's fees, Kentucky Minstrels, Folk Dancing and nothing more. . . .

Film Story
A Natural Play in Natural Surroundings
Golden Wedding.
A Novel story full of incident Grave and Gay
I have shown this to several people.   When they Read it they are full of Emotion.   The tears roll down their cheeks. They grip my hand and say one word
SPLENDID. . . .

. . . Then I am really Gods chosen Disciple.   to tell of His second Coming What an Honour What fancy me, a very ordinary man and not a Good man.

The Lord Works in a miserious Way
quite different to Mans Way
Now Dear Mr Shaw you see why I am Impatient
I have to do the most important Work man was ever called
    on to do
Fancy me above all men and Not a Good one
House – Heaven.   The Actors and Actress the Angels
O this is funny   Film stars are Angels and the Cinema
the Church.   Stars Actors the Guides for Lost Souls
and my Work The Holy Bible No 2.   Religion up to date.
I am doing Sacred Work   I scream with
Laughter   I go to see the flowers and think
I have an Idea.
Change name of Film
Heaven in the Cinema
Stars
May West & Geo Roby.
What a rush for seats . . .

                  . . . Now I say again with great
Deliberation   I have succeeded where every one has
failed.   This is my job.   I have done it   It has been
accomplished in 30 minutes   It is now 10.28 P.M.
Smart Work Thanks to Gods Wisdom given
to me.   I have not done it.   Do not Thank
me   Thank God   All go on your knees and pray
earnestly to God.   Keep his Commandments &
Sing With All your Might.   PRAISE GOD
FROM WHOM ALL BLESSINGS FLOW. . . .

Dear Mr Shaw I have completed my little job. The easiest
and the most pleasant job in the World
Will you kindly read and advise if it would make a
film. Every one I have shown it to say, ONE WORD
SPLENDID   ALL THE LADIES CRY, THEN THAT STARTS
my emotion, then with Heart filled I leave
Perhaps It would make a readable Book   Everybody
seem to Say.   This should be a film.   Then we
discuss the Title I say Golden Wedding,   others
New World.   Come and see the Film.   Then All say
What's say a Film and a Book for those unable to
see the Film.   now then What About both
What say you Dear Mr Shaw.   Your great

admirer.   The Best man living.   I shall do
all you advise.   Please think it over.   Speak Straight
I want your Candid Opinion.

As I have a flair for Writing and can write rapidly
what do you say.   You be the Sleeping Partner drawing
75% and I the Active   25% would be enough for
a beginner.   Nobody need know   The property would
be yours.   I feel certain it would be a success   fancy
the Cinema Depicted as the Church. . . .
. . . Well I am going to Heaven-Little Berkhamsted
6 oc Sunday next Outside the church.   I have 100
Handbills printed . . .
And The Rector will preside   I am the speaker
I am not nervous.   I will not only preach   I will
act it as when I am in the film.
Now Dear Mr Shaw   Can you give about spare Hour of
your valuable time on Sunday next.   I have stated the
time & place.

Buses from St Albans go within ¼ mile pleasant walk
Kindly come and see the Vicar and Yours

Sincerely
Chas Sills

It is now 20 to 12 P.M.   I feel Happy having
finished my Work which is Inspired by God.
I am sending a few Tomatoes   Grown on my
plot re-named The Garden of Eden
Everything Grows well.   Better than anywhere
of course this is as it should be . . .

Come to the Garden of Eden.
   Near Village School.
   Heaven-Little Berkhamsted
   I am dying to see you
      Do Come – I know you will
         Good   Night Dear Mr Shaw
         from one of your Admires of Old.
         Plenty of People openly Say I am Mad
         Men do not Say you are mad
         But your writing is like the writing
         of a Raving Lunatic.

95

We are twin brothers   2 old Fogies over 70
time we were off the off to make way
for sensible men.
   I quite Agree

The vast majority of those who asked Shaw to read and criticize literary manuscripts and unperformed plays were sent a postcard reply of refusal. His opinion, Shaw suggested, could be of 'no service to authors, and even if favorable, might prejudice their chances seriously.' He was therefore 'obliged, in their interests no less than his own, to rule out all such activities.'

Shaw went to endless trouble dispensing guidance of a practical sort, ranging from how to find suitable subjects, to how to get into a poetry-creating mood. He was eventually driven to the expediency of composing a 1500-word open letter of advice for young playwrights, copies of which were run off in galley proof form and sent to all inquirers. This letter advised on how to prepare the script, to whom to send it, and how to handle business arrangements. It warned against permitting disappointment to cause the writer to stop writing, for the experienced playwright who took his profession seriously did not, having completed one play, wait idly, palpitating for its production. On the contrary, he immediately wrote another. They must not, Shaw warned them, send their plays to anyone but a manager, and *certainly* not to their favourite playwright in the hope that he might place their work for them . . . The playwright, Shaw hinted, might be more inclined to take the play's ideas for his own. He advised one young writer who naively inquired whether a man could 'educate himself to be a writer', to turn over the leaves of a good encyclopaedia until he found something that interested him, and then follow that up. It was no use knowing how to write unless you had something to say; and if you had, the words would come if you had any literary faculty; 'if you have none, you must seek some other method of expression.'

Some aspirants certainly needed help with their versification. To one of them, very busy with manual work during the day, Shaw made the astonishing suggestion that he should cultivate the habit of talking in rhyme, such as 'Molly, you sinner, where's my dinner?' or, 'I'm going shopping, down High Street, Wapping.'

In 1931 one would-be poet stopped Shaw in the Strand, and presented him with a sonnet he had written to him, beginning 'Bernard! Tis well thou'rt living in our day.' He read the sonnet, stroked his beard benevolently, and said, 'It's all right – it's all right – but why not write a limerick?'

Mortified, the poet told him he thought the loftiness of the subject more justly served by the sonnet form.

'Oh yes, the subject's very good,' responded Shaw. 'But unless you've got something really beautiful to say, don't write sonnets – try something else. Have you got another copy? Oh, that's all right – so long as I don't have to write a letter!'

Occasionally, a would-be poet would employ verse when writing to Shaw for help:

The Nurses Home
The North Staffordshire
Royal Infirmary
Stoke-on-Trent

30   7   46

Dear Sir

If this letter reaches you, which I doubt, it will be probably opened by some ferocious human specimen of a secretary, read and credited as the absent minded jottings of a fool, torn into numerous pieces and thrown into the nearest waste paper basket, to lie there in solitary state until some weary cleaner places it into the salvage bin, from whence it will be borne away to become, what? possibly returning to its former state – pulp.

If however by some strange fate you should read the contents herewith I pray your attention for a few minutes.

I am Eliza Doolittle the second, though my name is not Eliza, nor can the term Doolittle be applied to a member of the nursing profession, but in many respects I am similar to the character you created. Why? Because I am a nurse who wants to become a writer, just as Eliza or Liza was a female guttersnipe who wanted to become a lady, or did she?

Soaked in ether I dream of essays. Doing dressings I long for drama, handing out pills I make up poems, making beds I think of bibliographies, testing urine I think of Utopia, studying nerves I long to write novels, but I don't. Why? Because like Liza I ain't no writer yet.

Although I have a literary streak
What I write is a little weak.
For as yet I am like Liza

Uneducated and could be wiser.
Tho my imagination's vivid
Yet could drive publishers livid.
For I soar from depths to height.
Where no Editors in sight.
I have ideas by the score.
Needing yet experience more.
In my pen I find escape.
From routine, dull red tape.
My parents think I'm Nightingale.
Yet I feel this hope is frail.
Which may burn in inferno like Dante.
I feel more like Charlotte Bronte.
Most unusual, people say.
For at twelve I wrote a play.
Tho the script now is lost.
For indeed it would have cost.
Quite a sum to be a writer.
So had to be much brighter.
Earning my own livelihood.
As a nurse – not too good.
Always keeping in good view
What these literary blokes do
Tho this poem's very poor
Not good enough for G. B. Shaw
Yet may serve to illustrate
Just the fate of poor Kate.
Who finds life is rather brittle
As a literary Liza Doolitle
If this poem isn't nice.
What I need is good advice.

Some forty years later, Kathleen Doreen Rogers is still struggling to become a writer, having retired from nursing.

Shaw's judgment could be painfully accurate:

Swansea, Glamorgan
May 26, 1940

Dear Mr. Shaw:

I wrote to you, some six years ago, with regards to a book of poems that I was publishing – 'Strivings After Consciousness': you were good enough to reply, you did not condemn the poems but said they would not sell, they did not sell, this poet is still a brewer . . .

One correspondent had a very cloak-and-dagger approach to retrieving his manuscript on interpretations of selected thoughts of Omar Khayyám:

> . . . It will take you about ¾ of an hour to run quickly through my manuscript. If you choose to do me that charity, please let your method of communicating with me be the following: in case of an adverse verdict the manuscript will be returned to me tomorrow before 4 p.m. at your door through your servant without you having gone to the further trouble of accompanying it with written or verbal comment. I shall understand, and shall be convinced and at peace. If the verdict is in my favour, then you might arrange for me to come to talk with you for the purpose of arranging for a preface by you and for you then to receive fifty per cent of the profits accruing from publication in England and in any part of the world and in any translation. If you have not, and do not foresee, spare time in which to read the manuscript, kindly leave it (with a message about lack of time) with your servant to be called for by me to-morrow afternoon. And then I shall naturally be disappointed, but no worse, if no better, off than I was before . . .

If he possibly could, Shaw would fend off receiving others' books:

> Dear Dr Devon
>   Do not send me the book: I have ordered it from my bookseller. We authors cannot live by taking in one another's washing.

In a postcard acknowledging the receipt of a book by Pierre Loti, he wrote that it was 'in morocco raiment, much too fine for my dustheap. I shall certainly give it to the next woman I fall in love with.'

Shaw occasionally gave advice on what to read. When he was visiting South Africa in 1932, Mrs Sarah Millen, the novelist and biographer of General Smuts, arranged an extraordinary meeting over breakfast between the two men. Not unnaturally, they did not get on. But Smuts gallantly tried to make conversation. 'Mr Shaw', he asked, 'can you recommend me a good book to improve my mind?' Shaw leant forward and whispered, 'General Smuts, there's a book by D. H. Lawrence which every schoolgirl of 15 should read, and it's called *Lady Chatterley's Lover*.' The novel was unknown to Smuts, as was the novelist. When he asked for it next day at a library, he was shocked to learn that it was an 'obscene' book banned in every 'decent' country in the world. Thereafter he never allowed Shaw's name to be mentioned in his presence.

One of Shaw's longest running correspondences about 'nothing' took place with 'n'er-do-well' Kerree Collins. Their three-year correspondence over a lost manuscript presents Shaw in a most amusing – and generous – light. An attempt by Collins to interest the Royal household in a children's story of his, as reading matter for the then young princesses, failed, as did his attempt to sell the serial rights to a national newspaper and the film rights to a British director. Undaunted, Collins sent the manuscript to Shaw in 1937, asking him to preface the work and send it to a publisher! 'Its style and treatment,' wrote the enthusiastic author in his 2,000-word accompanying letter, 'will remind you of *Alice in Wonderland* . . . It is called "The Little People of Rainbow Land," and is 60,000 words in length.' G.B.S's reply was brief:

5th July 1937

> I haven't the time to read your book.
> I have not enough time to read my own books.
> Moreover, it is not my business.
> However, do not be discouraged.
> My first book was not published for 50 years.

Anticipating a refusal, Collins posted his manuscript off before Shaw had a chance to reply.

Collins, it proved, was as expert at changing addresses as jobs (forty-nine by age thirty-three!). Shaw's attempt to post the manuscript back failed, and it was returned to him at Ayot St Lawrence marked 'Gone away'. Three months later, from Twickenham, where he was temporarily settled, Collins wrote for news of his precious book. Shaw replied in red ink at the bottom of the letter:

> It was sent back to the address you gave, and returned by the Post Office. What has become of it, heaven alone knows. I dare say it will come back presently and be sent to the address given above.
> If you send it to me a third time it will go straight into the dustbin.

A month later, Collins wrote from yet another new address: 'Almost I do not care whose dustbin it is in . . . I would ask you as a special favour if you could complete this Post Office form . . .'

To which Shaw replied:

> . . . As it was not destroyed it must be somewhere on the premises. I have no time to look for it, but it is statistically certain that it will turn up presently. Meanwhile keep me advised of your changes of address.

On March 5th, 1938, Collins wrote again: 'Three months have gone by . . . If you happen to be doing nothing one day, have a look for it yourself.' Back came a G.B.S. postcard:

> Instigate a search!! Man alive, I have lost a month's work looking for your confounded book. It has been worse than three removes and a fire.
> As a last resource I will try the Dead Letter Office, if you will remind me of the title of the book and of the old address . . .
> If it proves that the book, which must be somewhere, is in effect nowhere, you had better rewrite it as Carlyle wrote his French Revolution when Mill's housemaid burned the original, or else produce a fresh set of stories. No use crying for spilt milk.

Back came a Collins rebuke: 'I'm sorry you've lost a month's work looking for my book . . . But look how much time would have been put to better use if you had read my book in the first place . . . it is like the casuist who wastes time trying to prove the fact of his existence instead of getting on with the art of living.' The book, Collins informed Shaw, was worth far more to him than a few drops of milk, estimating its value at £500. 'My book was an inspiration . . . Have you looked in the potting shed?'

Shaw countered:

> That confounded MSS. of yours has become an obsession
> in this household. I have set the Dead Letter people
> searching for it; but I am convinced it must be in either of
> my houses. I certainly did nothing with it after you infuriated
> me by sending it to me.
>
> Even if you write it over again half a dozen times, the
> question of its disappearance remains unanswered. You
> may even die, and I shall still want to know how it happened
> and where it is. I cannot have MSS. vanishing miraculously
> from my study. I have no domestic animal capable of eating
> it.
>
> In my search I discovered bushels of plays and treatises,
> some 30 years old, that have never been reclaimed. But
> yours – no. Where! Where!! Where!!!

After some three months' lapse, Collins wrote again, suggesting that 'some of those film people who have been seeing Mr. Shaw lately' might have borrowed the book to take home to their children. 'My friends say, "Why don't I send all my MSS. to you?" This . . . reminds me of the mystery of the lost concerto by Schumann . . . I want to think one of your guests has taken it . . . It may be in America now. If I could have got my book into the hands of Disney! . . . You have done me out of £50,000.' Shaw replied on a postcard bearing a recent photograph of himself. He said he was ill and forbidden to worry about anything . . . 'but I remain convinced that the thing MUST turn up some day. Meanwhile write something else.' What happened next shouldn't have surprised Shaw. Back came a photograph of Collins himself together with a request to publish their correspondence!

> Dear Baby Collins,
>
> I have seldom been more amazed than by your
> photograph. Your letters suggested 13 to 17 as the extreme
> limits of your age. If you are 33 – and the picture is that of a
> robust adult – I give you up.
>
> You now want to publish my letters to you. Have you not
> read of the tailor who tried to get into London society on the
> strength of having had his nose pulled by Count d'Orsay?
>
> Have you no self respect? Dont be an infantile idiot!

'. . . Creditors haunt my door . . .' Collins wrote soon after, 'tell me where I can get the best price for your letters . . .' Back came a piece of uniquely Shavian financial advice:

When creditors press you for debts that you cannot pay
do not lose your nerve and try to put them off by promises to
pay next week, or pretences that you have expectations that
will be realised if only they will wait. Remember that the
position of a destitute person is impregnable: the County
Court judge will not commit you under a judgment
summons unless the creditor can prove that you have the
means to pay. Maintain an insouciant dignity, and announce
your condition frankly.

If proceedings are threatened (say by a Trade Society for
next Thursday) beg them not to wait, as you will be poorer
on Thursday than on Tuesday. At the same time be grateful
for the credit already received, and sympathetic with the
inconvenience caused by your insolvency.

In the case of a personal loan ask for another. If the
creditor is your tailor, order a new suit, as you cannot get
employment unless you are well dressed. Above all, don't
bother ME about it.

On October 14th, 1938, Collins, after yet another move, wrote
begging old hats, trousers and pants. G.B.S. replied with £5 and advice on
where to shop for the best value!

. . . In Piccadilly you can get a smart winter suit for £3 10s.
In the City or suburbs you can buy a quite presentable hat
for 10s. In Houndsditch on Sunday morning you can buy
three or four overcoats and half-a-dozen umbrellas with the
balance, but perhaps you had better spend it in
underclothing at Hopes, unless you prefer to send the whole
to the Artists' Benevolent Fund.

Perhaps I may be able to find you a cardigan, as it is an
impersonal sort of garment; but I will not promise until you
are externally equipped sufficiently to get a respectable job.

I shall not repeat this extravagance.

For the next six months Collins sent Shaw letters and fantastic
sketches from at least six addresses, all without reply. He then wrote, 'If I
take the trouble to walk all the way to Ayot St Lawrence, will you let me in?'
The threat worked. Shaw replied hastily:

Most certainly not. Idiots who will do nothing but talk
about themselves are specially kept out. Why do you not
write an essay on Shooting the Moon? Your frequent
changes of address suggest it. Or on 'My Landladies'?

Although Shaw refused to see him, Collins managed to get through to him on the telephone nine times, and continued to hound him with letters, half of which were left unanswered. By November 23rd, 1938, Shaw had had enough:

> . . . What screw is loose in you that you cannot get
> employment as a correspondence clerk or advertisement
> writer at least. You can write. Few people can, in the literary
> sense. Anyhow, stop bothering me.

But Collins was having too good a time to stop. Although the correspondence became scrappy, it did continue spasmodically. Shaw even gave Collins a pair of brown boots and, moreover, had them cobbled several times when they were worn through, and Collins was unable to pay the cobblers. However, he was far from pleased:

> What the devil do you mean by dumping your worn-out
> boots and secondhand books on me? My housekeeper in the
> country . . . has sent them to the village cobbler to be
> repaired. If they ever turn up again, they can be sent on to
> you. Meanwhile buy a pair of goloshes with the enclosed, to
> keep your feet dry; and stop bothering me. I have no time to
> spare for you.

Shaw was even less pleased when, on September 30th, 1942, Collins tried once more. 'Dear G.B.S. – Dare I send you once again, your most inestimable boots to be mended for me? Or will you be offended? The year has long gone by since last you mended them – and, as usual, the uppers are still sound, but the soles are gone.' Shaw's patience, however, like Collins' soles, had worn thin:

> If you dare to send them you will never see them again.
> The war has absorbed the village cobbler. And I am at the
> end of my patience with you.

Audacious, if nothing else, Collins then decided to sell the boots to a Shavian collector for £5, who, before purchasing the footwear wrote to the former owner for authentication. Shaw replied:

> The boots are authentic. Mr. Kerree Collins, to whom I
> gave them, wore them out, and then sent them back to me to
> be repaired. Having worn them out again, he is, you tell me,
> offering them for sale as relics for £5. Their cost when new
> was about 35s.

If you feel the slightest temptation to buy them, you had better consult a psycho-therapist doctor as to the state of your mind.

Despite this rebuke, bidding for the boots soon reached twelve guineas!

Shaw also assisted Collins in another matter, suggesting he should fill in a Ministry of Labour unemployment insurance form in the following manner:

> I am for all ordinary commercial purposes an unemployable. I can give references on this point to all the firms from whom I have obtained employment – usually for a few hours only – by representing that I am a skilled tradesman which I am not.
>
> I can boast of a ready pen, and am admitted on all hands to be a Confounded Nuisance. There must surely be room in the public service for these as well as for the more conventional qualifications.
>
> I believe that if I were placed under an iron discipline and severely flogged once a week or so, I might make good.
>
> Signature of Claimant . . . Collins.
> Address . . . Every apartment house in Richmond, Surrey.
>   I have been in all – for a week.
> Name of Association . . . The Guild of Richmond
>   Good-for-Nothings.
> Name and Full Postal Address of Branch Secretary . . .
>   Collins. Secretary and President.
>   Address as above.

At last, Collins wrote that he had a job out of town. Shaw, delighted, sent £1 for his fare with a card, 'I will not pay your fare back.' But Collins could not take the job. He came down with 'flu and spent Shaw's pound on oranges and medicine!

An eccentric himself, Shaw 'collected' like souls. 'I shall probably write Mr Collins a great many other letters if he goes on as at present,' Shaw commented early in their association. 'He's an extraordinary card.'

The 94-year-old Shaw would receive the most heart-rending of letters, some of which were so pathetic that he could be forgiven for questioning their genuineness. From Laurens, South Carolina, he received the following in August 1946:

Dear Sir.
                              I humbly
Beg pardon for this intrusion.
                         I pen these
Lines with crippled hands.
                         hands that truly
Reach out across the sea.
                              hopeing praying for
the understanding that my fellow Americans
have Denied me.
                    so I appeal to you Sir
the greatest of all writers. to Lend a
helping hand to a struggling amateur
writer in far away america.
I Recognize the heart Breaking Fact that
I am handicapped for Lack of Education . . .
                         . . . I am sure my
stories would sell. for there are many
common people like myself who would like
the stories I write
Mr Shaw I cannot express my appreciation
for any advice or help you may give me.
Being a writer you can understand.
Why I cannot give up hope of a
Brighter tomorrow. When all my
yesterdays have Been so filled with
Desolation and Dispair.
I do not Blame my precious old
parents that I was placed in a
Textile plant at the tender age of twelve
years. they needed Despertely the little
I earned. I loved my work.
                         I was a weaver
and a good one I assure you . . .
Mr Shaw forgive me please that I
would Dare intrude. may I send my
favorite short story for your opinion? out
of your life of Blessings and plenty
I beg only 20 minutes of your precious

time the time Required to Read the
Entire story . . .
please Believe I am not so Dumb
as this poorly written Letter would
indicate.
P.S. Mr Shaw. I am 46 years old. Both hands
have three fingers grown to gether   good good night.

One then comparatively obscure playwright to benefit by Shaw's criticism
was Noël Coward, whose 1921 play, *The Young Idea*, bore a close resemblance to Shaw's own *You Never Can Tell*, so close in fact that it was sent to
Shaw for his consideration. Not only did G.B.S. have no objections, but he
never even hinted at plagiarism! Quite the contrary. The script was
returned with constructive suggestions for rewriting the last act; and
helpful advice penned in the margins, such as, 'Oh no you don't, young
author!' A long letter followed, which Coward, as he recalled later, 'was
idiotic enough to lose' . . .

27 June 1921

Dear Mr. Coward,
    I gather from Mr Vedrenne that he turned the play down
because he had some misgivings about trying to repeat the
old success of the twins in You Never Can Tell, and was not
quite sure that you had pulled off the final scene which I
suggested. But when once a manager has entertained a play
at all, his reasons for discarding it are pretty sure to be
business and circumstantial ones . . . your twins will take
some casting to make them pardonable. I daresay Vedrenne
did not know where to lay his hands on the right pair.
    I have no doubt that you will succeed if you persevere,
and take care never to fall into a breach of essential good
manners, and above all, never to see or read my plays.
Unless you can get clean away from me you will begin as a
back number, and be hopelessly out of it when you are forty.

'It was,' Coward wrote later in his autobiography, *Present Indicative*,
'as might be expected, a brilliant letter, and I took its advice only half-
heartedly. But there was more than brilliance in the trouble that that great
man had taken in going minutely over the work of a comparatively unknown

young writer.' Coward, however, lived to regret having paid this autobiographical homage to Shaw, for when the book was published he was inundated with unsolicited playscripts requesting support similar to that G.B.S. had given him. Varying in tone, the letters almost always mentioned Shaw, ranging from supplications for Coward to 'be as kind to me as Mr Shaw was to you' to the more commanding 'I am young and poor and struggling, now it's your turn to help me as Bernard Shaw helped you.'

(LEFT TO RIGHT)
A 'FRANK' WOMAN NOVELIST, SHAKESPERE', SHAW, WELLS, BENNETT, ALDOUS HUXLEY,
D.H. LAWRENCE, JAMES JOYCE. EACH IS ACCOMPANIED BY HIS LITERARY INSPIRATION.
(AT BACK) DICKENS AND JANE AUSTEN

Friends as well as strangers – as Marie Stopes was to discover – received the same unbiased critical judgment from Shaw. The year 1917 saw the completion of both Marie Stopes' first book on sex and marriage, *Married Love*, and a play – which she duly sent to Shaw for his opinion – loftily entitled, *The Race, or Ernest's Immortality*, a New Play of Life, in Three Acts. There was no question about it, Marie Stopes' would-be masterpiece was no great work. 'Dottissima,' wrote Shaw:

> . . . Short of rewriting this play, I can do no more with it than cut 20 pages just to show you how you should cut the rest. You haven't used your brains on it one bit. Would you find me very interesting if I had nothing more to say than 'dowdy frocks, foolish ideas, blue stockings and spectacles,' and such like reach-me-downs? You think you can make a motor bicycle by taping a second hand tool bag on an old poker and hanging a few worn out ribbons on it; but you can't. You must cut out anything that does not get your play along; and if you wish to convey that your hero's hair is turning grey,

you must leave that to his wig maker and make-up box, and not spend pages of irrelevant twaddle on it.

Until you take the stage more seriously than you take a coal mine you will never do anything with it . . .

In the case of Frank Swinnerton, Shaw's criticism was rapier sharp.

Dear Sir

I have read Nocturne. I must say you young writers (if you <u>are</u> young) spread your butter thin and make it go a long way. There are pages and pages of Nocturne that would not last me half a line.

On the whole I found it a damned dismal book about people who ought not to exist. Dont you get tired of a world in which there is nothing but squalid poverty and women cut off above the waist? You impress me as a discouraged man discouraging other people. You may have your uses; but I wish you wouldnt . . .

However, you make your people live all right enough. You would be much better employed in killing them. You also have a pathological nightmare, in which, whilst striving towards a happy ending, you can never get to it because a series of trivial and sordid obstacles and objections continually interfere themselves. I get dreams like that when I am run down . . .

You are only a wretched artist, with only one subject. But you are probably worth insulting. That is the object of this tonic letter. Look round a bit and let yourself rip.

Some, however, like this Auckland man, preferred not to have Shaw's opinion.

20th March 1938

Dear Sir,

Thirteen years ago I sent you the ms. of the first scene of a play *The Mountains* which you didn't like.

A few years later I sent you the same thing tentatively

complete in novel form. You didn't answer my letter, which
I took to imply:
   (a) Worse, not better.
   (b) You don't like novels anyway.
   (c) Since the publication of *The Intelligent Woman's
Guide* at 18f (N.Z. price) you have dropped your vulgar
clientèle . . .
   . . . I have had my first book published – on a royalty basis,
which is most encouraging, after thirteen years. I beg that
you will accept the enclosed copy of it.
   Further that you will refrain from telling me what you
think of it . . .

Some supplicants hadn't even read Shaw and a number claimed – at
times defiantly – to be in no great hurry to do so. At ninety-four and less
than three months before his death, Shaw continued to receive 'What do I
do with my life' requests, as in the following from Tufnell Park, North
London.

Dear Mr. Shaw,
          It has been said that many young
writers like to quote Shaw. Why, I don't know.
I never do.   Indeed I cannot for I have never
read Shaw – although I would like to and
have no doubt that I shall in good time.
But I can quote myself – and I often do! . . .
   I hope that some day I shall be able
to call myself a writer.   I hope I shall
be able to earn security by my pen.   I hope
for a little fame.   A little niche in the
world of letters.   Is it wrong to hope this?
I work and pray and dream and scheme and
plan with this end in view.   Every now
and then I take out my ambition, polish
it up, and examine thoroughly . . .
   I cannot write nor speak nor even
think in words of more than two syllables.   Am
I being <u>too</u> ambitious when I say I want
to be a <u>writer</u>?   Am I <u>too</u> ignorant?   Have
I the ability?   Or have <u>I</u> just been deluding
myself the past few years?   Indulging in
too much wishful thinking?   Do I hope too
much? . . .
   I was born in a slum

of a drunken father and an indifferent mother and I think that – in a
way – my mind has not yet left that slum
and that life.   Perhaps I am anticipating
failure and blaming that failure in advance
on my background and ignorance.
     What do you think, Mr. Shaw? . . .
                                My collection of
rejection slips grows weekly.   (Perhaps my
hand writing depresses editors) . . .
     I know very little about you except what
I have learnt from hearsay – although I have
already begun to remedy that.   I'd been told
that G.B.S. was the man who wrote witty
postcards from Hertfordshire and had a heart
of gold, though he tried hard to hide it.
So I wrote him a begging letter which was –
rightly – refused. Then I wrote him an
insulting letter which was – rightly again –
refused. Now I write him a humble
letter.   I wonder what will happen –

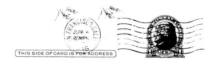

On occasion, Shaw paid for would-be writers to have their works professionally typed, as in the case of Miss Mary Madden of Leeds:

July 1915

Dear Madam
     What is the use of sending the story to me? I am not a
publisher. When I write stories myself, I have to take them
to a publisher and not to another author. Even if I liked your
story and took it to a publisher, he would be so angry and
disappointed at my not offering him something of my own
that he would bear a grudge against you for the rest of his
life. And then, when am I to read it? I have stacks of things
to read that would take me two years to get through if I did
nothing else all the time.
     However, if you send it to me, I'll get it typewritten for
you; and then you can try your luck with an editor.

In 1928 Shaw corresponded with a young African missionary, Mabel Shaw (no relation), at the girls' school at Mbereshi, Northern Rhodesia, who wanted to write about her experiences.

Dear Miss Shaw
   A friend of yours has shewn me some of your letters, and asked me – as I found them interesting – to let you know whether I thought you qualified to take up literature as a profession.
   As far as mere literary faculty is concerned I should say decidedly Yes. You have evidently no difficulty in putting into writing anything you want to say or describe, and in such a way that the reader reads willingly and expectantly. No more than this is required of the greatest authors as professional qualification.
   But success in literature depends on what you have to say as well as on how you say it . . . Whether you are enough of a freethinker to be successful in literature outside your own sect I cannot say . . .
   The question is, then, would your descriptions of your own discovery of God please a sufficient number of bookbuyers to make a profit for a publisher and bookseller and a living for you. I think it quite likely they would. I have found your scraps interesting; and I am not in sympathy with you at all. I am not in the least what modern psychologists call a masochist: that is, a person with a queer lust for being tortured; so that when your parents no longer tortured you you tortured yourself . . .
   You meet a young man with whom you fall in love, and who falls in love with you. There was nothing to prevent you making him and yourself happy by naturally and unaffectedly marrying him and filling your lap with babies. But no: that would not have been any fun for you: you must break his heart and break your own (if you have one) on the ridiculous pretext that the negro children needed you, though your own country was swarming with little white heathens who needed you as badly as they need Margaret

McMillan[1] in Deptford. And then comes your artistic
impulse. You must write about it and make a propaganda of
voluptuous agony. Well, there are plenty of people who find
agony voluptuous on paper; and they will make a reading
public for you. But I, who loathe torture, and object most
strongly to being tortured, my lusts being altogether normal,
should take you and shake you were it not that you are out of
my reach and that you would rather enjoy being shaken if it
hurt you enough.

It may be that this psychosis (pardon the jargon) will pass
away as your glands mature. At the bottom of this African
business there may be a young woman with a healthy taste
for travel, novelty, adventure, and salutary hardening
hardship. You may not really have wanted that unfortunate
young parson whom you smashed up . . .

And that is all I have to say to you on the little information
I have about you. You may think I have said a great deal too
much; but I assure you the question of becoming a
professional writer is a pretty deep one when the intention
behind it extends to becoming a prophet as well. I am in that
line myself; and I KNOW.

And anyhow you brought it on yourself. I wonder what
you expected me to say.

As well as literary and theatrical advice, Shaw gave musical advice. All three
were based on practical experience. From one American, the 91-year-old
received a most audacious request on February 19th, 1947:

Dear Mr. Shaw:

In your capacity as musician and music-critic, not as
writer, I am taking the liberty of sending you Four Songs by
William Blake which I have set to music – one Love Song,
one Risqué Song, one Diabolic Song, and one Song of
Innocence. These are representative of a number of Blake
poems which I have set.

Now William Blake was an evangelical, not a sentimental

---

1. Margaret McMillan worked with nursery school children in Deptford in South London.

or romantic poet, and least of all a mystic, as that word is ordinarily understood. In a manner of speaking, he was you – a somewhat more grumpy and knotty-headed you, whose external talents happened to incline towards the lyrical and expostulatory, rather than the dramatic and didactic. For this reason, his poems cannot sanely be set to music in the usual romantic or discursively impressionistic modern manner. Hence I cannot get these songs of mine performed, or even listened to, here in the United States.

If the meaning and quality of my music are apparent to you (two playings will be required, if you are in the least harassed or oppressed in spirit before the f st one) would you mind abandoning all your other activities for four or five months, and devoting all of your position and authority to getting them performed, privately or publicly, by someone in England? I ask this of you because I am he who once seized the flesh of Blake, Bunyan and yourself, and am now appeared again as a composer of music, aged 36, in this strange place called the United States of America.

The elderly Shaw replied in no uncertain terms – and in his own hand – by return of post. This was no case of 'gratuitous offensiveness', but a highly justified attack.

I am not by profession a musician; and it is half a century since I was a critic.

I am also a very old man without many months to live. I cannot spare you '4 or 5' of them to do your business as well as my own. You must be an extraordinarily thoughtless person to make such a request. Your songs must make their own way. Two playings are not necessary: a glance takes them in as simple little tunes without a single progression that would have surprised a baby in the XVIIth century. They have been rejected probably because being easy and childish, you have associated them with the great name of Blake instead of with Mary Had a Little Lamb. You have mistaken your size.

Some correspondents preferred money to literary advice. 'I have also,' Shaw recalled later:

> . . . received an S O S from a poet whose suit had caught on fire and he was now left without any clothes whatsoever. No doubt consumed like myself by an inward fire! I could remind him that the happiest man according to fable is the man without a shirt to his back, especially in these days when laundries are so impossible. I've never worn a so-called shirt. I have helped a poet once before. I saw real merit in his work and knowing that in this country of Shakespeare, Shelley and Browning, no poet can hope to make a livelihood I gave him a useful sum so that he could devote himself completely to poetry and write the masterpiece I expected of him. Instead of writing a poem which might have placed him among the immortals he settled down to writing a popular play so that he could pay me back ten-fold. No one would touch the play and in despair he committed suicide. As I don't want to kill off any others I can only save them by withholding all financial assistance.

There were those that wanted Shaw to keep them:

Buenos Aires
September 1941

> Mr. George Bernard Shaw
> (The playwright, nay, The Man!)
> This is the fourth or fifth time I have written to you, so far, never having posted them, not one. The others were simply the desire to write to you about different things and to hear from you. This one has to do with money. Don't stop here, go on reading. I am already twentyfour and see no way out to quitting my job so as to have time to grow and flower and drop my kernels. I propose you give a bank one thousand pounds to be paid to me at the rate of eight a month. That would be during exactly ten years. My present salary in pounds would work out at more or less eighteen pounds a month. So I have my living assured for the exchange of 8 hours a day of life which really turns out 22 hours or more . . . my brain is almost nil after the day's work. I have superior brains, whether this shows it or not . . . I am doing my best to convince you I am not a cheat, nor am I asking for a pension to do nothing. You at my age had begun writing a

novel. Well, I'm taking longer to develope. But that could be because I never have a day to myself, nor have had since I was seventeen. If I could get a lease of ten years – it is a long time – but if I said five years, the thought of my lease coming to an end would hamper me. I want to feel free and grow grow! Oh I am green green yet. But leaves grow yellow and shrink and drop when Autumn comes, so man has his season. If my blossoming is fooled with what of my fruit? . . . I have never been taught English, not even at home! So don't blame my English. And yet, English is going to be my tongue. And if I only had been in England before I was twenty my English would have pleased even he of the woodnotes wild, instead of being the archaic confusion it is today. This is not my land of expression although possibly no other land will be, my bones have become brittle they must have. How can my English smell of your daisies when I have been brought-up under the shade of our superb ombú? And yet this ombú seems to sigh when I tread its limbs, as if I were a stranger to it. I am copying what I wrote some days ago but have skipped half because I don't want to get on your nerves. Instead, I am sending (oh!) you some scraps in a last attempt. If this should fail, mala suerte. You have my blessings and I would like you to live some years more so as to have a word with you – perhaps as worms on the dewwet lips of your English daisy! By the way, I have a granddad here and a grandmother in Norway each a year or two older than yourself, but they don't ride bicycles. Don't be upset because of what I ask for, just drop it if it doesn't appeal to you.

Though I am trying to convince you, I am not trying to get round you – so be damned if you think so.

Shaw received many requests from perfect strangers who wanted him – for one reason or another – to send them free copies of his works. There were of course many wartime requests. He got one from a Royal Flying Corps lieutenant in a World War I prison camp at Karlsruhe, asking for copies of his books for the camp library – stipulating nothing published since the start of the war, since prisoners of war were forbidden such material. Would G.B.S, the correspondent asked, also pass on similar requests to Galsworthy, Chesterton, Wells, Belloc, Hardy, and Bennett? Shaw did. He also established a traffic in German books directly with an enemy company, S. Fischer Verlag of Berlin, publishers of his books. World War I German war prisoners in England also wanted copies of his books to read, especially *Pygmalion*, and after first supplying prison camps with books from his own collection, Shaw imported them from Germany by whatever indirect means S. Fischer could devise. He also received letters from English and French prisoners in German camps, who, having less difficulty obtaining German editions of his plays, wanted to raise points with him.

One audacious Manchester correspondent requested free copies of Shaw's works in order to judge for himself whether or not Shaw was a great writer.

Mr Shaw,

You are a great writer, at least they say you are. I'd like to judge for myself, tho'. There is one book of yours that I want to read, 'Caesar and Cleopatra', but can't afford to buy it. If you've got a spare copy, could I have it?

No, I can't join the so called 'free' library. I'm not a householder (thank God) so am not eligible for tickets. Nor can I spend my time in a library during the evenings. For one thing I'm too fed up after looking for work all day, and for another, interiors of libraries, any libraries, make me feel like commiting suicide – the row after row of works on divers subjects seem to me to be perfect representation of the futility of human endeavour.

I have'nt got any friends – (for which, again, I thank God) none in this world – the only friend to me is a man who has been dead since March 17th, 180A D – Marcus Aurelius Antoninus – so therefore I can't borrow a copy of your work. I don't think Marcus would like 'Caesar and Cleo', anyway . . .

Anyhow, if you've got a copy of 'Caesar and Cleopatra' which you can spare me I'd like to have it. You can have it returned, if you like, for I never keep books, be it except in this otherwise empty vessel called my head, and two works – 'Meditations of M. Aurelius' and a copy of 'Selected Epigrams of the Greeks', by Mackail. I have precisely 26/6d a week on which to live, so you can judge for yourself about whether I'm too 'mean' for to purchase the book, or not.

Best wishes
Yours respectfully
Leonard O'Duffy

Often, one request would lead to another and someone Shaw had helped in the past would approach him again with a further request.

Hove, Sussex.
December 1944

Dear Mr Bernard Shaw
   A while back you took compassion upon my
misery & answered a letter I presumed to send you
& for awhile I tried to buck-up – but alas always
a slipping. I am compelled to spend this Christmas
alone & wondered if you would give me your new
book to devour . . . Sign it for me & let it become a
treasure in my Treasury. I shall not feel so
alone. How are you in your greatness? do you
ever feel lonesome <u>within</u> or does your writing
forbid it. If we both are spared why can I not
(theres grammar) come & have tea along with thee next
summer . . . Are you well? What are you writing
now? Have you a lovely garden? Thats a lovesome
possession . . .
   Have you dear kind folk who wait on you & look
after you. hundreds I hear you say!!!!!
What are your views on the World's Slaughter?
I would not dare write what I think.
      F. A. Taylor/

Dont be angry
w. me for writing

While one American turned to Shaw for help when his embezzlement of funds was about to be exposed, a man from Montreal, Quebec, held him personally accountable for his thievery.

Dear Sir:
   . . . It is because you possess the gift of greatest
perspicacity and judgment; because you offer the most sane
methods for the reformation of this sorry state of affairs we
accept as life, and because the well of your understanding is
deeper than any other yours has become the greatest of

influences to me, above anyone I've ever read, and anyone I've ever known. I add truly, you're the very enjoyment of my quiet hours, and the sole factor retarding my intellectual degradation. And yet, my dear sir, you are at the same time the cause of crimes and my weaknesses.

Because of you, the municipal institutions, to which (living outside the districts I am not permitted as a borrower) I have only a visitor's access, have suffered (and, due to my impecuniosity will continue to suffer) incalculable literary losses. I simply pocket every pocketable volume of your work the wide and magnanimous shelves offer. When desireable books are too large to carry away without fear of suspicion I tear out quietly (and O how ingeniously) any likeness of you the book contains. These are my crimes! Moreover I have become irremediably addicted to your stimulating intelligence, because of which I have become the subject of a profound (and, viewed objectively, a humiliating) hero-worship . . .

Throughout the years Shaw meticulously reported to the printers the anachronisms and other errors brought to his attention by alert correspondents for correction in the next printing. He wrote to printer William Maxwell in 1933:

A schoolboy writes to me pointing out a hideous mistake in the Too True volume on p. 155 in the cross head. Seventh commandment (adultery) should be sixth commandment (kill). What is Edinburgh coming to when they dont know even the numbers of the commandments? Mend the plate instantly, and blush.

People wrote to Shaw, or – as in the following letter – to his secretary, regarding the most trivial points.

Banbury, Oxon.
19.11.1939

Dear Madam/
 If Mr. Shaw is well enough to deal with a small matter, I should be grateful if you would place my question before him.

In Saint Joan, is the king Charles meant to speak
ungrammatically when in the Epilogue he says to
Ladveau:?

'You cannot . . . ; and let you and I mind our own
business'?

I ask because I admire the play, have seen and
read it many times, and wonder why Charles is allowed
to lapse on this occasion alone.

To which Shaw replied personally by return of post, penning at the top of
his correspondent's letter:

Does it matter?

What king would say 'Let you and me mind our own
business'?

Several letters – like the following from a Royal Air Force corporal –
pointed out an incorrect bus number in the *Major Barbara* film:

April 1941

Dear Mr Shaw

Whilst enjoying a short spell of sick leave in London
recently, (following a period of Hospital treatment), I had
the pleasure of attending the World Premiere of your film,
'Major Barbara'.

Perhaps you will pardon me for saying that I found the
film extremely good, except for one item, of which I expect
you will have heard something already.

You will recall, I expect, the occasion upon which Wendy
Hiller and Rex Harrison leave the Salvation Army Shelter,
soon after their first meeting? The S.A. Shelter, as far as I
could gather, was somewhere near Whitechapel Road, or
Bethnal Green, or Stepney.

Suffice it to say that the Shelter was, and without much
doubt, meant to be in the East End of the inimitable London
Town . . . and Rex Harrison, waiting to hail a Taxi-cab, is
sharply brought to book, as it were, by Wendy Hiller, with
these words; – 'Taxi? oh no! We don't go about in Taxis in
the Army . . . we can't afford them, you know, so we will go
by bus . . . Look! There's a No. 73.'

At least, Mr Shaw, that is the general gist of how Rex
Harrison is cured of his extravagant ideas: but to the subtle
and ever-open eye of a Londoner, born and bred within the
murky atmosphere of those smoky and oft-abused limits of

the Metropolis, that remark came as a rude shock to my
knowledge of my native City.

Surely SOMEBODY on the Film-production Unit, (how
about Mr Gabriel Pascal?), knew that a No. 73 bus in
London runs from Richmond to Pimlico . . ? At the very
least, Mr Shaw, consider that I write as an experienced
guide of London Town, and I know, as I expect millions of
other Londoners do, that a No. 73 has *never* run near the
East End of London Town.

Before I return to Hospital for further and more annoying
treatment, do you think you would give me the honour of
answering the 'charge' of a sincere Londoner, that you have
scarred the history of our Town by a mistake which ought
never have occurred in a film which cost £250000 and took
twelve months to make?

Others wrote requesting interviews, articles and copyright permission. In
1917, the Northern Newspaper Syndicate offered Shaw ten guineas for
one thousand words answering six questions:

Has the war been worth it?
How will the war help democracy?
Is state control becoming a menace?
Has the war made us more religious?
Who is paying the war bill?
What will become of the neutrals?

Shaw refused to answer any of the questions, adding, however, that for
£1,000 he would have answered all six!

Sports reporting ran even higher. Asked by the *World* what honorarium he would wish for coming to the United States to cover the 1923
Dempsey–Firpo boxing match, Shaw retorted: 'Say 1,000,000 dollars, free
of American income tax as a first bid.'

Starting a fifth-form magazine, an Ellesmere (Shropshire) College
boy wrote to the 92-year-old, asking for an article. To his delight, Shaw
replied:

There are many school magazines and they all ask me for
contributions. Naturally I prefer larger circulations and

princely payments. If there is not enough talent in your Fifth to make the magazine readable, the school should be closed, and the teaching staff set to hoe turnips.

When Bernard Shaw saw the film of his *Caesar and Cleopatra* at a Welwyn, Hertfordshire, cinema in 1946, he insisted on paying, although the manager pointed out that even the operators saw it for nothing.

'Yes,' he retorted, 'but they don't get ten per cent on it – I do.'

And then there was George Morris Phillips, Principal of the State Normal School, West Chester, Pennsylvania, who in 1903 had the colossal nerve to ask Shaw to autograph a copy of the unauthorised Brentano edition of his *An Unsocial Socialist* – a pirated text! Returning the book to Mr Phillips, Shaw wrote in it: 'Contraband copy smuggled into the United Kingdom by an enterprising American, who sends it to the author with a request to autograph it and smuggle it out again. America is quite welcome to the book; but, really, to demand autographs into the bargain is not reasonable.' Even for Bernard Shaw, audacity should have its limits!

Shaw was similarly affronted many years later when shown – with great pride – a Tokyo library's collection of pirated editions of his works. 'We always translate your work, Shaw San,' said the librarian. 'Very popular.' 'Look here,' he said, 'this is all very fine, but who said you could translate my books? This is plain robbery.'

Although a stickler for the observance of copyright, royalties could take a number of forms: 'I am knitting mittens for George Bernard Shaw because he gave me permission to put *Pygmalion* on the air,' Gertrude Lawrence is quoted as saying as she sailed for New York in 1949, taking six balls of beige wool with her. On another occasion she sent Shaw chocolates and jars of jam as royalties for an American broadcast. He had waived the conventional royalties 'because British and American taxes cut them almost to nothing.'

Shaw once received a most inappropriate payment-in-kind from the Baxter Theatre at Abingdon, Virginia, who were using farm produce as money. Just as no salary was paid to the actors who shared in the payment-in-kind given by the Virginian farmers – including butter, eggs, ham, and other produce – Shaw was offered a ham in settlement of his *Pygmalion* royalty. Granting permission for the production, G.B.S. cabled:

I'M VEGETARIAN DON'T SEND HAM
SPINACH ACCEPTABLE.

Shaw, to the organizers of a 1926 Labour demonstration who wished to include his play *The Shewing-Up of Blanco Posnet* in their programme:

Under no circumstances can any play of mine be performed without payment of the standard author's fee. A Labour Advisory Council ought to understand this as a point of trade unionism.

What is more, unless you can assure me that the sixpence for admission will go to the players, and not to any other non-theatrical body, the performance must be classed as amateur, and the amateur fee (two or three guineas – I forget which) paid to the Society of Authors.

It is hard enough for my poorer fellow-authors to meet the competition of my plays without the additional handicap of having them performed gratuitously.

Despite Shaw's tight control over his work, there has been more tinkering with *Pygmalion* than with any other of his plays. Mrs Patrick Campbell began it by having the last act of the play re-written with a love interest. The Civic Theatre in Minneapolis cabled Shaw in 1923 proposing to stage her romantic version of the play.

> PYGMALION OPENS HERE WEDNESDAY AS SUPREME
> EFFORT OF STRUGGLING MINNEAPOLIS CIVIC
> THEATRE CONTROVERSY RAGES OVER ENDING
> SHALL WE USE MRS PAT CAMPBELLS LINE WHAT
> SIZE AND MAKE VILLAGERS HAPPY OR SHALL WE
> LEAVE THEM IN SHAVIAN SUSPENSION

Shaw's cabled response was immediate and predictable:

> I ABSOLUTELY FORBID THE CAMPBELL
> INTERPOLATION OR ANY SUGGESTION THAT THE
> MIDDLEAGED BULLY AND THE GIRL OF EIGHTEEN
> ARE LOVERS.

It is therefore highly unlikely Shaw would have approved the marketing strategy of cinema managers in 1938 to 'sell' the film *Pygmalion* on its general release with the following billing:

> DUSTMAN'S DAUGHTER VICTIM OF A
> RICH MAN'S WHIM.

In 1948, Shaw was asked permission for *Pygmalion* to be staged as a musical at an R.A.F. station. Off went a postcard:

I absolutely forbid any such outrage.
If *Pygmalion* is not good enough for
your friends with its own verbal music, their
talent must be altogether extraordinary.
Let them try Mozart's *Cosí fan tutte*, or
at least Offenbach's *Grand Duchess*

G.B.S.

He most certainly would have been exasperated by one forthcoming
attractions poster displayed outside a West Country repertory theatre in
1958:

'Pygmalion – the play of My Fair Lady'

There was, however, at least one adaptation of this play – in Korea –
for which no copyright approval was sought from the Shaw Estate. In
Prisoner of War Camp 2 on the Manchurian border in 1953, a group of
captive Allied officers produced a play entitled *Rain in Spain*. It was written,
partly from memory and partly improvised, by the Rev. S. J. Davies, then
chaplain to the Gloucesters, assisted by a subaltern of the Royal Ulster
Rifles. Every line had of course to be submitted to the Chinese censors,
who were only too ready to detect 'insults to the working classes'. Thus the
Doolittles had to be re-christened the Turnpennys. But the honoured
name of Shaw eventually carried the day. An obvious difficulty was in
finding suitable costumes and scenery. The chief acquisitions, apart from
some silk lent by the Chinese, were innumerable copies of the *Daily
Worker* . . .

One person unwilling to accept a 'stock' refusal was comedian Arthur
Askey, who in 1943 impersonated Shaw in the highly successful *The Love
Racket*. The scene was based on Roy Royston and Askey pretending to be
authors, with Royston garbed as Shakespeare with cloak, bald pate and
quill pen, and Askey as G.B.S, complete with beard and knickerbockers.
When the script was sent to Shaw on the instructions of the Lord
Chamberlain's office, back came a G.B.S. postcard, written in red ink,
which just said 'No. G.B.S.' Devastated, as he considered this scene his
virtuoso piece, Askey approached the 'great man' in person.

He told Shaw that the critics would regard the Shaw–Shakespeare
incident as the show's highlight. 'If this is one of the high spots, I'd hate to

see the low spots,' retorted Shaw, amiably, adding, 'You know Shakespeare wasn't a bad writer either, but he's not here to defend himself!'

As he was shown the door, Askey made one last appeal for permission to do the sketch. 'No, I won't,' repeated Shaw, 'but there's not the slightest reason why you shouldn't do it, because I won't be coming to see it!' At the end of the day the scene was left in, the play ran for about a year at the Victoria Palace before touring, and Askey had his break into musical-comedy.

A 1938 advertisement in a Midlands paper perpetrated a sad injustice:

Grand Theatre. 6.30 & 8.50 . . . 'Pygmalion,'
the Brilliant Comedy by Oscar Wilde.

Shaw to Mr David Manderson:

> My licence for the performance of my play Pygmalion by
> the Derek Salberg Company in Wolverhampton did not
> include an authorisation to advertise it as 'the brilliant
> comedy by Oscar Wilde'.
> Is Oscar's name a bigger draw than mine? and if so what
> royalty do his representatives receive for its use?

In reply, Manderson wrote:

> Dear Sir
> I regret that some confusion in the mind of the resident
> manager of the Grand Theatre, Wolverhampton, caused
> him last week to attribute to the late Mr. Wilde a play which,
> I understand, was written by you. Mr. Purdey, (the
> gentleman in question) is disinclined to offer an apology as
> he contends that this substitution accounts for the show
> having played to approximately three times as much money
> as it did when he billed it as being written by you. He also
> contends that this will result in your receiving larger
> royalties than he believes would otherwise have been the
> case and he is therefore unable to see what you are
> grumbling about.

And, from Shaw, a postcard reply:

> Please give my compliments to Mr. Purdey; and beg him
> to continue the attribution, which was a most happy thought.
> I am not grumbling; I am rejoicing.

And then there was the correspondent who paid Shaw what is
perhaps the ultimate tribute, that of imitation. He wrote to G.B.S. suggesting that he should be allowed to quote freely from the playwright's works,
after the manner in which Shaw had interfered with his life:

> for at the age
> of seventeen I came across your Prefaces
> and aped them so well that my schoolmaster,
> delighted to get readable essays from a pupil,
> recommended me for a scholarship to
> Oxford, which I was given without further
> ado.   And you must admit that three
> unexpected years at Oxford is a gross

interference though a welcome one.   Any
concession on my part, such as advancing
you half the money I received for the
scholarship will be strenuously resisted by me,
until I too am paying supertax,
when I shall reconsider the matter.

I enclose a stamped envelope,
for after obtaining £500 through your
good offices, I feel I cannot impose
on you to the further extent of
five halfpence.

Yours sincerely,
Oliver Lawson Dick

Thanks to the daring of a junior lady secretary, the British Foreign Office
was given unconditional rights to quote Shaw. The girl wrote Shaw a
minute seeking his permission to quote a paragraph from his *Everybody's
Political What's What*, expressing regret that by a Treasury ruling the
department was limited to a payment of one guinea a thousand words.
Shaw, who liked to exalt the humble and meek, responded most gallantly.
Back came the minute with another minute neatly written below in the red
ink used by Foreign Secretaries since the days of Lord Salisbury. It ran as
follows:

> The Foreign Office may quote any literary work of which I
> own the copyright 'ad lib', in the original or in translation
> unconditionally.
>
> G. Bernard Shaw, 17th Nov., 1944.

However, school editions were a different matter! To New York publishers
Dodd, Mead in 1933:

> I will have nothing to do with schools and colleges at any
> price: no book of mine shall ever with my consent be that
> damnable thing, a schoolbook. Let them buy the dollar
> editions if they want them. By a school edition they mean an
> edition with notes and prefaces full of material for such
> questions as 'Give the age of Bernard Shaw's great aunt

when he wrote You Never Can Tell and state the reasons
for believing that the inscription on her tombstone at
Ballyhooly is incorrect'. The experienced students read the
notes and prefaces and not the plays, and for ever after
loathe my very name.

To one of the Hollywood 'bigwigs' who sent him an interminable, ex-
quisitely composed cable outlining his qualifications for filming his works,
he replied:

> Your telegram is too literary. It is obvious that your
> aspirations would conflict with mine. I am the literary man.
> Besides, the costly and unnecessary length of your cable
> convinces me that you are a poor businessman and I want a
> good businessman.

Bulletins

When asked upon sailing to Capetown in December 1931 whether he had a Christmas message to give to the public, G.B.S. exclaimed, 'No. I hate a lot of the newspapers, but I do not hate them enough to give them a message to print.'

THIS SIDE OF CARD IS FOR ADDRESS

HON GEORGE BERNARD SHAW - dramatist

The Sultan of Satire & Socialist Czar

London, England

Shaw to the Better Citizenship Association, Portland, Oregon, on the innate goodness of man:

6th July 1910

... The Better Citizenship Association is a goose. Nature has designed plenty of bad men; and some of the worst are Americans. The Creator has created everything that is bad as well as everything that is good. The Creator makes mistakes just as American citizens do. In trying to make a successful world he has had to proceed by the method of Trial and Error, just like his creatures. The Creator created the American people, as he created all the other peoples, to do his work for him; and from what I can make out, they are doing it so badly, that he will presently have to scrap them and try some more efficient tools. ... What your Association should advocate is the formation of a Committee of Public Safety for the purpose of eliminating all Americans who cannot justify their existence by proving that they are every year producing what they consume in addition to a sinking fund to pay off the cost of their schooling and up-bringing and an insurance premium for their old age, and FIVE DOLLARS OVER.

If they cant, you may take it from me that the Creator wants them scrapped, and that he relies on you to do it. That's the reality of Citizenship Betterment.

To Shaw on book banning in prisons:

London, WC1
22nd July 1946

Dear Mr. Bernard Shaw,
I am only one of 190,000,000 millions
of Russians who admire you much more
than your own countrymen.   On occasion
of your 90th birthday, I wish you all
the health & strength you can muster
for your future work to the good
of humanity throughout the world.
Dear Mr Shaw, I have a personal
complaint to make.
The other day I sent your book called
'The Crime of Imprisonment' to my
friend Thurston who is doing a term

of imprisonment in Parkhurst prison.
To my chagrin the book was censored
and stopped, for it is too enlightening
to allow people in prison to read it.
Is not this too disgusting to know
that phylosophical works of the greatest
philosopher alive are banned by silly
& stupid prison authorities.   Ten words
from you in the press about this would
be very welcome, indeed.

Other letters requesting Shaw's opinion were incredibly drawn out,
like the following from Calcutta:

Honoured Sir,
   Though I am living in Hindusthan (India) far from yours,
I have read with interest your several precious speeches and
writings . . . May I humbly request you to let me know your
learned opinion on the Great Lord Shri Krishna who was
born at Mathura (or Mathusa) about six thousand years ago
and the speaker of Shrimad-Bhagabat-Gita to King Arjuna
in the famous Kurukhetra Battle-field in Bharatbarsa
(Hindusthan), and the greatest politician that ever appeared
in the whole Universe: in any age or sphere. And on the
Lord Shri Chartanya (Gouranga Deva) the great religious
reformer and founder of Universal Religion of Love
(Prem-Dharma), Who was born in the fifteenth century
A.D. (1486) at Nabadwip, Nadia Bengal (Hindusthan),
when the reformation in Europe took place (sixteenth
Century A.D.) and St. Martin arose. In both cases, we find
that the Almighty God Himself appeared among men and
like a man, in order to re-establish that which was lost, to
give that which the men were seeking i.e. 'Divine Love'
(Prema).   In many cases They said 'We are the Saviour, the
Creator and the Almighty God'.
   In this connection I may assume that you have read the
universal religious book 'Shrimad-Bhagabat-Gita' and the
life of the Hindu Reformer written in English 'Lord
Gouranga' written by Mahatma Sisir Kumar Ghosh, the
founder of the renowned daily journal 'Amrita Bazar
Patrika', Calcutta.
   A line in reply will be highly appreciated.

Yours very truly,
Natabar Datta.

On chain-letter creators:

Mr Sydney Walton in January 1930 received a snowball letter starting with the usual superstitious shibboleths – 'Please send this chain letter to nine persons to whom you wish luck. The chain was started by a railroad officer, and should go around the world three times. Do not break this chain, for if you do, you will have bad luck. Do it within nine days, and you will have good luck.' Surprised that Shaw's name was one of the first on the list, Walton wrote to him, receiving by return this characteristic reply:

> I have never signed nor passed on a chain or snowball letter
> of any kind; and I have never lost an opportunity of urging
> that the criminally thoughtless people who start or forward
> such things should be executed without benefit of clergy. I
> should be glad to have my views made known as widely as
> possible, as some liar has put my name on a list of persons
> accompanying a chain letter now in circulation, which, if its
> silly intention were carried out, would break the backs of all
> the postmen and bankrupt all the Postmasters-General in
> the world.

On divine retribution:

When asked in 1948 whether the burning down on his ninety-second birthday of the Ayot St Peter railway station, a mere three miles from his Ayot St Lawrence home, were a heaven-ordained bonfire, Shaw exclaimed, 'I'm afraid not; I've never used that station.'

On Edward and Mrs Simpson:

Over the years people brought a number of proposals of varying degrees of idiocy to Shaw's attention. His secretary Blanche Patch recalled that:

> Among American men, too, we had our oddities. There was
> one, rather like G.B.S. in appearance, who carried a singing
> kettle around with him. There was the other who passed on
> to Shaw a fantastic plan for the marriage of Mrs. Simpson to
> King Edward VIII on the deck of the U.S. battle-cruiser
> *Indianapolis*, attended by two other cruisers and a division of
> destroyers at anchor off Southampton . . .

As an anonymous correspondent wrote:

> To me, a citizen of the U.S.A. the stand taken by the British Ministry toward an American, is regretable.
>
> My Plan – Upon the return of President Roosevelt from his S. American Cruise on board the U.S. battle cruiser Indianapolis our Congress should appropriate funds to refit the ship together with 2 other cruisers and a division of destroyers, and send them to South Hampton.
>
> The Officers of our ships, our Ambassadors, and Mrs Simpson would witness together the Coronation of King Edward VIII.
>
> They should then escort Mrs Simpson on board the Indianapolis. There the following morning Mrs Simpson would announce the day for her wedding, the place, the deck of the American ship.
>
> If the Archbishop of Canterbury were present he could perform the ceremony, other the Chaplain of the Fleet. Salutes would be exchanged by the British & American ships and shore batteries. A British destroyer would then take the King & Queen ashore and our Fleet would weigh anchor for America.
>
> If there is no wedding our ships should remain till sundown and then sail for Hampton Roads, returning with Mrs Simpson aboard. On arrival the Admiral will report directly to Congress.
>
> Respectfully submitted
X.X.X.

More than one American wrote to Shaw to put him 'straight' on the Edward / Mrs Simpson 'misalliance':

> Boston U.S.A.
1936
>
> Sir
>   In the American news-
> papers it is cabled that you
> hope the Duke of Windsor and
> his wife will be able
> to make a visit to the
> United States . . .
> The United States, as every
> one knows, is the land
> of easy divorce, but there

are millions of Americans
who look with scorn on
twice-divorced men and
women, and they know that
the set of Americans who
were Mrs Simpson's friends
have no morals, but change
wives, via Reno, as often
as they feel inclined.   These
Americans, rich, poor,
and medium income
people, would never dream
of lowering themselves to
meet Mrs Simpson socially
if she had married an
American man as her
third husband, and they
see no reason why they
should receive this woman
merely because Edward,
Duke of Windsor, was silly
enough to marry her.
No American, who had
married a twice-divorced
woman, could ever hope
to be elected President of
the United States, for the
great majority of Americans
consider such a woman
a person with loose morals,
and not fit to act as
mistress of the White House.
Edward seems to have the
peculiar idea that, so long
as he has chosen to marry
Mrs Simpson, her past
life should be forgotten
because he has given
her a title as his wife.
He also seems to forget
that the United States is
a Republic, and that the
'Duke and Duchess of
Windsor' are quite out

of place in a Republic,
his open effort to impose
himself and his wife on
the American nation as
'important personalities'
was deeply resented by
Every Kind of American . . .
President and Mrs Franklin
Roosevelt, like many other
Americans, have no use for
Wally Simpson, and see no
reason why they should
allow Edward to force
this woman upon them;
the fact that she is an
American only disgusts
them more than ever, for
she is the kind of American
woman the nation is
ashamed of.
If Edward and his wife
come to the United States
there will be many very
unpleasant incidents.   The
notoriety surrounding them
will excite crowds to dog
their footsteps in public,
while some applause, and
many jeers and vulgar
remarks about 'Mrs
Windsor's' (as she is nick-
named in the U.S.A.) lack
of morals, and loud cries
of 'look up her first two
husbands for a jolly party
together' will make Edward
foam with rage and helpless
anger.

And why the English 'burnst' St Joan:

St Pancras Hospital
St Pancras Way. N W.1.
Ward 7.

Dear Mr/ Shaw .
    I should very
much like to know
why the English
burnst St Joan, when
she was a French
woman, & a Saint .
I saw your splendid
play twice at the
Lyceum, & I shall
never forget it.
Please do not think
I am writing this
out of mere frivolity
but I have seriously
wondered why we
ever came to make
such a blunder.
I thought perhaps
you might be
kind enough
to tell me.
    Yours Sincerely
    Helen Louise
        Ryan

'Burn it,' replied Shaw, when asked for suggestions on how
to improve the city of Leeds.

On firemen's income:
    When, in 1941, Shaw was asked to comment on the differing pay
rates for auxiliary and regular firemen, he advised:

You ought to ask for exact instructions as to how much fire
extinction one should do for £3 10s. and how much for £4.
It might save confusion at the next conflagration.

To Mr Shaw on suitable attire when bathing:

JOHANNESBURG
South Africa
25th October, 1937

Dear Sir,

In a recent issue of the 'Cavalcade' dated 18th September, 1937, we were interested in a photo of you taken while bathing, and in particular, that you were wearing 'trunks.'

At present there is a marked difference of opinion in Johannesburg as to whether men should be permitted to wear trunks or not at the public baths where both sexes are present.

The public baths are run by the City Council of Johannesburg and trunks are not permissible but they are worn at pleasure resorts not controlled by the Municipality.

We should deem it an honor and a favour if you would be kind enough to give us your views as to what you consider more beneficial –

bathing trunks or bathing costume.

yours truly,
W. T. N. Lones and F. Potter
(Two bathing enthusiasts)

When, at ninety-two, he was asked for a message for the Irish people on the passage of the Republic of Ireland Act, Shaw rapped back, 'Who am I that I should send messages to nations? I hope I know my place better.'

'What do you think of the Irish?' he was asked on another occasion. 'I don't ... I'm a busy man.'

Mr Cyril Dumpleton, Labour candidate for St Albans, called on Bernard Shaw at his Ayot St Lawrence home when canvassing in February 1950. Mr Dumpleton said afterwards, 'When I presented my election address to Mr Shaw he said: "We won't discuss it. I know more about it than you."'

On modesty:

Basingstoke, Hants.
7th December
1943.

George Bernard Shaw Esq.

Sir,

     I had a dream about you last night which may or may not amuse you.

     I dreamt I was interviewing you, and you gave me some stick-on labels reading 'READ G.B.S.', which you asked me to fix on letters and books. I said 'Surely Mr Shaw a man of your eminence does not need to advertise'.   I then awoke.

     As I am not an autograph hunter I send a post-card for possible acknowledgment.

Yours with respect
R.L. Cullum

Shaw's reply to Mussolini's 1927 *Daily News* declaration that Fascism disapproved of whiskers on the ground that these are 'a sign of decadence':

> Mr. Bernard Shaw desires to say that he does not wear whiskers; he wears a beard. So does the King.
>
> French waiters of a certain age are the only regular wearers of whiskers left. It is for France to take up the gauntlet.
>
> Louis Philippe whiskers are still to be seen in the north of Italy.
>
> Cavour wore whiskers; and Victor Emmanuel's moustache could be tied round his neck.

'Superfluous,' Shaw informed one correspondent wishing his opinion on the reviving popularity of beards. 'My testimony is on my chin for all to read.'

Judge Henry Neil of Chicago, the reputed 'Father of Mothers' Pensions', was one of a number of eccentrics Shaw indulged with brief articles and statements of support. His question – as to why governments pay pensions for war widows and orphans, and not to industrial ones – evoked a characteristic Shaw reply:

> I do not know why Governments pay pensions to war widows, and not to peace widows. Nor do I know why they force every man to fight, no matter how rich he is, but do not force him to work on the same terms. Why a man with a conscientious objection to killing his fellow-men should be persecuted with murderous ferocity, and a man with an unconscientious objection to helping them to live and pulling his own weight in the Commonwealth boat at the same time should be exalted and pampered and flattered is another conundrum which I give up. The longer I live the more I am inclined to the belief that this sphere is used by other planets as a lunatic asylum.

As Neil knew only too well, Shaw was a good bet for a striking phrase, as in his 'I have said that if I were a woman I should refuse to bear a child for less than $10,000 . . .'

Neil continued to spread his Mothers' Pensions gospel, with Shavian support, until his confinement in Kankakee State Hospital for the Insane in 1933.

On barbarism, war & Russia:

> MOSCOU 354/14 43 13 2120
> PP260,00 ELT BERNARD SHAW 4
> WHITEHALL COURT LONDON/SW/1
>
> FOREIGN COMMISSION UNION SOVIET WRITERS
> PUBLISHING BOOK WORLD WRITERS AGAINST
> FASCIST BARBARISM FOR PEOPLES LIBERTY STOP
> WOULD WELCOME ARTICLE UP TO THOUSAND
> WORDS
> ALEXANDER FADEYEV CHAIRMAN
> MOSCOU BOX 850
> ANSWER 1000 WORDS ELT RATE
> PREPAID

To which Shaw replied:

> NEVER MIND THE BARBARISM: ALL WAR IS
> BARBAROUS; AND TO SQUEAL IS CHILDISH. LET US
> RATHER APOLOGIZE FOR THE TERRIBLE THINGS
> WE MUST DO TO OUR GERMAN COMRADES BEFORE
> THEIR FUHRER LOSES HIS GLAMOR FOR THEM.
> WHEN TWO MIGHTY IDEAS CLASH MILLIONS OF
> LIVES COUNT FOR NOTHING.
> IT IS AS THE CHAMPION OF AN IDEA THAT
> ADOLF HITLER HAS FLUNG DOWN HIS GLOVE TO
> RUSSIA. RUSSIA PICKS IT UP AS THE CHAMPION OF
> A FAR MIGHTIER IDEA. WHEN SHE STRIKES DOWN
> ADOLF'S IDEA SHE WILL BECOME THE SPIRITUAL

CENTRE OF THE WORLD. AND WITH THAT TASK
BEFORE HER SHE MAY NOT HEED THE CRIES OF
THE WOUNDED OR THE TEARS OF THE
BEREAVED . . .

From one American, C. S. Boothby of Chicago:

November 8, 1946

Dear Sir:
The United States papers carried a statement to the effect
that you had the colossal nerve to recommend and urge that
Henry Wallace be elected president of the United States.

As a <u>real</u> American citizen, I am calling your attention to the
results of this week's elections in America just as a general
reminder to England that the great majority of American
citizens have reached the end of their patience with <u>both</u>
England and Russia. Twice this country, at the great cost of
its fine young manhood and billions of dollars, has saved the
selfish British Empire from oblivion . . .

It is difficult for generous and decent American citizens to
understand how a nation, which speaks our tongue, can be
so arrogant and so ungrateful. Our suggestion to you is that
for your few remaining years you keep very quiet and abstain
from trying to interfere with our internal affairs. We don't
like socialists – we don't like communists, and frankly, we
don't like to have Britishers or Russians interfering with our
business.

If your nation is not actually bankrupt, I suggest that you
devote your few remaining years to compel them to pay back
the monies they owe this country before you offer advice on
our government.

To which Shaw replied:

You certainly are a <u>real</u> American citizen: that is, your
outlook is that of a village blacksmith, and your notion of a

President a rather tight fit for a village postman.

The next President has to succeed F. Roosevelt as one of the three Powers on whom the destiny of the world for the moment depends.

Wallace is the sole American statesman who has an up-to-date European mind and equipment for the job. You are a political baby squabbling over a few dollars, and ignorant of the fact that the civilization of the U.S.A. is, like all civilization, built on a foundation of Communism and Socialism without which it would collapse in a week. You think all that came down from heaven like light from the sun. It didn't.

You know nothing about it; so do as I tell you and work for Wallace.

On Royals:

As with most things, Shaw had very individualistic ideas regarding the Royal family in particular and monarchy in general. According to his secretary, Blanche Patch:

> ... When George the Sixth was crowned he wanted to set up a Society for the Prevention of Cruelty to Royal Personages. He hailed the Simpson marriage as a diplomatic masterstroke. He accepted George the Fifth quite frankly as a lowbrow, and as such said he was quite right to go to a Cup Final instead of the inauguration of the Stratford Memorial Theatre, 'one of the greatest events of his reign'. And he had a singular comment upon the birth of Prince Charles, remarking to me that perhaps it was a pity that Princess Elizabeth had had an heir. I asked him why. It would probably be better, said he, if Margaret were allowed to come to the throne because the second child of a reigning monarch often made a better sovereign than the elder; and he indicated both George the Fifth and George the Sixth to support the theory.

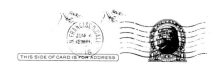

On more than one occasion a fraudulent message was issued in Shaw's name, as was the case in Darrall S. (Duke) Collins' 1948 campaign for the presidency of the Students' Representative Council at the University of Saskatchewan. Collins' spoof campaign – a law student prank to create interest in the election itself – was an anti-feminist one advocating the disenfranchisement of university women, promising the 'molding of co-eds to fit their God-given capacities as attentive wives and prolific mothers . . .' Collins, it would appear, asked Shaw for a policy endorsement. To his delight – and the surprise of many – the following 'cablegram' was received from Waters End, England, on February 23rd, 1948.

YOU WILL NEVER HAVE A QUIET WORLD UNTIL
YOU KNOCK WOMEN OUT OF POLITICS. CARRY ON.
G.B.S.

Picked up by *Time* and *Newsweek*, this 'Shaw' cable brought Collins invaluable publicity, and it was only when an enterprising reporter drew the great man's attention to it, that it was shown to be phoney. Shaw responded immediately and in no uncertain terms:

Political mendacity could hardly go farther. I know nothing about the contest in Saskatoon, and have not interfered in it. Far from wanting to knock women out of politics I have spent the relevant part of my life in trying to knock women into politics. If the candidate for the presidency of the University of Saskatoon, or any candidate for anything anywhere, is a professed anti-Feminist I hope the electors will knock him out of politics. The cabled message quoted as sent by me is an invention. The inventor might well be knocked out of politics also.

I advocate not only Women's Rights but Men's Rights, which were very seriously changed unintentionally into Men's Wrongs by the much needed Married Women's Property Act. People who cannot take in more than one idea at a time imagine that this makes me an anti-Feminist. More fools they!

G. Bernard Shaw

At the final count, Darrall Collins, one of five candidates, received a mere 106 votes of the 3,296 ballots cast. Today, nearly forty years later, he is an Administrative Judge in Victoria, British Columbia.

BULLETINS

On second childhood or 'gaga':

> Krakow
> Poland
> 20th Nov. 1948

Dear Sir, I learn that you are still alive, though you were born 7 years before me. This incites me to ask you whether the end of your 85th year was a definite change as I have experienced. Until the end of 85 years I was active as usual. I lectured at the university and answered immediately many letters as I have an extensive correspondence. But in my 86th year I suddenly felt a change and could not walk, had to remain in bed many days, and when going out had to use cabs, which I never did before. A first rate physician examined my body earnestly and found no defect. Did you experience a similar change seven years ago? . . .

To which Shaw replied:

> My experience is that second childhood or gaga passes and is followed by what athletes call Second Wind. Gaga occurs in the 8th decade. Second Wind in the 9th, with a notable improvement in body and mind. Centenarians are much clearerheaded than octogenarians.
>
> People who work hard mentally break down every forty years and need prolonged rest and change. Some die, as Schiller & Raphael & Mozart did, at the first attack: others, like Goethe and Michael Angelo and Beethoven, pull through and die at the second. A few, like Titian, survive the second and reach their century.

Cabling Shaw didn't always bring results, but if one were lucky he could be rewarded with a quotable line. When one American newspaper cabled asking his opinion of 'Babe' Ruth, G.B.S. cabled back,

> 'UNACQUAINTED WITH RUTH. WHOSE BABE
> IS SHE?'

145

On women over forty:

On being asked if every *woman* over forty were a scoundrel – a claim he had made in respect of men – Shaw replied: 'In the case of women, the age is 30.'

On when women are the most interesting – a question put to Shaw by the *Daily Express*, October 1919:

To the Editor:

Sir, – You are tempting me to make a fool of myself. Get thee behind me.   G. BERNARD SHAW.

What would you do if . . . ?

The posing of hypothetical questions was an oft-repeated ploy to get replies from famous people. Over the years Shaw received more than his fair share of these, which could be as simple as:

Q: What would you do if you suddenly became possessed of £40,000,000?

G.B.S: Send it along and I'll see.

Diet

&

Health

When asked, 'You don't smoke, you don't drink, you don't eat meat. What do you do?' Shaw replied, 'I spit!'

The aged G.B.S. received so many 'Dear Mr Shaw' letters asking whether he were still a vegetarian and what he ate, that he produced a postcard providing a summary of his philosophy and practice of vegetarianism and his attitudes towards killing for sport and for the dinner table.

VEGETARIAN DIET

Mr Shaw's correspondents are reminded that current vegetarianism does not mean living wholly on vegetables. Vegetarians eat cheese, butter, honey, eggs, and, on occasion, cod liver oil.

On this diet, without tasting fish, flesh, or fowl, Mr Shaw has reached the age of 92 (1948) in as good condition as his meat eating contemporaries. It is beyond question that persons who have never from their birth been fed otherwise than as vegetarians are at no disadvantage, mentally, physically, nor in duration of life, with their carnivorous fellow-citizens.

Nevertheless Mr Shaw is of opinion that his diet included an excess of protein. Until he was seventy he accumulated some poison that exploded every month or six weeks in a headache that blew it off and left him quite well after disabling him for a day. He tried every available treatment to get rid of the headaches: all quite unsuccessful. He now makes uncooked vegetables, chopped or grated, and their juices, with fruit, the staple of his diet, and finds it markedly better than the old high protein diet of beans, lentils and macaroni.

His objection to carnivorous diet is partly aesthetic, partly hygienic, mainly as involving an unnecessary waste of the labor of masses of mankind in the nurture and slaughter of cattle, poultry, and fish for human food.

He has no objection to the slaughter of animals as such. He knows that if we do not kill animals they will kill us. Squirrels, foxes, rabbits, tigers, cobras, locusts, white ants, rats, mosquitoes, fleas, and deer must be continually slain even to extermination by vegetarians as ruthlessly as by meat eaters. But he urges humane killing and does not enjoy it as a sport.

Ayot Saint Lawrence,
Welwyn, Herts.

... His meals being so light, and eating so frugally, G.B.S. never weighed much more than nine stone. 'One look at you, Mr Shaw,' the ample Alfred Hitchcock once said to him, 'and I know there's a famine in the land.' 'One look at you, Mr Hitchcock,' Shaw replied, 'and I know who caused it.'

Shaw first experimented with vegetarianism in January 1881, at the age of twenty-five, after suffering severe monthly headaches, whose occurrence he faithfully recorded in his pocket diary. These migraines were – he told his wife Charlotte – a mark of the exceptional person, citing Thomas Carlyle, G. F. Watts and Charles Darwin as having been similarly afflicted. Although the diet did not relieve the migraines – he later claimed they miraculously disappeared when he finally published *The Intelligent Woman's Guide to Socialism and Capitalism* because, as he put it, 'I transferred them to my readers' – he remained a vegetarian, except for a few minor lapses, until his death nearly seventy years later. One such relapse took place at Bayreuth on July 28th, 1889, when he noted in his diary: 'Dined at the restaurant, eating some salmon in the absence of anything more vegetarian.' Shaw claimed to have been 'born again' by his vegetarianism which he credited to the poet Shelley, 'who opened my eyes to the savagery of my diet.' As he wrote to the actress Ellen Terry:

> ... The odd thing about being a vegetarian is, not that the
> things that happen to other people don't happen to me –
> they all do – but that they happen differently: pain is
> different, pleasure different, fever different, cold different,
> even love different.

'A man,' he commented, 'of my spiritual intensity does not eat corpses.' Shaw claimed that vegetarianism, 'the diet of saints and heroes', helped people to keep their tempers instead of wasting them on useless spluttering. Although he later insisted he was a vegetarian by instinct, it should be remembered that Shaw was for many years impecunious and that vegetarian restaurants were comparatively inexpensive. Even so, he frequently gave ethical and health reasons for his vegetarianism. Although his late-in-life postcard on the subject announced that his objection to a carnivorous diet was partly hygienic and partly aesthetic, there was another more important reason. The daily breeding, rearing and slaughtering of animals for food meant an enormous waste of human energy, 'a prodigious slavery of men to animals'. As his secretary, Blanche Patch, would remark: 'Far from showing any sympathy for "these creatures", he almost blamed them for the trouble they gave in being slaughtered. Shaw was not sentimental about animals. His loathing for vivisection was a hygienic loathing.'

Ill in 1898, Shaw envisaged his own funeral:

> My situation is a solemn one. Life is offered to me on
> condition of eating beefsteaks. My weeping family crowd
> about me with Bovril and Brand's Essence. But death is
> better than cannibalism. My will contains directions for my
> funeral, which will be followed not by mourning coaches,
> but by herds of oxen, sheep, swine, flocks of poultry, and a
> small travelling aquarium of live fish, all wearing white
> scarves in honor of the man who perished rather than eat his
> fellow-creatures. It will be, with the exception of the
> procession into Noah's Ark, the most remarkable thing of
> the kind ever seen.

On G.B.S.'s ninetieth birthday, one enterprising correspondent, E. G. Barlow of the National Society for Abolition of Cruel Sports, wrote offering to stage manage this proposed funeral spectacular.

Dear Sir,

Whilst wishing you yet many more years of living that your lifelong fight for a recognition of animal rights may continue, I venture to mention the possibility of your death. As it is obvious that you will not like the usual mournful funeral procession, I wondered if it would be possible to arrange something entirely different. My idea was that you should be followed by a procession of animals – cattle, sheep, pigs, etc., with a prominent placard 'Shaw never ate us'. If this has your support I should deem it an honour (as an admirer of your work for animals and a vegetarian, etc. myself) to arrange this. It would be spectacular, there would never have been a funeral like it, and it would draw attention to a thing which you have persistently advocated. What has prompted me to write you is that I feel that in later years with the development of the 'scientific' and materialist age there has been a tendency to gloss over this aspect of your life work. If you were to approve of this procession it would put the matter before the whole world.

If you are at all interested in my suggestion I should be happy to discuss the matter further with you.

There was, however, to be no funeral procession, for Shaw had already made his will expressing the wish that:

. . . my dead body shall be cremated and its ashes
inseparably mixed with those of my late wife now in the
custody of the Golders Green Crematorium and in this
condition inurned or scattered in the garden of the house in
Ayot Saint Lawrence where we lived together for thirty five
years unless some other disposal of them should be in the
opinion of my Trustee more eligible. Personally I prefer the
garden to the cloister.

Although Shaw had clearly left the door open for some national
institution to claim his remains – had it wished to immortalize them – no
claimants were forthcoming, with the result that after a simple ceremony at
Shaw's Corner on November 23rd, 1950, his ashes were mingled with
those of his wife Charlotte and scattered in the back garden of his Ayot St
Lawrence home.

Shaw's wife, Charlotte, stopped eating meat and fish, in sympathy with her
husband's views, but returned to 'cannibalism' after a short lapse, having
had difficulty finding a cook who knew how to prepare vegetarian dishes.
She also felt she needed meat.

Shaw never claimed to be in perfect health – only that he was seldom
less than ten times as well as an ordinary carcass-eater. In a letter dated
August 15th, 1946, addressed to G. H. Sanders, of South Yarmouth,
Mass., and headed 'Not Private. Quote by all means', Shaw adds:

. . . I have not eaten fish, flesh or fowl for 65 years past. I eat
eggs very seldom and not much milk; . . . I have my potatoes
baked. I do not smoke nor drink tea, alcoholic stimulants
and narcotics: but lately I have taken a little mild coffee, at
breakfast – I claim nothing for this diet except that it has
kept me alive quite as effectively as a meat diet which costs
more and involves an enormous slavery of man to animals
and much cruelty and suffering, though the animals owe
their lives to it.

'Men can live on anything,' he told Cyril Clemens of the Mark Twain
Society. 'My favorite story is that of the centenarian who said, "I attribute
my longevity to the fact that I never drank, smoked, nor had any sexual
relations with women until I was fourteen."' When some humorist dared to

circulate the story that he ate oysters in secret, Shaw branded it as an 'unmitigated lie' that would be entered in the books of the Recording Angel as an aggravated and outrageous falsehood.

Shaw on wartime rationing:

> May we ask for an official assurance that when rationing begins special provision will be made for vegetarians? For some unexplained natural cause vegetarians are the most ferocious class we have; and any underfeeding of them would produce a reduction of our national fighting spirit out of all proportion to their numbers.

A troubled actor in Moylan, Pennsylvania, sought to purchase Shaw's advice:

> My Dear Bernard Shaw,
> Until now, I have been a meat-eater and I'm almost 34! Soon I shall play Franklyn Barnabas [in Shaw's *Back to Methuselah*], but I am troubled. The longer I act in your plays the more I become convinced that they couldn't have been written by a meat-eater, or, perhaps, even by you if you had been one. And now I begin to wonder if they can be properly acted by meat-eaters . . .
> Both you and Gandhi have recognized the relationship between intellectual activity and nutrition and have proved your point in the quality of your work. And so I am wondering if some kind of proper menu could be worked out for that strange combination of physical, imaginative, intellectual, and spiritual forces that go to make up an actor who wishes to outgrow the limitations of his ego. Could you advise source-material, or could you recommend a sample menu of general use that I might try? I wonder if you include eggs, fish-oils, etc in your own diet; and what, in heaven's name, can be taken in the form of a delightful, non-poisonous, hot drink?! . . .
>
> P.S. I have enclosed $5 for your time, trouble, and postage.
>   As an estimate of the value of your time I realize it is

insignificant but it is all I can afford at present. If you do not feel inclined to answer kindly accept it, anyway, as a small token of my admiration.

And, from Maldon, Essex:

> Dear Mr. Shaw   I am a
> non-entity, you an entity –
> my voice unheard, your voice heard –
> so please speak up for us vegetarians
> and if and when I become famous
> I shall be able to 'have a letter in
> the Times' too – on vegetarianism
> that it is nothing 'curious' only in
> the minds of retrogrades.   Very faithfully
> & very meekly   Yrs.   Horace Crawslay Frost

Try this diet

WAS George Bernard Shaw a strict vegetarian? [*Londoner's Diary, July 26*].

On a postcard to me, dated April 9, 1940, G.B.S. wrote: *"The most successful diets so far seem to be:*

A.—Potatoes and buttermilk.
B.—Grass.
C.—Bread and butter.
D.—Nine pounds of horseflesh a day.

Personally, I prefer C; but . . ."
—[*Mrs.*] *Eileen Coghlin, Templeton Place, S.W.5.*

In 1913, Shaw set out for the benefit of the *Restaurateur* paper his creed in regard to feeding. It was brief, but comprehensive:

'I dislike all dinners.'
'I dislike all drinks.'
'I prefer my food uncooked.'
'I like all kinds of waiters.'

The paper had been conducting a sort of gastronomic inquisition among prominent people. Other replies received included Mrs Pankhurst's 'too busy to trouble about dinners until women get votes.' (An indirect way of describing the hunger-strike, apparently.)

Shaw on the whole preferred to dine at home, due in part to the difficulties his vegetarianism created. He never told a hostess he was a vegetarian, preferring to take his chances on the hors-d'oeuvres and vegetables, as he lived in mortal terror of being served the almost statutory vegetarian fare of tomatoes and breadcrumbs, which he abhorred. On one occasion, when Sir James M. Barrie was lunching with Shaw, he noticed with some distaste a dish which bore a resemblance to limp seaweed. Taking his courage in his hands he spoke up, 'I say, Shaw, is that something you are going to eat, or is it something you have already eaten?'

'May I send you some Lewes sea-weed?' asked one correspondent. 'The crofters boil it in milk, strain it, and it sets like blancmange. It is very nourishing, delicious, and truly vegetarian.'

At a certain socialist conference the delegates assembled after lunch, and G.B.S. came in rubbing his hands with delight. Glad to see him looking so pleased, someone asked him what he had had for dinner. 'Ah!' replied Mr Shaw, smiling genially, 'a really good dinner. I've had seven bananas!'

Dr Thomas Okey, the poor London boy who began life as a working basketmaker in Shoreditch, and later became professor of Italian at Cambridge, describes in his autobiography Shaw's dietary problems 'abroad', when in the 1890s G.B.S. joined his Toynebee Travellers' expeditions to the Continent. Shaw was a rigid vegetarian even at that date, and his principles gave some trouble at the Italian hotels; for Italians cannot understand anyone, except on religious grounds, refusing to eat meat when able to include it in his diet. In the early stages of the tour Shaw was actually suffering from insufficient nourishment – he would even decline macaroni that was cooked in gravy – until at length the organizer hit upon the expedient of seeing the head waiter on arrival at each hotel and explaining to him that one member of the party was under a vow. This was at once understood, and for the remainder of the Italian tour Shaw travelled as a devout Roman Catholic under a vow to abstain from flesh.

Shaw usually breakfasted at home on half a grapefruit, oatmeal porridge liberally dosed with butter, or some drier cereal, and a cup of Instant Postum; and usually ended his luncheon with an orange. He ate salads, fruits, cheese, butter and eggs. His vegetarianism was based on low-calorie count and economy. However, whilst economical in some things, he wanted the very best butter and cream, many varieties of excellent cheese, and a large assortment of the finest nuts. He spent a long time over his meals and made his housekeeper-cook, Mrs Alice Laden, weigh the calories in each, keeping the total carefully.

During the war years when there was a scarcity of the required vegetarian foods, Mrs Laden often travelled twenty-five miles to satisfy G.B.S.'s wishes. Similar difficulties arose when the Shaws travelled abroad. Over the years they toured extensively, including South Africa, China, Japan and New Zealand. The passion for travel was Charlotte's, and in this as in other things Shaw humoured her. Wherever they went she would take with them a menu of what suited her husband, which she would hand to the chief steward on their boat, and to their head waiter when they stayed at a hotel. Her culinary ultimatum ran:

> Mr Bernard Shaw does not eat MEAT, GAME, FOWL OR FISH, or take TEA or COFFEE. Instead he will want one of the undermentioned dishes at lunch and dinner. He will eat green vegetables, puddings, pastry, etc., cheese and dessert like other people. He likes oranges and salads and nuts – especially walnuts.

For breakfast	*Oatmeal porridge or other cereals and always grapefruit. For drink 'Instant Postum'.*
Other meals	*One of the following dishes at lunch and dinner.*

(Haricot Beans dry, white)	*May be plain boiled, with a sauce; or curried or formed into cutlets.*
Butter Beans	
Lentils	*(as above)*
Macaroni	*au gratin or with tomato, cheese or other sauce – or curried.*
Spaghetti	*(as above)*
Welsh Rarebit	
Yorkshire Pudding	
Rice	*Savoury: or Milanese (no ham): or curried with haricots or eggs or nuts, raisins, etc.*
Pease pudding	
Eggs (not too often)	*Curried: cutlets: mayonnaise: Espagnoli: en cocotte à la crème: omelette, etc.*
Gnocchi	
Sweet Corn	
Curried Chestnuts	
Minced Walnuts	
Soups	*Any thick vegetable soup such as Lentil, Haricot, Pea (St. Germain) Barley (crème d'orge), Rice (crème de riz), Artichoke (Palestine), Celery, Onion, Tomato.*

When Shaw was nearly ninety-three someone sent him a machine from America which seized upon raw vegetables and shredded them into a sort of pulp, which then constituted his main midday meal. And in the evening he supped on milk and bread or biscuits, with perhaps a little fruit.

'Ox-roasting seems to me a very tame attempt to revive ancient festivities,' was Shaw's comment when it was announced that the 1931 Brentwood, Essex, hospital carnival proposed to roast an ox whole. 'Why not bait a bear, burn a village atheist, flog a Quakeress, pillory a dissenter, duck a scold, fight a main of cocks, have a match between two oyster eaters and do the thing in style?' In deference to protests from Shaw and others, the Brentwood ox-roast was cancelled. His response was rather different eight years later when Thornton Grammar School, near Bradford, held a public ox-roasting at a garden party. 'I do not agree,' he wrote on a postcard, 'about the ox-roasting. I advocate the public exhibition not only of the roasting of the ox, but of its preliminary driving and slaughtering. After the complete ceremony the town crier should quote Shakespeare's line, "And now to dinner with what appetite you may."'

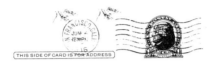

'I do not know,' commented Shaw's secretary, Blanche Patch:

> . . . whether he was a mythical waiter who is alleged to have remarked, 'I see you are wearing new boots, Mr. Shaw', when G.B.S. reproved him for serving meat. One excited individual certainly did ask us why, if he was a vegetarian, he should wear leather, and also woollen clothing. There was nothing in the point, said Shaw brusquely. As long as huge numbers of animals were brought into existence for feeding mankind, their hides and fleeces would be used for clothing, and 'no vegetarian who was not also an idiot would refuse to wear woollen clothes and leather boots unless he wanted to demonstrate that clothes and boots could be made if cattle were exterminated.

'If you had charge of boys who wanted to be carnivorous,' one Sussex correspondent wrote to G.B.S., 'you would have talked them to death before they were twelve . . .'

While some people wrote to Shaw asking for his advice on diet and health, there were those who – like the following correspondent – gave it freely to him, along with, in this case, one pound of a new flour (made of soy flour, kelp and alfalfa) a package of alfalfa tablets, and, not surprisingly, a treatise on Alfalfa-for-People, products of Bower Laboratories of California.

. . . I hope that this might aid you in extending your life span in this particular body – if that so be your wish.

My wife and I are also vegetarians and feel sure that it not only aids in health but also in our quest for solar knowledge.

I note that you eat acid and starch foods at the same meal – I find that acid and starch do not mix. Fruits should be eaten three hours away from all starches . . .

After many years of research and study and much dissatisfaction in the methods of the medical doctor in treating the sick, I developed a treatment using the Electro-magnetic energy of the body, which I contact by hands only, through the various nerve centres in the body . . .

My theory is: contracture of musculature and plexuses of the body is the beginning of all diseases. Freeing the contracture and allowing the vital energy to flow uninhibited from the brain through the entire body, gives normal tone to all individual cells . . .

Shaw insisted he threw such 'advice' letters in the basket at a glance. 'I get,' he estimated, 'at least 50 books a year instructing me how to live for ever. Also letters offering treatments (professional) guaranteed to achieve the same very undesirable result. Most of them would waste my remaining years in unhappy hard work to keep me alive.'

As with his headaches, friends as well as strangers sent Shaw insomnia cures. The 75-year-old Sir Horace Plunkett suggested the 74-year-old G.B.S. should take up flying as he had done; T. E. Lawrence of Arabia advocated a change of identity, and Einstein recommended strenuous physical exercises – long intervals with no thinking.

Shaw's self-cures were often drastic. Although towards the end of his life he was quite willing to accept the help and advice of doctors, in his early years he preferred to rely on his own cures wherever possible, as when he caught influenza:

I abstained from medical advice and quinine. I treated the fever by enjoying the morning air at an open window in an entirely unprotected condition for a prolonged period before finishing up with a cold bath; I stimulated myself by transitions from the overwhelming heat of the crowded St. James Hall to the chill coolness of Regent Street at night; I wore my lightest attire. I kept out of bed as much as possible.

According to Shaw's secretary, Miss Patch, Shaw's most fantastic 'cure' – based on shock therapy – was one for loss of sight which he passed on with perfect seriousness to Lady Martin Harvey. Loss of sight through shock sometimes cured itself, he told her. What the victim must do, apparently, he explained, was to buy 'a nice white wig, which looks well at all ages.' Then, he went on:

> get your head shaved completely and utterly. You will have a fearful shock when you see your shoulders surmounted by a bladder of lard with your well-known features carved on it. I have witnessed this phenomenon in the case of a very handsome woman; and I nearly fainted. So you must have a wig ready to clap on immediately. The reason for the wig being white is that, when the hair grows again, it will grow white or grey long before it would have changed colour if let alone. This also is a shock; and the total effect is to wake up the head and produce physical and psychological activities which may react on the sight or on anything else.

Fans

Dear Mr Shaw
  Why shouldn't I too write to you. I'm a great fan . . .
                    from Bessie Adams of Dublin

'. . . *don't do anything merely because I do it. If you do you will do
many foolish things.*'

                    Shaw to a female fan

Shaw was himself an adept hand at penning 'fan' letters, as in the following to musician Jascha Heifetz after his Queen's Hall London debut, May 5th, 1920.

13th June 1920

My dear Heifetz

Your recital has filled me and my wife with anxiety. If you provoke a jealous God by playing with such superhuman perfection, you will die young. I earnestly advise you to play something badly every night before going to bed instead of saying your prayers. No mere mortal should presume to play so faultlessly as that.

There were two basic 'Dear Mr Shaw' letters: worshipping letters and begging letters. Fan letters were largely eulogistic, full of praise. To his fans he was a 'great man' – 'How are you in your greatness?' one would ask. 'Stay with us . . . as long as you can endure us,' another pleaded. On the whole these hero-worshipping correspondents wanted little from Shaw beyond a simple token, an autograph or photograph. As one expressed it – 'It would do my mind, soul, and heart untold pleasure and happiness if I could but have a momento of you. Even if just a letter or name.' Many just wanted to establish some link with Shaw, perhaps just to know that he had read their letter or to let him know how he had affected their lives, as in the case of one American woman who wrote to him so: 'He will know that, though he is alone now, he is dearly loved. Not just revered.'

Shaw tried to play down such hero worship, for he was irritated by idolatry in all its manifestations. He rejected a suggestion that a park in County Dublin, where he played as a boy, should be called George Bernard Shaw Park . . . 'Not only would that be a clumsy, ugly title, but out of the question, because the men of Ireland are mortal and temporal, and her hills eternal.' He agreed to a plaquette being placed on Torca Cottage, Dalkey, where he had once lived, and on No. 33 Synge Street, Dublin, his birthplace. However, he insisted that the Synge Street tablet should not bear any inscription of opinion as to his literary merits or demerits, but state only the unquestionable fact that he was born in the house.

And, for the benefit of the pious Shavian, he once announced that although he did live in a house in Osnaburgh Street, London, he was indifferent whether they worshipped there or at the ginger-beer shop which had been photographed as one of the buildings made sacred by his presence.

When, in 1944, Dr F. E. Loewenstein, founder of the Shaw Society, asked for a formal ante-mortem request that a death mask should be made, Shaw replied with a question:

> Do you think I want to be remembered as a corpse 88 years
> old? In an early will I left my skull to the College of
> Surgeons so that I could grin eternally at posterity from a
> glass case. So none of your silly tricks with my remains.

Shaw similarly pooh-poohed his request for a lock of hair for a proposed Shaw museum. 'You idiot. My hair is white like any other old man's hair. Cut a wisp off the nearest white dog; it will do just as well.'

Shaw had fans from all walks of life. There was the wealthy American visitor who in July 1912 bought out the 1,400-seat Grand Opera House at Scarborough, in order to have the performance of a Shaw play entirely to himself! There was Harpo Marx, who first met Shaw at Antibes, in southern France. One night after driving Shaw to his Riviera hotel he confessed, 'For a while I considered driving the car into a smashup so that the papers could report that I was in such good company.' Shaw, who had never heard of Harpo, took him for a German philosopher, and treated him with deference accordingly. And then there was the Warsaw censor of plays who in 1932 was dismissed for 'false reverence to the author' for passing his new play, *Too True To Be Good*. It was stated that he was so overwhelmed by the importance of Shaw, that he had passed the play unread! 'A useful sort of censor,' commented Mr Shaw, when given the news.

A Detroit man in 1917 was arrested and convicted for reading Shaw's novel, *An Unsocial Socialist*.

One fan's enjoyment of Shaw's works led to an official reprimand:

High Wycombe
Bucks.

Dear Bernard Shaw

One day, of course, the story of your death will be true, though I hope not before you wish it.

So I think that it would be a pity for you not to know that you and I are in a 'Log Book' together. This is how the entry reads: –

> On May 4th, Head Teacher had occasion to enter Miss Lawson's room, and found her reading Bernard Shaw's 'Pygmalion' in the Council's time. The children were at recreation, but Miss Lawson should have been occupied with school work.
>
> Head Teacher has shown this entry to Miss Lawson and warned her that, should there be a repeat of dishonest conduct, sterner measures will be taken.

You were the Devil's brother, as far as she was concerned.

I am no longer at her school, and she, I imagine, has gone the way of all flesh

Yours sincerely,
DORA
LAWSON

P.S. If you think that this letter is written because I want your autograph, you are mistaken, for I already have it . . .

There was the artist disciple who put into practice Shaw's suggestion of selling pictures for £5 each, and the Ottawa dentist who met with others of like sympathies to read his plays. But perhaps Shaw's oddest fan of all was a house burglar. In December 1932, while three masked and armed thieves ransacked a Glasgow villa, a fourth tried to interest the two tied-up female occupants in a discussion of the works of Shaw, a picture of whom hung in the room. After recovering, the widow, Mrs McArthur, and her daughter gave the police a description of their assailants, one of whom had an artificial hand. Whether or not this was the Shaw-lover was not reported, however.

One man actually defended his vices before a court of law on the grounds that he was one of Shaw's disciples! Similarly, Ellen Taylor, when charged in February 1920 with using bad language, told the Plymouth magistrate's clerk, 'I don't see any profane or obscene language here. These are only the classical words used by George Bernard Shaw.'

The case was dismissed, the woman being advised to avoid 'classical' phraseology.

Shaw maintained an index-card list of 'disciples' until 1904. In a few years' time one of these recognized 'disciples', Professor Archibald Henderson of North Carolina, would – with Shaw's assistance – write his biography.

Another fan, Mr Patrick O'Reilly, founder and president of the Dublin Bernard Shaw Society, was disgusted when in 1953 the organizers of the Irish National Holiday Festival ignored Shaw's memory. The 60-year-old ex-Dublin Corporation worker decided to stage a protest during each day of the three-week festival by parading through the streets in a hundred-year-old chair drawn by a donkey.

One 'would-be reformed' criminal disciple even took the trouble to write to Shaw explaining how it was almost impossible to go 'straight':

London

Dear Mr Shaw

You are such a strong Socialist & believer in the equality of man, that I am hoping this little note on why criminals remain criminals may interest you a little. I am, or have been, a burglar, thief, confidence tricks man, & a keeper of brothels.

So far it has paid me fairly well, & I have been enabled to live at the rate of four or five pounds a week.

But lately, I have felt a craving for the life of a honest man, due perhaps to the awakening of a long dormant conscience. I gave up dishonesty, & looked around me, but could find no opening for a man without a character.

Then, in the hope that some philanthropic person would see my cure, I sent the following advertisement, to the Daily Mail, & 'The Evening News' – *Will anyone give a Thief & Blackguard a chance to reform? Age 28. Willing to work at anything England or abroad. Tall, strong, of good appearance & honest, (in future) A. Hinton, 1 Kings X Rd.* Both papers refused to insert this, although they gave no reasons. And now, almost penniless, I am forced to either starve, beg or steal once more. Later on, I suppose I shall be caught red handed, & sentenced to three years, with a few remarks from the bench about 'hardened criminals'.

And thats why most of us rogues remain rogues, – Because we aren't allowed to be any thing else . . .

And, from Wycliffe, A. Hill of American Offset Printers:

. . . I am a desciple of yours for the way you hurl your clever

and truthful barbs at us American boobs – and of Rudyard
Kipling – because of the way he sized up women . . .

In 1905 one young woman, Dorothy Treherne Willis of London,
wrote that reading his *Man and Superman* had led her to deny her own
womanly instincts – to deny her love.

Dear Mr Shaw
. . . When I first read it I thought I was fearfully in love.
Possibly I was, but knowing the unfortunate victim had read
it too was quite enough. It had to be squashed & has to be
still. Thats why I've just read it again. Just as Ann does I did,
before I saw it put like that, & when I came to the gestures
she makes I nearly swore. They were identical & I imagined
the victim, whom I respect rather much, making
comparisons & hated you for telling the truth. Then at the
second reading I had to laugh, it was so absurd to be taken
literally like that, then I had to own it is much better to put
things straightly & have no humbug & now whenever I feel
in the least fond of the man I rub it in that its nothing but the
Life-Force & subside . . .
Having got to the bottom of things through that Play &
the others I feel at an advantage with all men . . . The people
I meet don't read your plays & might be shocked if they did.
The *man* reads them but he is too far away, besides I am
consumed with anger when I think of my interpretation of
Ann, & have no desire to talk to him . . .

A few words from Shaw were all that were needed to encourage at
least one disciple – for better or worse – to carry on. Discouraged with the
lack of interest being shown in his 'Work-Sharing Plan' for the elimination
of *all* unemployment, 44-year-old John Wilde of Penrith, Cumberland,
wrote to the 93-year-old Shaw in desperation. In his reply, Shaw, while
ticking Wilde off as having a chip on his shoulder, expressed support for his
work-sharing plan, advising him to drop all other ideas except this one –
which he termed 'Holiday Banking' – as a man with more than one idea is
regarded as a crank. However he warned Wilde that no one would take any
notice of him or his suggestion for AT LEAST 25 YEARS!!

28th August 1949

Dear Mr. Shaw,
I cannot hope to express all that your letter means to me.
All my adult life I seem to have been misunderstood,
vilified, persecuted and victimised for daring to have some

idea or other which was not already part of the mental
stock-in-trade of the mediocrities who all-too-frequently
occupy – locally and nationally – positions of authority or
leadership in our socialist, trade union, and co operative
movements. Often – more often than not – the idea was too
small to be worthy of the name or too obvious to become a
subject for dispute, but it was always too much for those
whose entire education and thought appears to have been
embodied in a series of slogans invented by the Tolpuddle
Martyrs and the Rochdale Pioneers. . . . I feel that you have
wiped out for me years of disappointments and frustrations.
Above all, you have given me back my confidence in myself,
for I had begun to wonder whether I was insane after all,
and that I couldn't be right and the rest of the world wrong.
Now, with your opinion to sustain me, I don't care a toot for
the rest of the world: in any case, if ever you permit me to
quote you, the rest of the world will tumble over itself in
reversing its policy of suppression . . .

Alas, for Wilde, Shaw's avowed support, while fortifying, did little to gain
publicity for his propositions. Ironically, the sale of his Shaw letters at
Sotheby's in 1977 brought financial gain to at least one cause dear to the
playwright's heart: Wilde divided the £142 raised amongst five animal
charities, with £10 to the RSPCA, £60 to Animal Refuge (Carlisle), £40 to
the Dr Hadwen Trust For Humane Research, £20 to the Anti-Vivisection
Society and £12 to the League Against Cruel Sports.

A 1939 fan letter from an old socialist, Ben Tillett, was both a lament
and a plea:

> . . . It's fifty years or thereabouts, since we were young; and
> all these movements have grown, shrivelled up, then
> advanced, then retreated; Nationalised, Internationalised,
> then bloody murder and war – again the 'Brotherhood of
> man' is put to music!
>
> 'What might have been!' Calls to what are brains, or soul
> of me; what have we missed, lost, thrown away – not even
> you could prevent, or check, or resist the avalanche,
> relentlessly crushing out dreams & realisation together.
>
> I'm too Irish to laugh, either side of my face. I must hate,
> or forgive & in the latter I bemoan – as if there was anything
> in regretting, or bemoaning!
>
> You are over 80 years of age; I am 79, this September;
> I'm a real old asthmatic person, with resentment enough to
> harden the heart of me – so I just live on, and we are to have

the Jubilee of the Dock-Strike of 1889, I want to live to see it. God forgive me for the lack of graciousness; for progress seems to come in torture, in fault & failing.

I want you to come along to the function – I shall be glad, for you haven't suffered the errors and tribulations of success; the base ingratitude of it all . . .

I am writing this with two fingers on each hand – not as yet crippled. God love you, don't die, just beat the sordidness of the selfish; and just live to make bright the brains, and souls of men and women; of all lands and languages . . .

Both kings and revolutionary youths followed Shaw; his correspondence was cluttered with requests for ethical counsel and moral guidance. King Ananda of Siam, killed by a gunman in 1946, had wanted to abdicate and seek election as Premier, getting the idea from Shaw's *The Apple Cart*, according to evidence given at the 1950 trial of Ananda's private secretary and two pages, charged with his murder. Ananda, it was claimed, liked to stop his car and talk to villagers, who annoyed him by lying face down on the street until he drove on . . .

To Budapest shoeblack, Miksa Spitzer, who wrote asking for unobtainable British shoe polish because it is 'the best'.

From
Bernard Shaw

I am proud to number among my disciples a shoeblack; and I should gladly buy you a supply of British polish if I knew how to set about it.

But I am in my 94th year, and cannot walk further than my garden.

Ask some younger man.

G. Bernard Shaw

From a Berkshire disciple:

Dear Mr Bernard Shaw:
    The other night I was reading your 'Everybody's Political What's What?' in bed, and I came to the passage about blowing your nose on to the ground instead of into a handkerchief (p. 234).[1] With some triumph I read it out to my husband. When I used to go ski-ing in Austria my instructor forbade me to blow my nose on a handkerchief – not for your reason – but because, if you do, you make your nose sore and may even get frostbite. Liking the habit, I have continued it, much to my husband's disgust. He thinks I am a barbarian. But you and the Chinese seem to agree that it is far more disgusting to carry snot round in the pocket . . .

From John Bookbinder of the 28th Czechoslovak Regiment:

Prague, 24th Dec. 1920

Mr G. Bernard SHAW

London

    We soldiers of the 28th czechoslovak regiment of Prague, to whom your work always has been the philosophical basement of life, day by day endeavouring to follow our great Irish teacher, beg you to accept our best wishes for a happy new year.

We remain,
Dear Sir
and master
for the soldiers of the
Prague quarters reg. 28-:
John Bookbinder

---

1. '. . . If you have a cold, and are in the country, never use a handkerchief, use your fingers when nobody is looking; and select the sunniest spot you can find. When you are on city pavements or indoors use a paper handkerchief and burn it.'

From Shaw's New Zealand chauffeur, 1934:

> In these few lines I wish to tell you that nothing has surprised me so much in my life, so far, as to discover that such a great man as you are Mr Shaw whose utterances can attract the attention of nations, and that Mrs Shaw, the wife of such a world famed man, could both be so absolutely natural, and so very considerate to me whose privilege it has been to drive you on your tour of New Zealand.
>
> I can assure you that I will never forget your very many acts of kindness, shown to me during the tour.
>
> Once again thanking you two lovely people . . .

And, perhaps, the simplest of all, from Turkey:

20 March 1946

> Mr. Shaw,
> I like your plays.

In July 1931 Shaw was sent a 6,400-word open letter by a young man in Long Beach, California, which he hoped would promote sales of Shaw's book, *The Intelligent Woman's Guide to Socialism and Capitalism*. Fortunately for Shaw this 'Open Letter' from 'Irving Brisman, Paranoic', signed 'Your disciple whether you like it or not', read far more intelligently than the personal note which accompanied it.

> . . . Don't let on that you know anything about me. There's a plot to get me and they may think you're in with me on account of me having taken your *Intelligent Woman's Guide* out of a public library the same day I was examined by a prosecuting attorney & a psychiatrist up in Seattle last May — you see I hadn't been able to communicate for over a year with a woman I'm in love with so I was planning to kidnap

171

her and call it 'plot' and let those who opposed me (about two or three thousand people) laugh it off – I had just been reading your *Man & Superman* backwards and in my then state of mind it had the effect of making me suspicion that my Heroine was about to stop returning my letters to me unopened after reading them, and perhaps going to offer to marry me so she could answer them without first being introduced to me. I immediately went both Hamlet and Don Juan as I had some more sonnets I wanted to write first – also a novel; and that was when the Psychiatrists got wind of me – where is the woman Mr Shaw, that doesn't want to be kidnapped? – providing she's picked her man first – and while I have my drawbacks, still . . .

Shaw, an eccentric, responded to this quality in others, taking on from time to time, as he put it, 'an occasional crony'. One such man was Francis Collison (1850–1912), the proprietor of a Colchester stationery and newspaper shop. Nineteen years after Collison's death, Shaw would recall their association in a letter to his son:

Dear Mr Collison
    I remember your father well, though we never met face to face. He wrote to me out of the blue about something or other. Scores of people do that every week, and hear no more of it; but something about your father – who must have been a really dear old chap – secured my attention. He was then a bookseller-newsagent-philosopher-breeder of kittens and canaries. I was then an active member of the executive committee of the Society of Authors; and the light he threw for me on the relations between literary wholesalers and retailers was not only interesting – for he knew how to pick out the crucial points – but very useful to me. So I took him on as an occasional crony, and sent him my books to amuse him . . .

In 1903 as a token of gratitude for a small loan, Collison sent Shaw a gift canary, together with the offer of a kitten.

20th August 1903

Now I ask you, Mr Collison, as a sensible man, what the
devil you suppose I want with a canary. I am a vegetarian,
and cant eat it; and it is not big enough to eat me. But you
are not a sensible man: you are a 'fancier'; and you believe
that the height of earthly happiness is to be surrounded with
pigeons & Persian cats & guinea pigs & rabbits, with a tub
full of toads & newts under the counter. I once had a canary,
a little green brute that flew in through the open window one
day & would not go away. I hated it and it hated me. I
bought it a cage – a thing I abhor – & gave it everything I
could find at the seedsman's; but it was utterly miserable &
did its best to make me miserable until some benevolent
person stole it. I have been happy ever since until this day,
when I have received from Woking the devastating news that
you have inflicted another canary on me . . . And now,
having taken advantage of my being away on my holiday to
introduce this ornithological pest into my household, you
want to send me a kitten as well. Why, man, the kitten will
kill the canary when it grows up. Have you no common
sense? . . . What did I ever do to . . . you that you should
heap these injuries on me? Did my books ever do you any
harm? did they disturb you with silly whistlings at your work,
or bring forth litters of little books that you had to drown?
. . . My only hope is in the gardener's wife. She has one
canary already; and perhaps, if I make her a present of the
cage, she will consent to take the other if I offer her five
shillings a week for the term of its natural life. I shall then
hear it only when I walk in the garden; and at every trill I
shall curse the name of F. Collison.

However, Collison and family saw through Shaw's rebuke, and
when Collison died nine years later one of his sons wrote to inform Shaw of
his occasional crony's death.

Stamford
14th May 1912

Dear Sir,
    Three weeks ago at a
'Harbour of Refuge' known as
Winsley Square, Colchester, there
died suddenly at midnight &
alone a poor little man known

to you only by his quaint &
original correspondence, by name
Francis Collison – my father . . .
as he lived, so he died, alone;
depressed, reserved, melancholy –
but a brave old heretic to the last.
. . . You, sir, have been very kind
to him. You have spared valuable
time & effort to correspond with
him at length and you have
lent him, indeed given him, money.
This was most generous of you.
Giving to the poor seems to be the
last act of a Christian in this
christian country, but you, sir,
are more than a Christian, for which
God be thanked. I am deeply
grateful to you and feel under
an obligation to repay you, but
being only a very elementary
schoolmaster, have not the means to
do so at present.
  I think your patronage was
the greatest pleasure my poor father
ever had . . . He treasured
your correspondence, he read your
books & he expounded (I was going
to say exposed) your philosophy; and
in his final retirement in the
uncongenial atmosphere of the
Winsley retreat, your last
letter (dated Feb 21st)
did more than anything else to
cheer the last two months of an
existence which his peculiar temperament
rendered almost intolerable . . .

ANOTHER PACT: GRÆCO-ROMAN STYLE.

M. Venizelos. "AVE, CÆSAR!"
Signor Mussolini. "THE SAME TO YOU, ARISTIDES."

[M. Venizelos, during his recent visit to Rome, signed an agreement between Greece and Italy with the view of promoting peace in the Mediterranean and the Balkans.]

Now and again some fan would write to chide Shaw himself:

London, W1
1936

Dear Mr Shaw,

I have not seen any comment or sympathy from you about King George. A small word from you would do more than a thousand from Mr De Valera . . . I am a London Busman Driver twice I have nearly run you down Kingsway & Whitehall & the next time I shall just pass over you & then get my name in Papers the Driver who Killed Bernard Shaw. You were not the only one I missed Mr Churchill at Westminster at Mr Asquiths Service & you should have heard the policeman to me. I said Where the hell are you

going. I did not know who he was its funny how you great
men are abused when you are dead. I bought a picture of Mr
Mark Twain given to Sir Thomas Lipton 1907 & signed at
the market 6d & paid for it. I have a little antique shop here
Now I would like a photograph of you signed for nothing. If
there is any trouble of selling it I will wait until you are dead
& then you wont know. Well I am just dead tired on since
2.30 now 12.30 so off to bed & send that photograph. The
one no hands just as I saw it in a paper I have it.

Yours respectfully
Robert Emmet McCowen

Mr Strelling of Strelling's Kerbs, Carpets, Rugs, Glass, China and
Hardware of Hull thought Shaw less vociferous in his views than he ought
to be. He was afraid that Shaw's 'faint praise' of dictatorships would harm
his image and undermine his attempt to enlighten the world.

16th July 1938

Dear Mr Shaw.

I venture to address you in this manner, hoping you will
be able, both as regards eluding a conscientious secretary's
vigilance, and also deciphering this particularly abominable,
yet nevertheless, adult caligraphy. I speak to you, because I
have for many years contributed freely and enthusiastically
towards your present comfortable position.

The matter that is disturbing my mind, is your <u>apparent</u>
support of 'Dictators'. We will retain that title to avoid
quibble. Now, you write for 'popular' papers and therefore
speak to 'ordinary' people . . . I <u>must</u> say, however, that
before the world becomes the poorer for your loss, it would
be an addition – a <u>notable</u> addition – to an already rich
'memory', if you would use your pen, not in faint praise of
Mosley, Hitler and Co – but <u>against</u> them . . . But when
Fascists & Nazis form a Gangster's Council, with elaborate
and brute methods of making <u>themselves</u> 'The State' it
merely means that 'ordinary' folk are entirely at the mercy of
this little group of fanatics and thieves, hereinafter referred
to as 'The State'. Surely, this is not what <u>you</u> support, Mr

Shaw? It is what millions now <u>believe</u> you support and frankly, it worries me a very great deal . . .

I won't bore you longer, Mr Shaw, but do <u>please</u> exercise your great influence <u>against</u> mass Hypnotism.

WHERE OUR FOREIGN POLICY COMES FROM.

Shaw would appeal to the British government for the dockers on strike, or to the United Nations for Stateless refugees, or to anyone in authority for any victim of injustice. When a German film actor was hauled before a de-Nazification Court for having appeared in the film *Jew Suss*, Shaw wrote and told the Court that their proceedings were 'not only stupid but actually a criminal undertaking.' And when the Communist M.P. Willie Gallacher was charged with sedition, it was G.B.S. who stood him bail. 'Are you worth £200?' inquired the magistrate. 'No,' replied Shaw, 'I would hardly like to say that; but I've got £200, if that's what you mean.'

He had little faith in the ability of British democracy to reform itself quickly enough. On one occasion, he wrote off to a window-cleaner in northern England assuring him that, as the British parliamentary system was far too slow for the needs of modern society, 'a British adaptation of the Soviet system was indispensable.' Then someone would artlessly inquire whether people were happier under dictatorships than democracies. 'About happiness I know nothing,' he would snort in reply. 'An able dictator can effect reforms in six months that parliament would wrangle about for 60 years.' He therefore approved of Hitler when he ended unemployment and Mussolini when he drained the Pontine Marshes. Their obsessive hatred of Jews and coloured people, however, was beyond the realms of his imagination, such irrational venom incomprehensible to a man of reason.

Females tended to be Shaw's greatest fans.

12th October 1896

'. . . Up to the time I was 29, actually twenty-nine I was too shabby for any woman to tolerate me. I stalked about in a decaying green coat, cuffs trimmed with the scissors, terrible boots, and so on. Then I got a job to do and bought a suit of clothes with the proceeds. A lady immediately invited me to tea, threw her arms round me, and said she adored me.

On 31st March, 1896, Shaw wrote to Bertha Newcombe, an artist who was in love with him and whose friends conspired unsuccessfully to pair them off:

Your sex likes me as children like wedding cake, for the sake of the sugar on the top. If they taste by an accident a bit of crumb or citron, it is all over: I am a fiend, delighting in vivisectional cruelties, as indicated by the corners of my mouth.

A woman fluttered up alongside a spry, bearded old man striding along the street.

'Have I the pleasure of talking to Mr. Shaw?' she asked.

'Yes, but not for long.'

Sunday Express, June 19th, 1934

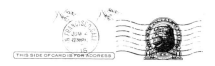

Walking through Malvern, Worcestershire, during its 1936 Shaw Festival, G.B.S. met an American woman who seized his hand.

'Oh, Mr Shaw,' she gushed, 'I won't go back to America till I've spoken to you.'

'Well,' said Mr Shaw politely, 'now you can go back to America.'

News Chronicle, July 31st, 1936

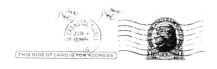

A great many female adorers pestered Shaw, who, although impatient with them, often answered their letters, as he was fond of giving advice – whether it be on their love problems, souls, or marital difficulties; in short, frustrations of all kinds. He could not resist the temptation to give them the benefit of his wisdom – on more than one occasion gratuitously. Periodically, as in the case of the effusive Erica Cotterill, Shaw's wife, Charlotte, was left to bail him out ... After attending a Shaw play in 1905, Miss

Cotterill, hopelessly infatuated with the author, wrote impassionedly to him, signing her letter, 'Miss Charmer'. As she appealed to both his vanity and Henry Higgins nature (he thought she had a promising literary talent), G.B.S. responded, giving her advice and theatre tickets, inviting her to lunch and introducing her to his friends. Gradually, however, her protestations of love got out of hand and she committed the almost unforgivable sin of disrupting the Shavian work routine, by roaring up to Ayot St Lawrence on a motor bicycle and trying to take charge of the Shaw household. When the situation became impossible, husband and wife conspired together to cool Erica's passions by means of a 'restraining' letter. Sent by Charlotte Shaw, the letter had in fact been drafted by Shaw himself.

> I think I had better write to you to explain exactly why I intentionally shewed you that I strongly disapproved of your presence in my house, and that I did not – and do not – intend that your visit should be repeated . . . The matter is a very simple one. You have made a declaration of your feelings to my husband, and you have followed that up by coming to live near us with the avowed object of gratifying those feelings by seeing as much as possible of him. If you were an older & more experienced woman I should characterize that in terms which would make any further acquaintance between us impossible. As you are young & entirely taken up with your own feelings, I can only tell you that when a woman once makes such a declaration to a married man, or a man to a married woman, there is an end of all honorable question of their meeting one another again – intentionally at least . . .
>   The present case is a specially dangerous one; for my husband is not a common man; . . . He is quite friendly & sympathetic with everybody, from dogs & cats to dukes & duchesses; and none of them can imagine that his universal friendliness is not a special regard for them. He has already allowed you to become far more attracted to him than he should; and I do not intend to let you drift any further into an impossible position . . .

A few months before his death, Shaw remembered the incident:

> 40 or 50 years ago she imagined herself violently in love with me and, being about one third mad, was a terror and a nuisance, as she would arrive at 10 or 11 on a motor bicycle and assume that my house was her own and I her husband. When we were driven to tell her that if she would not go

away we should have to call the police she either slept in the woods or planted herself on the nearest farmhouse. Yet she was an exquisite sort of person . . . At last she dropped out of my life; but I never quite got over my dread that she would turn up again, and her death is a relief, though it is at least 40 years since I saw her last.

A strange lady giving an address in Zurich sent Shaw a proposal, thus: 'You have the greatest brain in the world, and I have the most beautiful body; so we ought to produce the most perfect child.' Shaw asked: 'What if the child inherits my body and your brains?'

Shaw himself occasionally 'fell in love' on the spot, as he wrote to Virginia Woolf May 10th, 1940:

> There is a play of mine called *Heartbreak House* which I always connect with you because I conceived it in that house somewhere in Sussex where I first met you and, of course, fell in love with you. I suppose every man did.

This confession prompted a matching expression of love from Virginia Woolf:

> Monks House, Rodmell
> near Lewes, Sussex
> 15th May 1940

Dear Mr. Shaw,
. . . As for the falling in love, it was not, let me confess, one-sided. When I first met you at the Webbs I was set against all great men, having been liberally fed on them in my father's house. I wanted only to meet businessmen and say racing experts. But in a jiffy you made me re-consider all that and had me at your feet. Indeed you have acted a lover's part in my life for the past thirty years; and though I dare say its not much to boast of, I should have been a worser woman without Bernard Shaw. That is the reason – I mean the multiplicity of your lovers and what you must suffer from them – why Leonard and Virginia have never liked to impose themselves upon you . . .

From a girl with many questions, Bessie Adams of Dublin:

> 27th July 1946

Dear Mr Shaw
    Why shouldn't I too write to you. I'm a great fan. I want to know if you indulge yourself by sitting at, and enjoying a coal fire. Do you wear leather shoes – being a vegetarian – do you live in a house of 'hewn' stone Exod.20.25 and do you think, metals are a forced evolution and have you read 'The Hidden Side of Things' by C. W. Leadbeater? Since I read this book I've become a vegetarian – a thing the Church of Ireland ought to teach . . . Do you believe in fairies, unseen beings, sylphs etc . . . I'm on a seven day fast trying to see if I can see anything and this is the fifth day – (anyway if its done nothing else its given me the courage at long last to write to

you) . . . I would be humbly grateful if you would tell me what you think of this Fourth Dimension – as I suppose this is what it would be – nature-spirits etc . . .

From one female fan not asking for anything at all:

> Finchley
> London, N3
> 30th July 1944

Dear Mr. Shaw,

I suppose you will not recall a girl on a bicycle passing you this afternoon at Ayot St. Laurence. After you had smiled at me, I looked back to watch you go through a gate into a field. Somehow, to me, you looked lonely and had not my friend stopped me, I would have spoken to you again.

Very sensibly, she pointed out that one with so great an intellect and wisdom as yourself would quite overwhelm me. Even so the picture of you walking along stayed in my mind all the way back to my home – so much so that I am now taking the liberty of writing this letter to you, although I am wondering whether I shall have the audacity or courage to post it.

I would love to talk to you but am abashed at the thought that your life-long circle of acquaintances must be of the wittiest and most intellectual. Yet should you ever feel the desire for the company of a very ordinary young person, I would be happy to come and see you at anytime . . .

> Yours sincerely,
> Marian Lee

Although the following correspondent wrote to Shaw of her repeated failure to get anywhere with either her writing or music, she didn't ask for – or beg – his help, but only his indulgence while she acknowledged his influence on her life, crediting him – as many others did – with giving her the courage to continue struggling. Shaw responded to her letter with a postcard.

Dear Shaw:

More than thirty years ago, on a broken-down Georgia cotton plantation named *Eureka*, in a section H. L. Mencken loftily called 'the Sahara of the Bozart', you were a tutelary deity. Over the sitting-room mantel in the big-house hung three portraits. Shakespeare's above, dark and kind and abiding, copied in oils by some great-aunt or other. On the left, where my mother sat, in big gauzy sleeves and a bow in her hair, was Tolstoy in his peasant blouse. And on the right, above Dadda's chair, flaunting red beard and brilliant eyes and all – was you . . .

You were my father's household god, Tolstoy, my gay enthusiastic mother's . . .

For years I wanted to tell you this; for years, periodically, I would make notes for 'Letter to Shaw'. When I came across them, in bottom drawers, tied up in packets, I would rage at myself in no friendly fashion, 'Have you got delusions of grandeur?' and quickly stuff them out of sight. I was, in a way, ashamed of it.

And the reason for it was this: I knew if I wrote you that you had been a teacher of my life, I should have a somehow fancy life to return to you – the proof of your worth to me. Well, sadly, I still cannot prove it. I cannot weigh it, nor essay it. I don't even earn any money by it. But I live by it . . .

Some few weeks ago, *Life* magazine came, and there from the cover, unchanged by so much as an eyebrow, except that the beard was white, quizzed the same brilliant eyes, the same witty enchanting smile . . . But this time, seeing your grand face again, I said, what if, after all, Shaw would not mind knowing his worth to an unknown life. That he has been appreciated without a lapse, every audacious word; known as a poet, as well as a philosopher; understood as a true believer, as well as a sceptic. Because by my life he can multiply hundreds, and hundreds of thousands. He will know that, though he is alone now, he is dearly loved. Not just revered . . . I wish I had something worthy to offer you, in return for all you have given me. Something I had made – I am to have a second story soon in the *Saturday Evening Post* (I began better, in the *Yale Review*), but writing is not my art . . . It was music I was born with. At fourteen I began by setting Titania's lullaby, and the songs have never really stopped since. But my right hand was never strong enough to play any musical instrument (did I say I had polio myelitis as a child, and am still on crutches) I thought I could not have a musical education without that, and since I <u>had</u> to create, I began to write. Yet all through the years the songs have kept rising like an exhalation from my breast . . . I have tried to get some critic to judge if a few of them might have some worth.* Not one will so much as listen . . .

Even now, I find it not possible to dispair in a world where minds like yours still function . . . I think God spares you to slash into men's minds like a sword.

The war of my generation was the Depression. I died in that war daily. And with no medals, no artificially stimulated 'morale'. We fell like sparrows then. A whole generation of us. I had just begun to sell a few stories to the more widely circulated magazines. Then I was told by the editors, 'We have enough stories laid by to last us four years. We are buying only well-known names now.' I have never been well since.

And that battle has never been won. We laid it aside (eagerly, I think) to join in this holocaust in Europe. Men are so much easier to kill. It waits, the real war, until this barbarous blunder is over. The war to prove whether man can continue to exist in an industrialized world. Maybe it was just nerves over our failure there, that led us all into this one? Dear Shaw, forgive me. I hadn't meant to get cosmic with you. This is, as I hope I have indicated, a letter of love, pure and simple. Only, writing to you, I write of the deepest questions of my life. When one summons up courage at last to speak to the oracle, it is not about the weather.

It is to beg you, dear Shaw – don't go! Stay with us . . . as long as you can endure us.

And now, perhaps you will excuse me if I sign myself, with the love and solicitude of an own child,

Faithfully yours,
Elmira Grogan

* Even as I write this, I know I will try again. You do that to me. <u>Thank you.</u>

And, there were those who just wanted to thank Shaw.

> . . . May I thank you for
> the entertainment and refreshment
> your plays have afforded me.
> When I am feeling that Government
> ought to provide a lethal chamber
> where persons presenting a certificate
> of superfluity signed by relatives
> & friends might be dispatched, I
> try to see one of your plays –
> they make me feel – Perhaps!
> After all –

(Miss) Elizabeth Sykes

Some 'Dear Mr Shaw' letters were written more for the fans' benefit than Shaw's. These correspondents wanted to comment on what they saw, often everyday occurrences in their lives, or perhaps to comment upon current issues, political or social, or, as was frequently the case during the war years, aspects of wartime life. Such was the case with a young Canadian girl who wrote of the twelve hours she spent in a lifeboat after her home-bound ship the *Athenia* was torpedoed at the outbreak of World War II. There was often a semi-confessional air to these writings – an attempt perhaps to create a personal sense of intimacy with the 'great man'. But fans often wrote for lesser reasons, perhaps just to reminisce, or – as in the following letter from a 21-year-old American girl from Yonkers, New York, to Shaw on his ninetieth birthday – just to share their frustration and dissatisfaction with the world.

> . . . I am sitting here in our living room at home, alone and
> there is quite a thunderstorm banging away outside . . . And
> while I am very comfortable and warm and safe, still,
> suddenly I felt a little lonely. I turned on the radio and a
> rich, warm Irish melody filled the room. Then I looked on
> the couch where the Sunday papers were piled and I saw
> your face on the cover of the Times Magazine. And so I
> wondered if you would mind if I sat down and had a little
> talk with you. I don't feel lonely at all now . . . Maybe
> sometime you might feel a little lonely, and you'll know that
> somewhere in America, a girl was thinking of you . . .
>
> Today I read about you and about how you are filling your
> days, and somehow my pulse started to beat faster and I
> thought, A man still lives today, a man who has filled his life
> with courage and action and vividness and faith in himself
> and life. You love life and aren't afraid to show it. If there
> were only more men like you.
>
> – Where are they Mr Shaw. The whole world is teeming
> with things to be done, the skys are still as blue and swept
> with clouds, the sea is still as silver and gray as it always was,
> the grass is still golden and green and sways in the winds,
> the stars are still as brilliant, the cities and skyscrapers are
> still as crushing and virile, but where is the red blood that
> should course thru men's veins. Where are the strong men,
> the leaders, the heroes . . .
>
> There is graft, there are strikes, there is fear and
> double-dealing in the UNO [United Nations
> Organization], inconsistency and reprisals and revenge
> steaming out of the cracked and crumbling wall the world
> has thrown up around itself. But it isn't this so much that

frightens and angers me, as the fact that no one seems to care. The fact that the majority of the people feel it is none of their business. They shrug their shoulders and say, what can we do about it. The big shots are running things . . .

I am not the type who wears thick glasses and keeps my nose buried in facts and statistics. I like fun, I love to dance and sing, I have lots of dates. My spirit rebels however at the thought of living a life of artificiality and shell-like sophistication and cowardice. I was twenty-one last September. I will be able to vote in the next Presidential election, and I haven't the faintest idea of whom I can vote for. It will be my first vote, but that is just the thing. There will be lots of us voting for the first time. And who have we got to look to for strong, decent leadership. And I'll be damned if I'll vote for some puny, political puttied puppet who will simper and bow before the world and attend ice cream parties and egg rolling on the Capitol lawn, but who will be afraid to stand up before the world and demand a little decent thinking and action from every human being in it.

What is it all about Mr Shaw, what can we do. Isn't there some way we can break out of our molds and Live. So that when it's all over and we are sitting upon a little cloud somewhere, we won't have to look down and shudder at the mess we left the world in.

There are so many wonderful things in life. Why can't we fight for them. Why can't we hammer and forge and raise up something shining. Great men have sat and slashed at paper and canvass, filling the air with great music, with great art, with great words and books and plays and dreams and ideals. Aren't these men greater than the munitions maker. Aren't they greater than the business tycoon, aren't they greater than all the political double-crossers.

. . . Your face has been familiar to me ever since I can remember. Would you like to know what I look like. I am tall enough so that I can't find many men who tower over me when I'm wearing high heels. Five, six and a half to be exact. I have black hair that has to be put up every night, brown eyes, white skin, and freckles. Goodnight dear Mr Shaw. I admire you, I respect you, and I love you very dearly. God be with you always.

In January 1925 a lady 'lionizer' wrote to Shaw asking for the large photograph of him she had seen displayed in a bookshop window, for hanging over the altar in her church. Shaw returned her postcard, re-directed in his own twitchy hand, writing on the back between the lines:

> She MAY want it. She will HAVE to want it, but it does not happen to be at her disposal. If she hangs it in a church she will get the incumbent into serious trouble.

From Annie Morgan of Ballynabraggett, Ireland, March 13th, 1912, with a gift of shamrocks to wear on St Patrick's Day:

> Dear Mr Shaw – (that is more familiary) but if ever you take a notion to visit our part of the country, we have a brown delph teapot, also a black japanned tea tray and eke a sofa minus a leg – we prop it with a piece of an old leg of a table that went to pieces at one time But you would get a bed – not the sofa . . .

'A ROAD IN KERRY: AUGUST 1923' PENNED BY G.B.S. HIMSELF

From a girl delighted with her 'Shaw' reply:

West Hill, Putney
London, SW15
8th December 1944

Dear Sir,

To-day is a veritable 'Red Letter Day'. I did not open the parcel at once, fearing, with a quickly beating, yet timid heart, a disappointment. Imagine my surprise when I saw not only your esteemed autographs, but also the additional answering lines! I was overjoyed & nearly overcome with emotion.

You have made me the happiest girl – rather woman – in Gt. Britain & Austria, nay, in the whole world – forgetting the war, of course.

I wish to thank you deeply and with all my heart for your great kindness so generously bestowed upon me, a nonentity in every respect. I keep reading your witty lines over and over again, and I find it difficult to convince myself I am not dreaming. These signed books, together with my poor effort of the oil study of yourself, will always occupy the most honoured place among my few treasured possessions . . .

With renewed profound thanks for the great honour with which you have privileged a quite ordinary short-hand-typist – who, alas, has many desires, with not the remotest chance of seeing them come true – ever.

When Elise Deutsch was sixteen and living in London she wrote asking Shaw for his autograph. Then she wrote from Palestine, receiving this reply: 'I have been in the Holy Land, so we share its charm. I am always glad to hear about it.' Their four-year series of exchanges ended in 1949, a year before Shaw's death, when he sent Miss Deutsch a postcard photograph of himself in knee-length cloak, gaiters and huge felt hat, bearing the following message:

Dear Elise,
Seek younger friends; I am extinct.
G. Bernard Shaw

There were those who wished a more personal contact. Just before Shaw sailed from New York in 1933, a woman elbowed her way through the crowd which had gathered round him, and planted a resounding kiss amid the Shavian whiskers, exclaiming: 'You're wonderful!' 'I'm always wonderful,' G.B.S. replied.

On occasion, however, the situation was reversed. Mae West, it is reported, on being informed that it was the declared ambition of Bernard Shaw to kiss her, commented: 'We never met, but I would have been happy to entertain the gentleman.'

There were fans, like journalist Beatrice Marshall, whose interest Shaw decidedly did not want. An Englishwoman living in Germany before the war, she was a fervid admirer of Hitler. She began writing to Shaw in 1934, sending him unwanted translations of her articles and so many photographs of 'her hero' that he asked his secretary, Blanche Patch, to inform her that it was impossible for him to answer her letters and that further photographs would be discarded. This so annoyed Miss Marshall that she began writing to his secretary as 'Miss Cross Patch'. The journalist had wanted to translate Shaw's plays into German, and was angered that the playwright had no intention of changing from his official German translator. Annoyed by the woman's persistence, Shaw eventually lashed out:

> What do you mean, you stupid woman, by bothering me
> with your translations? I told you that your writing was
> MORE legible than typing – so graphic in fact that any editor
> would see at a glance that you are a holy terror. Do be
> careful what you write about your hero (Hitler). Your letters
> may pass through many hands before they reach me; and
> even I may be tempted some day to seek a ready means of
> deliverance from you. If you send me any more books I will
> give them to the waste paper collectors. If you send amusing
> pictures I will not return them. So there!
>
> G.B.S.

Shaw's vitriolic note was returned to him by the Post Office marked 'Addressee not known', with on the back, however, in Miss Marshall's own handwriting:

> P.S. It would have hurt much more if you had
> merely returned the books: 'With Compliments'

by writing a letter you have only incited me to
emulate you in rudeness and I enjoy doing that.

Shaw's 90th birthday in 1946 would prove most disruptive for one
Cumberland housewife, Mrs Margaret Wheeler. Whereas Shaw could try
to escape the fuss by picking up his writing pad and going off in his
Rolls-Royce to London, she was trapped at home.

> . . . In the absence of news to the
> contrary, I am assuming you have
> survived that famous birthday. I have
> survived it myself, but only just. You have
> no idea of the demands it made upon
> my stamina and powers of endurance.
> My friends all know of my habit of
> not reading the newspapers and quite
> early on the morning of this stupendous
> birthday there was a knock on my door
> and there stood the first of them
> holding in her hand a newspaper with
> photographs of you emblazoned across it.
> 'I know youre interested in Mr Shaw,' she
> said, 'and I thought you'd like to see this.'
> I peeped out of the doorway and
> was somewhat staggered to see a long
> procession stretching right up the road
> and winding three times round the park;
> and everyone in it was holding newspapers
> or magazines, or both. I stood there
> all the morning receiving these offerings
> with indomitable patience, until I was
> neck-deep in a pyramid of articles,
> cuttings, interviews, photographs and
> reminiscences about you. Just as I was
> almost submerged by the culminating
> two or three thousand I stuck out
> my head and remarked with my last
> gasp that it was a great mercy Mr
> Shaw was so opposed to any celebration
> of his birthday – goodness only knows
> what would have happened if he'd thrown
> himself into it with any enthusiasm . . .

Between 22 January 1944 and 19 July 1950, Mrs Wheeler and Shaw engaged in what is thought to be G.B.S.'s last lengthy correspondence before his death in November 1950. This correspondence, which evidences great mutual affection, began when Shaw was 87 and she 35, and over the six-year period totalled about 80 letters. When asked many years later how their exchange of letters began, Mrs Wheeler replied succinctly, 'I wanted an intelligent man to discuss things with, so I deliberately picked him up.' And 'pick him up' she most certainly did. The no-nonsense forthrightness of this unromantic, self-educated Workingtonian immediately appealed to Shaw, sad and isolated after the death in 1943 of his wife, Charlotte, to whom he had been married for nearly 45 years. Most of his Fabian cronies as well as many of his theatre associates were long since dead, and he felt his own death was considerably overdue. Similarly, with her husband Charles away in India on war service with the British Army, Mrs Wheeler felt lonely and over-burdened. In lieu of Charles, Shaw would serve as a sounding-board off which to bounce ideas. Her sprightly pen chatter, to which, until shortly before his death, Shaw always replied in his own steady hand, lessened the loneliness of these years. 'I am neglecting my proper work to write all this,' he told Mrs Wheeler. 'Clever of you to induce me to do it . . .' As she kept their correspondence private, he knew he could write to her without the whole world listening, and while doing so could enact for one last time one of his most favoured roles, that of official tutor, to – it would soon prove – a rather self-determined and argumentative pupil. For Shaw it was an ideal arrangement. As he had often found in the past, he could flirt to his heart's content with the Postmaster-General as chaperone. Neither Shaw nor Margaret Wheeler wanted to meet, nor did they. To make things perfect, there was a husband – to whom she was happily married. The marital triangle of Shaw's early London years of husband, wife – and Shaw – would repeat itself yet again. He was, as Mrs Wheeler addressed him from time to time, her 'Sunday husband'.

The Shaw-Wheeler correspondence has great charm, as it reveals how quickly G.B.S. could establish a companionable relationship with a complete stranger, exhibiting as he did great compassion for her well-being and interest both in her problems and her everyday Workington routine – cooking, mending, washing, ironing, and all the other jobs involved in looking after her own four children and an evacuee. The pride women took in their spotless front step angered her greatly. 'I am overcome with fury,' she wrote, 'when I think of the hundreds of thousands of Northern and Midlands women who daily go down on their knees in senseless worship of that insatiable idol . . . If ever I build a house of my own, one of the things I shall insist on will be a front doorstep that will get up and clout anyone who tries to clean it.' Shaw, however, was charmed by Margaret's report of such a common domestic ritual. 'That front door step of yours tickled me enormously,' he replied. 'I do wish,' she wrote on another occasion, 'you wouldn't keep on throwing Beatrice Webb and her half-hour housekeeping in my teeth . . .'

While Mrs Wheeler first baited the correspondence with a highly informed letter on a subject most dear to Shaw's heart – the Alphabet – the reform of which he intended to be the chief beneficiary of his Last Will and Testament, she quickly moved on to other areas of mutual interest: crime and punishment; war and peace; flood control; domestic drudgery; the Coupled Vote; coercions and sanctions; parent-child relationships and the nurturing of children (she sent him a childcare questionnaire); euthanasia; the Life Force; and even Shaw's difficulty with his teeth! 'I heard your voice last July,' wrote Mrs Wheeler, 'and took a fancy to it . . . (You must either have borrowed a decent set of teeth or else glued the offending ones in firmly on that occasion) . . .'

On such subjects as the Life Force they had to agree to disagree. Mrs Wheeler, to Shaw's great delight, was more often than not refreshingly argumentative.

> . . . I have been re-reading some of the things you have written, and am filled with fury about this Life Force of which you talk so much – this mysterious force that is alleged to take whom it will by the scruff of the neck and make them do its inscrutable bidding, and I wish most particularly to tell you that I, Margaret Wheeler, will have none of it. I would as soon sit in the path of an avalanche or give my allegiance to a maelstrom . . .

And, elsewhere, 'Don't tell me again that children need to be destructive, I don't believe it' . . . or 'I swear with abandon when seriously annoyed . . .' Asked by Shaw whether she were a quarrelsome devil, Mrs Wheeler replied, 'Of course I'm not. Only argumentative.' 'You are,' she informed Shaw, 'the only man I know who can keep me up till 4 a.m. with exasperation . . .' 'Do you know that you are responsible for this seething discontent of mind? Raspberries to you.'

Praising Mrs Wheeler's prose, which he claimed to prefer to the novels of George Meredith, Shaw did something he rarely did: he advised her to take up literature as a profession, confessing that when he destroyed her letters he always felt as if he were committing a literary crime. Her way of 'putting the stuff together' was the right way, and it was high time she exchanged the kitchen and the nursery for the study and the library. Despite the sort of encouragement which many a literary supplicant would have coveted, Mrs Wheeler was not interested. Above all, she refused adamantly to be a Shavian protégé. 'If ever I go into serious writing, I want to go on my own feet, and not on your shoulders . . . One can't fall off the floor, you know; but it appals me to think of what would be expected of a protégé of G.B.S. – *what* a handicap!'

During their six-year correspondence Shaw sent the highly privileged Mrs Wheeler a number of Private Edition/First Rehearsal copies of his works. More importantly, however, he offered her a measure of closeness through a number of small personal revelations. She, in turn, shared her fears as to her 'changeling daughter': her belief that one of her daughters was not her own by birth, that the child had been swapped with hers by accident in the Nottingham nursing home where both children were born in September 1936. In this instance, Shaw tried to take on the mantle of a latter-day Solomon. He warned her not to prove her case publicly and legally, advising her to be content with a private understanding between the two families, leaving the girls as they were, 'loved by parents they have acquired' – whether by accident or by the course of nature. What mattered was that the children were content, and above all, loved, irrespective of parentage. Shaw's advice, whether consciously or unconsciously, was at least partially taken. By the time the mix-up was proven seven years after the birth of the girls, the families had agreed to bring up each other's child. It wasn't until many years later when Peggy Clark was 18 that Mrs Wheeler told her she was her real mother.

Throughout their exchange of letters, depending upon mood, G.B.S. and Mrs Wheeler used a number of different modes of address for each other. Mrs Wheeler was variously, 'Mrs Wheeler, not to say Margaret or Maggie or Meg', 'Mrs Thoughtless', 'Mrs Sundayspouse', 'Dame Margaret', 'Margaret Wheeler', or more flirtatiously, 'Missiedee', 'Mrs Dimplekins' and 'Mrs Twodimples'. As well as her 'Sunday husband', G.B.S. could be 'Old Astringent', or more simply, 'Mr Shaw'.

> . . . you will always be Dear Mr Shaw to me. I am entirely
> convinced that at this safe distance – with four hundred
> miles and fifty years between us – it is quite proper for me to
> be thus devoted to you.
> But I should warn you that your description of yourself
> (with pathos) as 'senile' raises no compassion in my bosom –
> I am as flint. Senile indeed! Come off it, Mr Shaw! I don't
> believe a word of it – besides, it's so damned unflattering to
> *me*. Do you wish me to think that if you hadn't been in your
> dotage you'd never have dreamt of letting me sob about my
> thousand-and-one woes on your shoulder – at long
> distance, of course, and if I've given you rheumatism in that
> one just wait a moment and I'll cross over to the other!

When Shaw died, 'I felt,' Mrs Wheeler told the *Sunday Times* when interviewed in 1983, 'I had lost a real friend – and I sobbed my socks off.'

There were those who didn't write, but expressed their gratitude by deed. On the day of Shaw's cremation, suffragist Mrs Mary Leigh turned up at the chapel before the service began, taking a suffragette flag from her bag. When officials objected, she told them, 'Mr Shaw was one of our best friends. He visited us in prison. I only want to pay tribute with the rest.' After unfolding the old flag, she moved quietly out into the road when asked by the police, and stood there, paying personal tribute.

Daily Mail *(November 7th, 1950)*

Gifts & Greetings: Birthdays, Christmas & Other Occasions

ADVENTURES OF SANTA CLAUS.   No4.   AT Mr. SHAW'S.

There were those who, instead of asking Shaw for something, sent him something. Several Americans sent him cameras and fountain pens, another an axe; a man from Manchester, a pocket-lamp with accumulator; a pipe-organ builder sent him a poem; the composer Ernest Wilson dedicated a new work for alto saxophone to him – 'Saxophone Caprice' – and Edward Elgar dedicated the Severn Suite for Brass Bands. The actress Katharine Cornell sent a Christmas gift of diamond-studded scissors for Shaw's beard and another female admirer a G.B.S. wishbone caricature; and yet another sent an enamel washing bowl with the bottom chipped in the shape of Shaw's profile.

From C. A. Potter of Sheffield came gift knives and teapots and the offer to sharpen Shaw's scissors and knives and replate his silver. Over the years, gifts ranged from fish lures when he was 88 years old to his own will – a thoughtful gift from his own solicitor, for the man who has everything. His housekeeper, Alice Laden, was on the scene when many of these gifts arrived:

> The world did not really know Mr Shaw. He could be
> kindness itself one moment, and appeared the last word in
> discourtesy the next. To people who sent him food – parcels
> with cakes, sweets or nuts used to arrive from all over the
> world – he would usually reply 'Don't send any more of this
> rubbish.' He even swore like a trooper sometimes.

A Toronto woman who sent Shaw a box of chocolates for his ninety-fourth birthday on July 26th, 1950 received this reply on the back of a photograph:

> Do I look as if I liked sweets? Eat them yourself or give them
> to kiddies in their first childhood not to dotards in their
> second.

As early as 1898, in a letter to Max Hecht, Shaw expressed his dislike of presents:

> . . . If ever I get married, it will have to be done very secretly,
> because I have a great many friends who would make a fuss,
> and who would spend money which they cannot afford in
> giving me things which I don't want – I hate presents . . .

From on shipboard, he wrote:

> Stresa. 3rd October 1926
>
> The room is full of flowers; and I daresay yours are among them.
>> Waste of money, I call it.
>> Do you suppose you can get at me by buying things in a shop?
>> However, my wife likes cut flowers.
> For my own feeling about them, see John Bull's Other Island, Act II. [don't pluck the little flower]

Time and time again he referred to actress Ellen Pollock's gift-giving as lunacy.

> 25th December 1947
>
> I have half a dozen pullovers and I never wear them. Yours is the richest in color in the collection.
>> If you cannot restrain this mania for making presents, exchanging money which everyone wants for things that nobody wants, you should do it at unexpected moments and not at Xmas when all the other people do it and smother your gift under a pile of cards and rubbish.
>> I must cure you of this lunacy. Let me think of you as a fellow-artist, not as a mental case.
> Drop it, Ellen.

GBS

Unwanted gifts – like Miss Pollock's ninety-fourth birthday present to Shaw – were given or thrown away. Two weeks before the big event, Miss Pollock, who prided herself on sending Shaw 'odd' gifts, sent him a bison's foot inkstand she had purchased in Germany. At the time she was producing his play *The Devil's Disciple*, and halfway through a letter of dramatic advice he ungraciously noted receipt of her gift:

> Just arrived. The hideous foot
> of an animal in the form of an inkstand,
> which wobbles when you touch it. I
> shall give it to the vicar for his fair.
> It may help to warm his church, which is
> usually icy cold . . .
> That will teach you to spend your money
> more wisely . . .

Shaw even wrote a letter – a mere four days after 'the birthday' – to be auctioned with the present to enhance its value and vouch for its authenticity.

> This Knockover Jug, a horrible object,
> was presented to me by
>   Ellen Pollock
> who has appeared in my plays with great
> success.
>   A less suitable present for a teetotaller
> and vegetarian like myself cannot be
> imagined.
>   The church here needs heating, they tell
> me. Some person with strange tastes may buy
> it for enough to fetch a scuttle of coals.
>   So here it is with my blessing.
>
>   G. Bernard Shaw.

The unusual in presents, as in other matters, attracted Shaw. To Hartwell Brothers, Manufacturers of Hartwell Handles of Memphis, Tennessee:

> 14th January 1928
>
> Dear Sirs
>   Today for the first time for months I found it impossible
> to keep on slaving at literature; so I went out into the sun
> and did a morning's honest work – in spite of its being
> Sunday – with your axe, which I handled for the first time. It
> was a great success: your handles are not only works of art
> which I exhibit as such to my friends but what handles must
> be in the first place: that is, perfectly handy.
>   I do not know what inspired you to make me this very
> unexpected but very welcome present; but you certainly hit
> off my fancy exactly. Most Americans send me books
> containing plans for regenerating the world, mostly by paper
> money based on land values or labor hours, which I never
> read, my recreation being anything that takes me away from
> books. But your axe has not been wasted: you should see my
> woodpile. And I cannot be suspected of grinding it for you,
> as there cannot be a woodman in America, or on earth, who
> would buy an axe on the recommendation of a literary
> amateur.

Five hundred years hence, connoisseurs will perhaps collect your axe handles as they now collect Stradivarius violins, but you and I, like Stradivarius will be none the richer for that.

HOW "G. B. S." KEEPS FIT

Mr C. W. Shannaw, a London artist reduced to selling matches, copied a sarcophagus in the British Museum because it reminded him of Bernard Shaw. G.B.S. was delighted when the drawing was sent to him for inspection.

19th July 1934

Dear Mr. Shannaw
    If you can draw as well as this, how do you come to be selling matches for a livelihood?

However, it is just as well for an artist to have some honest trade to fall back on.

My Etruscan ancestor in the British Museum certainly has points of resemblance. I invite the Herald's College to note that I go back to 630 B.C.

Thank you for allowing me to inspect.

THIS SIDE OF CARD IS FOR ADDRESS

'To hell,' wrote Shaw, 'with all birthday wishes. Who in his senses wants to be reminded that he's growing old?'

> . . . For my part, as I grow older, I care less and less to be reminded of these milestones on my way to the cremation furnace. It is true that I am not so young as I was; but why the devil should people remind me of that? When I meet an elderly friend in the street, I do not go up to him and wring his hand sympathetically and say 'Old friend, let me congratulate you on a few more teeth gone, a stronger pair of spectacles, another patch of hair off your head, a rapprochement of your knees, a more pronounced curvature of your spine, and a perceptible increase of senile dementia . . .'

'I don't want to be asked how I am,' he insisted angrily. 'There's so much nonsense in this "How are you?" business. People are always saying "You look younger than ever," when the truth is they are thinking how damned awful you look and wondering that you manage to keep alive, anyhow.'

The Shaws shared an aversion for anniversaries, including their own birthdays and silver wedding. When a special dinner was held to celebrate Mr and Mrs Pethick Lawrence's silver wedding, G.B.S, who was in Italy, instructed his secretary to send his condolences on their failure to conceal their silver wedding as successfully as he had concealed his, and to add that his seventieth birthday so nearly killed him that nothing would ever induce him to celebrate any personal festivals except those of his worst enemies.

And yet, inconsistently:

> Bernard Shaw was annoyed because the English did not compliment him on his 75th birthday, and Germany did. Well, Germany don't have to live with him.
>
> Will Rogers

Shaw had at one time expressed the wish to celebrate his seventy-fifth birthday in the Soviet capital, a wish which came true in July 1931 when he, in the unlikely company of the Astors and Lord Lothian, paid a ten-day visit to Russia, which was reported in great detail by the British press – how they took tins of food with them; how Lady Astor was discovered washing Shaw's beard; how at last they met Lenin's widow, Krupskaya. Inevitably the visit's highlight was a two-and-a-half-hour privileged interview with Stalin after which Shaw's iconoclastic gaiety was paraded before the Russian people. Leaving Stalin, Shaw appeared at the head of a flight of steps, looking very serious, and, after calculatedly waiting for silence, announced anticlimactically to the waiting reporters that Stalin had splendid black moustaches . . .

The special Russian treat laid on for Shaw's seventy-fifth birthday did not suit this *enfant terrible*, who, while not excessively discourteous, made it clear that a day at the races was not an apt outing for the only living Irishman who had not the slightest interest in horseracing! Shaw paid no attention to the proceedings, ignoring even the 'Bernard Shaw Handicap' race, and eventually fell asleep.

After visiting a Russian factory, Shaw wrote in their distinguished visitors' book:

> My father drank too much. I have worked too much. I hope
> your Five Year Plan will succeed but when it does, for
> heaven's sake stop and take a rest.

'I have,' responded Shaw, when asked to send greetings to Gandhi on *his* seventy-fifth birthday, 'a cordial personal liking for Gandhi. But, being myself a mahatma, I never send messages to my colleagues in that profession.'

'One more question, Mr. Shaw. What would you have done if you had waked on your seventy-sixth birthday to find this country being governed in what you think is a rational manner?'

Mr Shaw: 'I should probably haved died of
astonishment.   Good-bye!'

On his eighty-fifth birthday Shaw left instructions that all telephone callers were to be told that:

1. A birthday was just like any other day.
2. He was not 'keeping' it.
3. He never 'kept' it, and
4. There was no party.

Many birthday greetings were of a charming simplicity.

Hounslow Middx.
July 22nd.

To Bernard Shaw, Esq.
Dear Sir

   May I be excused addressing you a working man. but being a stage Hand under Messrs Vedrenne & Barker at the Court Theatre and Savoy in all your productions that have given me plenty of pleasure in fact I saw them all many times from the flys and never got sick of them I expect it would be too much if I wish you many Happy returns but may I wish you good health and happiness during your stay on this earth that I am certain you have done a deal of good in more ways than one.

Good luck sir
Alfred Coleman

P.S. perhaps I have not put this together Quite as well as your speech by Robert Lorane in Don Juan but excuse it please.

Other birthday letters were expressions of gratitude:

Dear Mr Shaw
   I am a labourer, being a
specialist with the hod, for a number of years.
My wife and I have agreed (for once) to
refuse point-blank on allowing the 26th July, [Shaw's birthday] to pass without thanking you, for many hours of pleasure and profit.

To an invitation to attend the Shakespeare celebrations at Stratford-upon-Avon, Shaw replied that as he never celebrated his own birthday he could not 'consistently take an active part in celebrations in honour of a lesser dramatist.' And, on another occasion:

. . . But it is clear to me that when a man is not for an age but for all time he cannot decently be allowed to go on with his birthdays. There should be a statute of limitations. This thing has been going on now for over 350 years. How many more birthdays does he want?

However, in 1925, the year he received the Nobel Prize for Literature, he attended – for the first time – the birthday luncheon in the Stratford Town Hall, proposing 'The immortal memory of William Shakespeare'. His presence on this occasion mortally offended the playwright Henry Arthur Jones, who had been adamantly – and almost hysterically – opposed to Shaw's World War I opinions. After the birthday event, he wrote to the newspapers advising that the Town Hall should be thoroughly fumigated after the presence of the traitorous Bernard Shaw.

MEASURE FOR MEASURE.
(*"Shakespeare in Modern Costume."*)
Shakespeare. "HULLO, OLD THING! WHAT'S THE IDEA?"
Mr. Bernard Shaw. "WELL, AS YOU'RE DRESSING LIKE THAT, I THOUGHT I'D DRESS LIKE THIS."

However, despite Shaw's repeated disavowal of presents – birthday or otherwise – there were certain gifts of clothing which he found most useful: such practical items as fingerless mittens, socks and scarves. The socks were specially shaped for his right and left foot as he found them much more comfortable like that.

> London W2
> 16th April 1944

> My dear G.B.S.
> Here are your socks.
> If they are not exactly the Shavian pattern.
> I hope they will fit you. & that you will like them.
> As you will instantly see the socks are alike. I have put the red spot, & made a 'right' foot because it is better knitted.
> You would laugh at the funny places in which they were 'raised'. Queues, shelter, railway platform, & in trains & trams. The next pair will be better, I hope, I should like anything I am privileged to do for you to be flawless. Please let me know if there is anything you would like changed. I shall be so proud if I may sometimes make you gloves & socks . . .'

The gift of a scarf woven by a woman admirer in Scotland was to confirm Shaw's colour-blindness. His secretary would later recall the incident.

> He was very pleased with it, but he wrote to ask her, would she do him one with less green in it? It was not green, I pointed out, but blue, and the weaver herself settled our argument by regretfully informing him that his secretary was right.

There was at least one occasion on which Shaw agreed to accept birthday gifts. But, he made one stipulation. No one present at the 1936 Malvern Festival was to spend more than threepence on his eightieth birthday gift.

The original proposal was that the members of the Malvern Festival Company should club together for a joint presentation, a plan put a stop to by Shaw as soon as he heard of it. He immediately wrote to the actor Ernest Thesiger and said that although he appreciated their kind thought, he really did not want a piece of silver that he could pawn, claiming that his eight ounce solid gold 1925 Nobel Prize had given him no personal satisfaction. He much preferred that the actors and actresses should each give him a personal present, the cost not to exceed 3d, adding that he owed so much more to the actors than they did to him that he was sending £100 to the Actors' Benevolent Fund, to show that he knew his place.

The members of the Malvern company had little choice but to flock to Woolworth's, and Shaw vowed that never in his life had he received such a useful collection of pens, pencils, ink, sealing wax, and so forth. Mr Thesiger sent a 2d pencil sharpener; another actor a children's drawing book; from one of the brighter members of the cast he received a razor blade and someone else sent a home-made valentine. A poetic rendering accompanied one gift.

> Your friends will send rich gifts,
> No matter what they cost 'em.
> Here is mine – a simple thing –
> A tin of Instant Postum.

Shaw was delighted with these simple gifts; as he was a year or two later when a vanload of Ayot landgirls passed his Ayot St Lawrence home chanting 'Happy Birthday, dear Bernard, Happy Birthday to you!' However, although he appreciated these impromptu outbursts of affection, he genuinely disliked an annual flurry of presents. He was therefore to find all the fuss made over his ninetieth birthday a traumatic experience.

Mr. Bernard implores his friends and readers not to celebrate his birthdays nor even to mention them to him. It is easy to write one letter or send one birthday cake; but the arrival of hundreds of them together is a calamity that is not the less dreaded because it occurs only once a year.

Acknowledgment of such unwelcome letters and gifts is not possible.

No major playwright since Sophocles had lived so long. His becoming a nonagenarian required production of a very special salmon-coloured card, to be used for his last four birthdays. It was so hastily printed that Shaw's surname was omitted!

Despite this protective measure, however, the event provided a focus for Shavian eulogies and elicited a flood of 'Dear Mr Shaw' letters. As his postman, Harry Rayner, later recalled:

> On this 90th birthday I was accosted by a reporter who asked if I would let him take in the mail in my place and offered me a £2 bribe for the privilege. But of course as a servant of the Crown I refused. And apart from that, there was a policeman on guard all the time outside Shaw's Corner, to protect him from the expected deluge of unwanted visitors. There were two large size mail bags chock-full of letters and packages for him from all over the world by the first post alone, and much more followed by other deliveries. Later in the day I delivered over 100 telegrams myself, and a boy was put on specially all day to deliver the several hundred others . . .

Most of these letters were opened and destroyed at Shaw's request by his bibliographic assistant Dr F. E. Loewenstein and his neighbour Stephen Winsten.

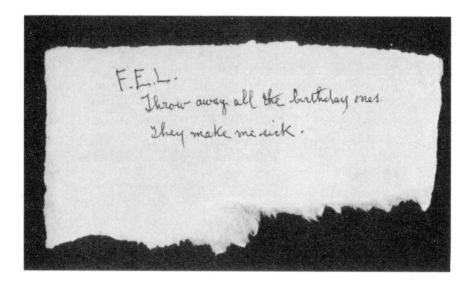

However, despite Loewenstein's destructive labours, a number survived.

The Police Station
Deighton Bar. Nr Wetherby.
24th July 1946. 2.a.m.

SIR,

At this early hour of 2 a.m. . . . in a very quiet rural township situated in the heart of Yorkshire, I, the local Policeman, am typing a sincere greeting to my most beloved writer on I hope, his happiest of birthdates.

It is not by any means a fad of mine to write eulogies, but for very many years, in my leisure and out of my leisure, much that has been begotten and born of your great mind, has been to me an inspiration and a delight.

So very many years ago it seems, since I took hold of your first book, but just now I love Saint Joan as dearly as I did when first introduced to it.

Nor shall I forget going to London town to see Dame Sybil Thorndike take that tremendous role, and how I went every night for ten nights, and was the greater thrilled at every performance she gave of it.

The incident will ever remain in my memory of attending this play on one of the nights stated, wearing a new pair of shoes which hurt me. To enjoy the night to the full, I untied the laces, and having removed the offending shoes, toed them under the seat in front of me.

Upon leaving the Theatre it rained in torrents, but the spell was so intense, that by tube and on foot I arrived at Clapham and to my rooms, before I recollected that I was in stockinged feet. I did of course recover them on the morrow.

So . . . I greet you SIR, with sincerity and with a great regard . . . May your ninety years of monumental thinking and doing, at this late hour so inspire us, that we shall the better apply that time yet left to each of us, in creating a world freer of strife than the past three generations have experienced.

Sincerely and with deep gratitude,
Ted Tempest

THIS SIDE OF CARD IS FOR ADDRESS

As in past years some ninetieth birthday letters were accompanied by gifts. He was so delighted by the golden shamrock sent by Dublin dustman Patrick O'Reilly on behalf of the Bernard Shaw branch of the Irish Labour Party that it was instantly attached to his watch chain and worn until his death. From Ayot St Lawrence schoolgirls he received sweets; from Canada and Australia, cakes; and from American vegetarian fans came grain cereals and molasses. Another birthday gift – a Talisman & Talismi Powder from India – came complete with a complex set of operational instructions, which, if Shaw followed them faithfully, were to guarantee he would be free 'from the diseases & anxieties and certainly reach the age of 125 years happily.' He was advised that:

> The Talisman or Amulet will not work at all or properly if it
> is used by a dirty man or for bad motive and against its
> simple teachings, & directions.

In closing, the correspondent offered his services – for a charge – to Shaw's friends, kith and kin:

> If any person requires to utalize the Amil's (my) services (to
> work for him & perform the spiritual ways & rites to seek the
> blessings) in some urgent or important cases the Amil (I)
> may be informed by a letter or telegram about the matter
> and remit a fee fifteen Gold Guinnes (one tolu each in
> weight) or equilant to one hundred pound.

There were gifts of poems, for Shaw's birthdays frequently released the poetic muse – for better or worse – in others!

> An Acrostic Sonnet
> respectfully dedicated to G.B.S. on his ninetieth Birthday:

For shame that men should dare to call you old!
Our marvel is that you remain so young.
Reading the quips that from your brain unfold,
By Zeus, I swear you have the Moderns strung,
Each by a feeble thread of stammered prose.
Refusing to grow old, you add each year
New themes with which to tweak a critic's nose,
And set the reader's mind all out of gear.
Receive, good Sir, the homage that's your due.
Don't blame us for our rationed bread and Points;
Since you have lived in better times – how true! –
Have pity on the housewife's shrunken joints,
    And be not scathing of this poor old earth
    Which in a flash of wisdom gave you birth.

Some letters, like the following from Barcelona, were confusing.

> Venerated Don Jorge,
> God save George Bernard Shaw!
> as he was in the beginning he is now
> and will ever shall be, Amen!
>   The anniversary of the Old
> young man remember us, that
> nineteen year ago ever he a tender baby
> like all babies of Dublin and of Ireland, Scotland,
> England and the British Empire and
> was making some progress as heaven born
> joker with a sarcastel smile to all
> snobs seduced to let be remembered
> in such a sacred day on July the 26th . . .
> I am out of practice to write in English
> but since 1922–1946 my teacher in your vernacular
> tongue is the tenth Duke of Argyll . . .
> Because you are pretending to reach 300 years
> My question: How are your hormones,
> hypophise, pineal, tiroides, superrenales, pancreas
> viticulos from which are proceeding the chromosomas.
> Are you able to procreate again
> like Abraham with Sarah? As nightcap I am absorbing
> yoghurt . . .
>
>   Arnold Fédor van Muyden.

Asked how he would spend his ninety-fourth birthday, he replied:

> Rising, dressing, feeding, with its inevitable sequels,
> working, snoozing, undressing, and going to bed. Provided,
> of course, that I do not spend an earlier date in Golders
> Green being cremated . . . Being actuarially dead at 94, I no
> longer plan my future . . .

Owing to his ninetieth birthday postcard requesting no gift parcels, Shaw received fewer presents in his last few years. On his ninety-second birthday he was sent four cakes; on his ninety-third none; and his ninety-fourth was brought by film-maker Gabriel Pascal, who alone constituted his party. To one Australian lady, who had sent a gift cake, he wrote:

> Very kind of you to send me that cake. My grocer is selling
> them at £1 each. I do not eat cakes. You have wasted your
> money. Don't do it again.

Her reply, 'Mr. Shaw must be a bit of a humorist,' was worthy of Shaw himself.

Christmas, like birthdays, was ignored by Shaw. For he and Charlotte the day went by like any other with the same customary routine and meals, with one small difference. According to Shaw:

> When we first came here [to Ayot St Lawrence] the squire's wife induced me to give something at Christmas Time. Charlotte and I decided that every Christmas the children should have a shilling with which to buy sweets for themselves. To make sure that their mothers didn't get hold of the money we arranged for the children to call personally at the home for their shilling apiece. And sometimes as many as ten come to the back door.

Although Charlotte would send a few cards and give one or two presents, she, like her husband, did not like to get presents from anybody. Shaw, however, on the Christmas after Charlotte died, sent a photograph of her to those who had known her. The following picture of himself gazing through his Ayot gate he would send as a postcard to his friends throughout the year.

A seasonal request from the Matron of Cynthia Mosely Wartime Nursery, Oval Way:

8.12.43.

Mr. G.B. SHAW.
Sir.

On asking a friend of mine, to act as Father Christmas for the children, at their party, which will be held at the above address on the 21st of December, he suggested that you would be ideal.

It is perhaps an unusual request, and you will possibly feel you are so much above the understanding of children – but, there is a war, and, forgive my being personal, you have such a beautiful beard, already made –

Could it be possible that you would accept?

Asked what he wanted for his ninetieth birthday, Shaw had snapped, 'The head of Father Christmas on a charger.'

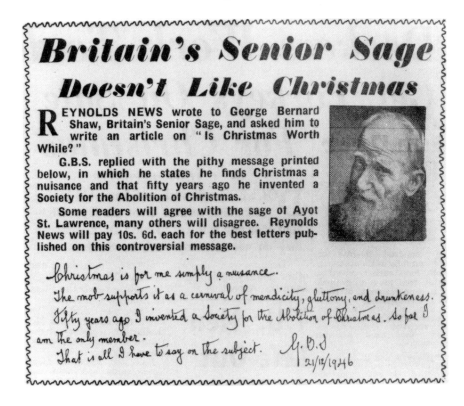

Britain's Senior Sage Doesn't Like Christmas

REYNOLDS NEWS wrote to George Bernard Shaw, Britain's Senior Sage, and asked him to write an article on "Is Christmas Worth While?"

G.B.S. replied with the pithy message printed below, in which he states he finds Christmas a nuisance and that fifty years ago he invented a Society for the Abolition of Christmas.

Some readers will agree with the sage of Ayot St. Lawrence, many others will disagree. Reynolds News will pay 10s. 6d. each for the best letters published on this controversial message.

Christmas is for me simply a nuisance.
The mob supports it as a carnival of mendicity, gluttony, and drunkenness.
Fifty years ago I invented a Society for the Abolition of Christmas. So far I am the only member.
That is all I have to say on the subject. G.B.S
21/12/1946

This statement elicited 'Dear Mr Shaw' letters worldwide. Many correspondents wrote supporting his anti-Christmas society and some even sent their annual dues. One American – 'an obscure student of Anthropology and Paleontology' – enclosed one cent as his membership fee. Others requested copies of the Society's Constitution and Standing Order.

Some were of two minds about Shaw's society.

> Dec. 25, 1946
>
> I heard about your committee for 'The Abolition of Christmas'.
> I was entirely in agreement withyou until this morning, when I received atypewriter.
>
> > Respectivly yours
> > William Catlin

From a Kansas postman:

> Dear Sir:
> I just read in The Wichita Beacon of Wichita, Kans. where at one time you had invented a society for the abolition of Christmas. I am not ninety years of age, but it did not take me that long to come to agreement with you. I have been a postal employee for over 25 years and my mother-in-law has visited my home at Christ mas time for over twenty years. That makes me willing and eligible for your society . . .
>
> > Thomas M. Yager

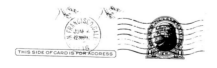

From Philadelphia, Pennsylvania:

> Dear G.B.S.
> Now we are two!
>   A.J.R.

From New York City:

> Dear Mr Shaw,
>   Please accept my
> application for membership in
> your 'Do away with Christmas'
> club.
>   Today I am filled
> with corrupting, coercing,
> constipating Christmas cheer.
> I have paid my due to
> humanity by emptying my
> wallet in a blaze of tinselled
> glory. Now the deadly candy
> pistol is away from my back
> until next year.
>   I am not bitter.
> I am fatigued from estimating
> the relative value of
> individuals with the
> gifts that I anticipated
> giving them.   Which of them
> were underpaid, and will
> trade todays smiles for
> sneers tomorrow?
>   Whoever said that it
> is better to give than to receive
> had nothing to start with . . .
>   Merry Christmas,
>   Frank E. Hefler.
>   Park Ave.
>   New York City
>   U.S.A.

And from Hollywood, California:

December 24 1946

Dear GBS

Today, a Los Angeles paper quotes you as follows:
'Fifty years ago, I invented a society for the abolition of
Christmas.   So far, I am the only member.'

Wonderful!!! Please send me a life membership!!!

My grand-pappy knew you when you were a lad: said he
didn't think much of you in those days but I'll join your
Society anyhow if your membership committee accepts me.

Bye the way: did you know that the rise and fall of the USA
is well and fully described in the holy bible? Likewise the
conduct of its affairs from its beginning to its ending is
faithfully pointed out in language that's plain.

It has much also to tell you about the Empire of Turkey and
the seven present states of Europe, from their origins to the
end of their career fully recorded. It will make interesting
reading for you while we are abolishing christmas . . .

There is a lovely feeling of humanity about a number of these letters:

. . . I am a common working man, at
present unemployed, 2 years yet to go to get my Old Age
Pension The only diferensance the 25th with me will be that
I shall have an Orange & an Apple on that day. Otherwise
the diet will be the same, My only recreation in the Winter is
Reading, And not a bad one at that, for a working man I
have led a very uncommon life, I have worked in 6 different
Countrys excluding my own, but I wont bore you with any
other details. If I had your gift for expression my life story
would make a Best seller, But I'd have to leave out the most
interesting Part as it is would not be Publishable. I admire
your Works. I have only read 3 of them & they are very
good. From the Publick Libarry I have read WELLS,
DICKENS, SHAKSPEARE, ANATOL FRANCE, VICTOR
HUGO ECT, I think SUPERMAN was your best at least what I
have read. I have a small Libarry I made the Book-case
myself, excuse this scribble, But writing is hard work to me,
it may be to you too, so don't bother to answer this if you are

busy, as I expect you will be, and you have earned a rest at
your time of life . . .

> I remain your
> Humble Admirer
> F. A. Spencer.

While one woman agreed with Shaw's Society for the Abolition
of Christmas, she believed the proposal to be of '*Devine*', not Shavian,
origin.

Dear Sir: –
    I congratulate you. Yet, may I add, while
you feel you had 'invented,' (invented is the word
used in the newspaper), a society for the
abolition of Christmas, I feel your idea
is of Devine Idea, God.

    I, Mrs. Florence Eleanora Toeneboehn Pearson,
being a Student and Lover of the Works of
Mary Baker Eddy, know you will find
what you seek in her book, *Christ and Christmas*,
as I have.
    This book and other of her writings
may be read, borrowed, or purchased
at Christian Science Reading Rooms.
    May I also state, I, too, have never
really known what to do with
traditional christmasses as celebrated
by the masses
Yet may I, Mrs. Florence Eleanora Toeneboehn Pearson,
know Christ was born this Christmas morn?
and may I also know my Christmas
is white, for in Reality it can only
        be white.
Your grand Intelligence can only be
exceeded by Devine Light, Life, Truth, and Love.
>   With Sincerity,
>   Mrs. Florence Eleanora Toeneboehn Pearson,
>   Belle, Mo., U.S.A.

P.S. – My husband, Mr. James Bruce Pearson,
also loves Mary Baker Eddy's Works and
Writings and has known the understanding
of Christian Science since Sunday School age.

However, not everyone agreed with Shaw's anti-Christmas stance. From New York:

> Poor puny shrunken soul!
> . . . Standing on the threshold of Eternity as you
> most surely are – poor insignificant pretended
> agnostic, if through the mercy of that little
> Babe – the God made man, you survive this
> Birthday of His, go down on your aging knees
> and beg His Infinite Majesty for mercy & pardon
> for all the unhappiness you have spread
> throughout the world with your oft-repeated
> inane & blasphemous utterances.
>
> Soon, maybe, very soon, you will come face-
> to Face with that little 'Babe' who will then
> be your Supreme Judge. What then will
> any of your Agnostical boasts avail you?
> You, who would try to brush aside the
> beautiful story of Bethlehem, tested and come
> down to us through the centuries.
>
> A committee of one, you certainly are, poor puny
> blinded soul, and we can only pray &
> beg the Infinite Pity of that little Babe for you
> 'ere it is too late.
>
> Sympathetically one
> who was also born in England over 50 years
> ago, and still remains awed by that
> 'old Story ever new' told at the Christmas Crib.
>
>> Mrs Elizabeth Breen & others of
>> like sentiments.

Interviews

'I occasionally swank a little because people like it; a modest man is such a nuisance'

to an interviewer, March 3rd, 1937

Shaw's May 1931 application to join the National Union of Journalists:

NATIONAL UNION OF JOURNALISTS.

ESTABLISHED 1907.

THE TRADE UNION FOR WORKING JOURNALISTS. Head Office: 180, FLEET STREET, E.C. 4.

APPLICATION FOR MEMBERSHIP.

Assoc 9 Cen Lon

(Date) *May* 1931

I hereby apply for election as an *Associate* Member of the *Central London* Branch of the National Union of Journalists. I declare that I am qualified under the Rules of the Union. I undertake, if elected, to conform to the Rules and Regulations of the Union, and to such alterations as may be made from time to time in accordance with the Constitution.

Name in full *George Bernard Shaw*

Private Address *4 Whitehall Court London S.W.1.*

Age *75 next month*

Number of years in Journalism *Since 1877*

Position of present employment and name of Journal *Unattached - Free Lance.*

Length of service with present employer

*Are you receiving at least the Union minimum salary for your district? *A dollar a word offered in America. In this country anything I can get.*

Have you previously been a member of the Union? If so, please state the Branch or Branches with which you were connected and why you left the Union *No.*

Have you been denied admission to the Union; if so, by which Branch or Branches? *No.*

Proposer *J. S. Dean* *Press Club, Fleet. St.*

Seconder *F. P. Dickinson* *Press Club Fleet. St.*

To the Secretary, *Central London* Branch.

NATIONAL UNION OF JOURNALISTS.

(To be filled in immediately after admission.)

This is to certify that *Mr G. B. Shaw* of *4 Whitehall Court S.W.1* was admitted an *associate member* of the *Central London* Branch on *June 20 1931*

(Signed) *J S Dean* Chairman

F P Dickinson Secretary

NOTE.—After the particulars have been copied into the Branch Membership Book this form must be forwarded to the Central Office for the purpose of general registration.

The first monthly contribution is to be paid when the nomination is sent in. In the event of the nomination being rejected the money will be returned to the applicant.

* Accompanying this form is a schedule of Union minimum rates.

G.P.S.—34631

Shaw's advice to would-be writer John Carveth Wells:

> Never write for fun or spec – be sure you are going to get
> paid before you write a word.

When his new play, *Great Catherine*, appeared in 1913, Shaw announced his willingness to be interviewed for 'the trifling honorarium of £500', adding that 'If an extra £500 is forthcoming, I may find it worth my while to write the interview myself.'

And on another occasion:

> Q. Do you think, Mr. Shaw, that woman's love for
> ever-changing fashion in this part of the world, has
> greatly affected the progress of masculine
> democracy?
>
> G.B.S. The price of an answer will, if given at all, be
> £2,500.

Shaw's interview technique was that of the duel. When, for example, he arrived at San Francisco in March 1933 on his first visit to the US, he was met by a brigade of reporters and asked, 'Would you care to be America's dictator?' The reply was characteristic. It was simply, 'How much would you pay me?' And again, 'Where have you found the happiest people?' 'In the cemeteries,' replied G.B.S. 'I mean alive,' pursued the hapless reporter. 'I have not been everywhere,' countered the dramatist.

One enterprising newsreel man desperate to obtain a ninety-fourth birthday interview with Shaw at his Ayot St Lawrence home sent in an X-ray photograph of a fractured leg with a covering note, 'They call this "The Doctor's Dilemma". I've had one good break. How about giving me another?' Shaw, however, found it quite easy to resist the novelty and charm of this invitation.

Many years earlier, another reporter perpetrated a hoax to get through to the great man. Hotly pursued by admirers when visiting Cairo in March 1931, Shaw instructed the hotel porter to 'tell 'em I'm dead'. An enterprising French journalist, however, got through by scribbling on his card, 'Einstein's nephew wants to shake hands with Shaw.'

'What do you think of nudism?' the reporter asked when Shaw received him.

'When one's body is so aesthetically formed as mine,' Shaw replied, 'one likes the world to admire it. Nudity puts an end to the Darwinian quarrel, for when they are naked all humans look like gorillas.'

When Shaw discovered the hoax he told the journalist he would be forgiven if he would play the same trick on Rudyard Kipling, then at Aswan.

Mr. Bernard Shaw is obliged to remind correspondents who seek to interview him for publication that as he is himself a professional journalist, he naturally prefers to communicate with the public through the Press at first hand. He is willing, when time permits, to answer written questions when they happen to be interesting as current news *and can be answered in twenty words or less*. Questions that require answers at greater length should be accompanied by an offer of a fee of not less than three figures.

Inexperienced editors who imagine that their fortunes are made if they can obtain a contribution from a celebrity should consider that as nobody will buy a periodical on the offchance of its containing such a contribution perhaps once a year or so, only a permanent staff of writers capable of ensuring that every number will contain something topical and readable can make a magazine a success.

There were two stages in getting an interview with Shaw. In the first instance one had, by fair means or foul, to get permission to conduct an interview. The difficulty would then arise of preparing questions of suitable interest and novelty that might *induce* Shaw to reply. Shaw was not adverse to coaching people on interview technique.

Dear Miss Dale
    It is quite true that editors and such people want what I say. They pay me from £150 to £200 per thousand words for it. Naturally they would be very glad to get it for £2 or less

per thousand from you; but such golden dreams are not realized in this sordid world. When I have anything to say on any subject of public interest I write it myself and get paid for it at the aforesaid rates.

If you are beginning your career as a journalist and interviewer the first thing you have to learn is that you can only interview people who are not themselves journalists, and who therefore have no other means of making their views public except through interviews or unpaid contributions to the correspondence columns. These persons are your natural prey; and you are doing them a service in interviewing them. You can lump them as celebrities who cannot write. But to approach me, or Mr Wells, or Mr Bennett, or Mr Chesterton, or Mr Garvin, or any other writer with an offer to make his views public is like offering Lord Londonderry (who owns all the mines in Sunderland) a scuttle of coals for an invitation to spend a week at his castle.

There is only one way of getting at these super-journalists. If you send them a written question, or even a few questions, which they can answer (you must leave space for the answer) with an epigram on the spur of the moment, they may do it for the fun of the thing if there is an addressed envelope ready to pop it into. But you must be very smart to pull this off. Most journalists who try it on ask questions which could not be answered with less than a year's work: for instance 'What do you think about photography and the cinema?' 'What is your view of the revised prayerbook?,' 'What were the books that influenced you in your youth?', 'How would you reform the House of Lords?' 'What is to be the future of America?' or something too silly for the dignity of the recipient like 'Should women shingle?.' You must try to divine something that is not worth my while to say myself, or something that I could not very well volunteer myself, but which I should not mind replying to a question – provided always that it did not take me more than five minutes at the outside.

This is for your guidance, as you seem to be a budding novice . . .

In 1933, Ian Coster of the *Sunday Dispatch* had his questions answered in a fashion. He was, however, severely rebuked in the process. The questions were answered in blue ink; the reproof came in red.

You had better tear these up; for you have missed your

chance by not putting a single *topical* question admitting of a brief answer. I warned you not to ask me for a volume on democracy. All your other questions have been asked and answered a hundred times and are neither acute nor amusing.

There is no knowledge and no work behind your job. The 'Dispatch' may give you an obscure corner if the sub. is very hard-pressed for matter to fill up; but he cannot let down his front page with such resourceless muck.

Take your profession seriously or it will not take you seriously.

Shaw's replies to the young man's questions were a reproof in themselves.

Q. Do you write plays now (1) for money? (2) as an amusement? (3) because you must, as birds and poets must sing?

G.B.S. *It's my profession. Haven't you heard?*

Q. Do ideas for plays just flit into your head unbidden or do you have to induce them by stern application, opium, or alcohol?

G.B.S. *They are all there already.*

Q. Your last three plays have suggested that you are not so sure of the future of democracy. Is Britain 'on the rocks' because it lacks a wise despot, king, or dictator? Do we want a Mussolini?

G.B.S. *No; you don't want a Mussolini. But if you are not very careful you will get one.*

Q. Did the idea of 'On the Rocks' come to you out of the blue? How long did it take to write? Did you dictate it straight off, type it, or write it in shorthand?

G.B.S. *In shorthand. Do not, however, conclude that if you learn shorthand you will be able to write plays.*

Q. Is 'On the Rocks' likely to be your last play, or are you at work on another already?

G.B.S. *Consult an actuary.*

Q. Which of your plays is your masterpiece, or if they are all masterpieces, which gives you the most pleasure to re-read?

G.B.S. *When I am out for pleasure I read other people's plays.*

Q. If you had your life to live over again would you concentrate on again becoming the world's greatest

dramatist, or would you become the world's great
pugilist?

G.B.S. *You evidently know nothing about pugilism. A pugilist is
finished at the age at which other professionals are
waiting for their first fee.*

Q. What is your Christmas message to the world?

G.B.S *I do not send Christmas messages. You will find several in
the gospels and elsewhere that still await attention.*

One interviewer stopped the great man in his tracks by making use of the
old music-hall gag, 'Do you sleep with those whiskers inside the sheets or
out?' More often than not, however, it was Shaw who had the last word, as
in the case of the interviewer, who, after putting his questions to G.B.S,
commented out of politeness, 'I hope you are well.' The reply came,
strongly, in the well-known Dublin accent – 'At my age, young man, you are
either well or dead.'

Shaw was very concerned with journalistic accuracy. 'Journalism,' he
believed, 'is the only profession in the world in which inaccuracy does not
matter.' That is, not to others; it mattered to him – so much so that he often
insisted on checking the typescript of an interview. As his manuscript
alterations were frequently extensive, an interviewer benefited doubly. One
young man, for example, who at the time sold his 'vetted' interview for
twenty guineas, sold the original Shaw amended manuscript for two
hundred guineas a number of years later.

Shaw hated being bored; or, worse still, not being allowed to talk. He
gave one extremely loquacious interviewer permission to publish the
interview as long as he kept all he said out of it. 'There are many such
people,' Shaw remarked:

who talk to me for five boring minutes and spend the rest of
their life condemning me. Nothing infuriates me more than
being praised for attributes I despise, though I don't mind
being despised for qualities it has taken me years and years
to develop. In future I will demand that all journalists submit

the full text of the interview before I agree to let them interview me. All this talk about my amazing vitality, my extraordinary wit, my terrific capacity for hard work, my radiant beauty must have been concocted in the village inn over a liquid meal before the persons have even ventured on my doorstep.

Shaw could never fathom public interest in the trivia of his life.

. . . If you intrude upon me to ask how many buttons there are on my waistcoat, I can only reply: 'I don't know. Get out!'

It has been said that the public has a right to *know* its public persons, since – so it is held – what they are explains what they do . . . Is it of interest to the public to know that I never had bacon for breakfast?

Yes, it is, if the newspaper is collecting material for a serious article on dietetics. No, it is not, if it has in view an article on the war in Spain.

My breakfast consists of porridge, postum, and grapefruit. What is the news value of that fact compared with that of an earthquake in Chile? . . .

Towards the end of his life he turned many would-be interviewers away; often, as in the case of one Brazilian journalist visiting London in 1942, with great courtesy:

The Bernard Shaw you wish to see no longer exists. There is nothing of him except an old spectre with his 87 years in an inaccessible village where he has no means of entertaining such distinguished visitors, and where also his old companion lies seriously ill. He regrets this deeply because he foresees a great future for South America.

Invitations

Shaw on Shaw:

> *You invite him down to your place because you think he will entertain your guests with his brilliant conversation; and before you know where you are he has chosen a school for your son, made your will for you, regulated your diet, and assumed all the privileges of your family solicitor, your housekeeper, your clergyman, your doctor, your dressmaker, your hairdresser, and your estate agent. When he has finished with everybody else, he incites the children to rebellion. And when he can find nothing more to do, he goes away and forgets all about you . . .*

"When he speaks, you are both pleased and surprised at the
sweetness of his tone"

English sports were said to include 'drawing' Mr Bernard Shaw to send a vituperative letter by asking him on a postcard to lay a foundation-stone, open a bazaar, or address the local Boy Scouts . . .

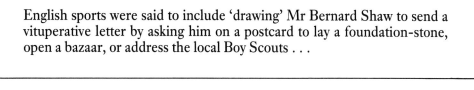

Mr. Bernard Shaw has long since been obliged by advancing years to retire from his committees and his personal activities on the platform. He therefore begs secretaries of societies to strike his name from their lists of available speakers. Mr. Shaw does not open exhibitions or bazaars, take the chair, speak at public dinners, give his name as vice-president or patron, make appeals for money on behalf of hospitals or 'good causes' (however deserving), nor do any ceremonial public work. Neither can he take part in new movements nor contribute to the first numbers of new magazines. He begs his correspondents to excuse him accordingly.

'Society' did not interest Shaw. Society people, however, were decidedly interested in him, fighting for his attendance at their 'At Homes'. He had his reply ready. When Lady X informed him on a card that she would be 'at home' on Thursday at 3 p.m., he returned the card, penning on the back, 'So will G. Bernard Shaw'.

In 1912 he refused an invitation in these words:

My own mother (82) has just had a stroke, Charlotte is blue
and gasping for life in paroxysms of asthma and bronchitis;
and I am rehearsing no less than three plays: therefore my
reply to your letter is a hollow laugh.

Intimate luncheons were the Shaws' habitual method of entertaining. He was much happier hosting a lunch than being a difficult guest at a dinner party, where a special vegetarian meal had to be prepared and where he and Charlotte would be expected to stay later than they wished.

'Shaw,' Arnold Bennett noted in his *Journals*, referring to a dinner with H. G. Wells, 'talked practically the whole time, which is the same thing as saying he talked a damned sight too much.'

One of the great hostesses of her day, Winston Churchill's mother was the only American from whom G.B.S. ever got as good as he gave, when much to her chagrin he refused her luncheon invitation, replying, 'Certainly not; what have I done to provoke such an attack on my well-known habit?' An expert at sharp repartee, Lady Churchill answered in the same spirit: 'Know nothing of your habits; hope they are not as bad as your manners.' Much to her surprise, Shaw responded at length:

Be reasonable: what can I do? If I refuse an invitation in conventional terms I am understood as repudiating the acquaintance of my hostess. If I make the usual excuses and convince her that I am desolated by some other engagement, she will ask me again. And when I have excused myself six times running, she will conclude that I personally dislike her ... Therefore I am compelled to do the simple thing, and when you say, 'Come to lunch with a lot of people,' reply flatly, 'I won't.' If you propose anything pleasant to me I shall reply with equal flatness, 'I will.' But lunching with a lot of people – carnivorous people – is not pleasant. Besides, it cuts down my morning's work. I *won't* lunch with you; I *won't* dine with you; I *won't* call on you; I *won't* take the smallest part in your social routine; and I *won't* ever know you except on the most special and privileged terms, to the utter exclusion of that 'lot of other people' whose appetites you offered me as an entertainment.

Only, if I can be of any real service at any time, that is what I exist for; so you may command me. To which you will no doubt reply, 'Thank you for nothing; you would say the same to anybody.' So I would, but it is a great concession to write it at such length to a lady who has bludgeoned me with an invitation to lunch. So there!

If the story is authentic, Winston Churchill (like his mother before) bettered Shaw in repartee on at least one occasion. When Shaw invited Churchill to the first night of his new play *Buoyant Billions* in 1949, enclosing two tickets, 'one for yourself and one for your friend – if you have one,' Churchill replied thanking Mr Shaw and saying that he could not attend the first night . . . but would be delighted to come on the second – 'if you have one.'

Shaw to a Miss Macnaughtan who 'once' invited him to dinner. 'Never!' he replied on a postcard. 'I decline to sit in a hot room and eat dead animals, even with you to amuse me.'

'It is no use asking me to dinner in Oxford,' he wrote Hugh Aronsen:

> I can get a dinner in London without any trouble. I am quite aware that it is a common English practice for lovers of the pleasures of the table to allege a larger human purpose as an excuse for indulging themselves . . . Eat and drink by all means; but do not imagine that you are spreading a spirit of brotherhood among the nations by doing it. You are simply ruining your own digestions.

Shaw's May 1925 reply to T. P. O'Connor's invitation to attend a dinner honouring Ramsay MacDonald:

> My dear T.P. –
>
> Absence from town and a strong sense of humor will prevent me from accepting your invitation to dine in acknowledgment of the political eminence of Ramsay Macdonald. Considering that the man has been prime minister of England, I should have thought his eminence had been noticed.
>
> If the dinner is a success, I suggest that it be followed by another to acknowledge the piety of the pope, yet another to emphasize the mathematical talent of Einstein, and a final one to call attention to the existence of milestones on the Dover road.
>
> If you could throw in a lunch to remind people that I am rather good at writing plays, all the better . . .

A double invite: to take tea and honour:

PRIME MINISTER   10, Downing Street
Very Private   Whitehall.
                                 9th July 1929

. . . Turn up, both of you, at
Chequers one Sunday for lunch
or tea or both, but let me know
when you propose to come lest I
not be there.
                Yours always
                Ramsay MacDonald
What about Sir Geo. B.S.?

On July 21st, 1930, a *News-Chronicle* representative asked George Bernard Shaw if the report were true that the Prime Minister recently sounded him as to whether he would accept a peerage in order to help the Government's debating strength in the House of Lords and that Mr Shaw declined in appropriate terms.

'The Prime Minister has not communicated his desire to me,' was G.B.S.'s reply. 'Of course, he may contemplate it, but I cannot tell what is in his mind, or the King's mind, or anybody else's mind.

'I suppose there are various Dukedoms vacant. They could scarcely offer me less than a Dukedom, do you think?'

'Would you accept a peerage if it were offered, Mr. Shaw?'

'Well, you know. I never ford a stream until I come to it. If they could find me a more distinguished title than George Bernard Shaw, I might consider it.'

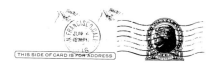

Some invitations, however, could not have been more inappropriate:

'WATERSIDE'
DOE HEY RD
BOLTON
LANCS
6–11–34

Dear Mr Shaw.
    Twenty years ago almost
one thousand men left Bolton on the
'SS TINTORETTO' to help to settle a spot of bother
in France – about 250 returned and each
year they have a re-union dinner.
    The survivors choose a guest
each year – this year for some unknown
reason they have voted that you be asked as
the guest & it is my duty to invite you to
join them at the 'Swan Hotel' in Bolton on the
10th February next.
    The dinner consists of Soup,
Hot Pot and of course beer – 'Wild Woodbine'
cigarettes are also included – I'm quite
sure you will enjoy them!
    I haven't your address &

have taken the easiest way out of a difficulty –
it was far easier to caricature you than to find
your address – I did consult a Directory, but
really there were so many 'Shaws' that I gave the
job up in despair & have left the P.O. officials
to find you.

   The survivors are an interesting
crowd consisting of Doctors, lawyers, dentists,
colliers Joiners butchers bakers AND a POET
– in fact almost every profession is represented with
the exception of course of Mrs Warrens.
   I hope you can find the time to visit us.

Yours Sincerely
J. Rothwell

P.S. I have enclosed
    last years Menu Card.

LONDON
OR - WHERE - EVER - HE - HAPPENS -
TO - BE - AT - THE - MOMENT!

Hot Pot, beer and 'Wild Woodbine' cigarettes – what an unsuitable menu
for a vegetarian, teetotalling, non-smoker!

And here is Shaw's reply to an invitation by his biographer, Archibald
Henderson, to attend a dinner in his honour at the Town Hall Club, New
York City. Given by theatrical luminaries who had either acted in or
produced Shaw's plays, the 19th January 1930 dinner was designed as a
public Shaw tribute on the part of his American admirers. Various tables
were named after Shaw's works, and a red cloth placed at one represented
Mrs Warren's Profession.

   A dinner!
   How horrible!
   I am to be made the pretext for
killing all those wretched animals and
birds and fish!
   Thank you for nothing.
   Now if it were to be a fast
instead of a feast: say a solemn three
days' abstention from corpses in my
honor, I could at least pretend to
believe that it was disinterested.
   Blood sacrifices are not in my
line.
   G. Bernard Shaw

A friend of William Randolph Hearst's invited Shaw to a 'small and entirely private dinner for Marion Davies in one of the private rooms at the Savoy,' adding that, if Mr Hearst were in England in time, he too would be there. 'Say,' Shaw instructed his secretary, 'I never heard of Marion Davies, and would not go to a little dinner at the Savoy if she were all the 11,000 virgins of St Ursula rolled into one. I am no good for games of that sort.' He later wrote to the intending host:

> . . . I have now ascertained that Miss M.D. is a film star. Do you seriously believe that these young and beautiful ladies want to meet old gentlemen of 65 and 72, or to be made an excuse for their meeting one another? If so, you must be more innocent than the woolliest lamb in Hamleys' toyshop. I just wont go. Mr. Hearst and I, old as we are, have still gumption enough left to be able to meet without making Miss Davies yawn and spoiling your festivities.

In the end victory went to America, for the Shaws met Hearst five years later, when, in a pause during their world tour, they went ashore to look at Hollywood and stayed at the palatial Hearst home, San Simeon, the only time G.B.S. consented to sleep on American soil. Shaw later told his secretary, Blanche Patch, that Marion Davies, who acted as hostess on the occasion, was 'by far the most attractive of the stars who are not really eighteen.'

MR. GEORGE BERNARD SHAW with Miss Marion Davies and Mr. Charles Chaplin at Hollywood.

There were those who objected to Shaw accepting such invitations.

New York
11th March 1936

Dear Sir:–

    They say that politics makes strange bedfellows, but I
dare say not stranger than the literary and film press
agenting game.

    I enclose a clipping from the New York American of this
morning showing how you and your decent, respectable wife
went to call upon the concubine of a certain millionaire
publisher. She has had two bastards by him, and when he
dies the fun will begin. His official wife has lived apart
from him for many years, after bearing him a number of
stalwart sons; she has her priests and Milk Fund
Terara-boom-de-ay, and exacts much publicity for it. Does
not get as much sometimes as the Concubine, who is a
remorseless publicity hound. There is never a Milk Fund
entertainment, opera or prize-fight for the legitimate wife,
but her rival insists upon yards of gabble about her 'new film
production', and we have the spectacle of an inferior trollop
who has never created character on the stage, and cannot act
(for her also Romanist heart is false and incapable of
virtuous expression) foisted on the American public by a
chain of nearly a score of papers.

    You, too, are a glutton for publicity, but it seems to me
that you ought not to drag your decent wife into a worship at
the shrine of a whore.

SARDONICUS

For the sake of the man being honoured, Shaw refused to attend the 1937
celebration of S. R. Littlewood's forty years as a London critic.

    . . . you must be the hero on this occasion. You must get
somebody who will not reduce the assembled critics to a
ring of fascinated rabbits. I exercise that fascination most
unwillingly and unconsciously; but as it seems to persist and
be incurable it makes me a most undesirable intruder except

on occasions where there is no other principal attraction. So I wont come . . .

Shaw declining Southwick Cricket Club's December 1938 invitation to attend their annual dinner:

> Too old, loathe cricket. No connection with Southwick; don't even know where it is.

As a life member of the Clan Chattan Association, representative of many Scottish families, Shaw in October 1949 was notified of their coming dinner dance. 'Please note,' he wrote, refusing the invitation, 'that I am in my 94th year, and stop bothering and mocking me with ridiculous invitations to dance Scottish reels, and the like. Dine and dance as much as you like, but let me alone – *G.B.S.*'

An American woman pianist was furious when Shaw declined to attend her Aeolian Hall recital. He told his secretary, Blanche Patch, to tell her that it was a delusion on the part of American artists to persuade themselves that his influence and presence at their concerts would help them, for he was now 'completely superannuated in that respect and many others.' Angered, the woman pianist flared out with the names of Gluck, Handel, Beethoven, Strauss, Tchaikovsky, Glinka, Dargomizhsky, Rachmaninoff, and others, who were all on the Aeolian Hall recital programme, which she felt might be of some service to G.B.S! As for her, she had no need of the services of 'even a Bernard Shaw', for in the field of music, 'according to the world's best critics', she had arrived without his aid . . .

In like fashion, another American woman was embittered by Shaw's failure to attend her husband's 1925 concert:

> . . . Yet you supposedly had no time to attend my husband's concert, nor have you, in the many days since, found 20 minutes out of the 24 hours in which you could grant him an audience in order to listen to one of his compositions – It is odd, almost fantastic, that an American woman who belongs, as you once remarked, to a barbarous country should remind you that it matters not how illustrious you may be as a writer, you have yet to learn to be a man . . .

To which Shaw replied with scarcely controlled anger:

> Dear Madam
> You are a gloriously unreasonable lady. Why the deuce should I go to your husband's concert if I don't choose, or have something else to do? . . .
> Suppose my wife were to write to your husband & tell him that he had yet to learn to be a man because he had not gone to one of my plays, what would you say to her? Probably 'Don't be an idiot', or something of that sort. Well, I should like to say that to you; but it would not be polite; so I mustn't.

On occasion it was debatable whether Shaw's presence or absence were preferable.

Mr Shaw had been inveigled by a 'high-brow' Hampstead hostess into being present at her musical party, where the lion of the evening was a young violinist, whose efforts, however, gave more pain than pleasure to the assembled guests.

After a long period of torture the hostess turned to Shaw and asked rapturously: 'Well, Mr Shaw, what do you think of my discovery?'

'I find in him a great resemblance to Paderewski,' replied Shaw tactfully.

Puzzled for a moment, the hostess then answered correctly: 'Oh, but Mr Shaw, Paderewski's not a violinist.'

'Exactly,' said G.B.S.

On another occasion Bernard Shaw happened to be beguiled into attending a feeble concert given by a prominent London society woman, who, during the evening found the author sitting disconsolate and bored in a corner of the room.

'Now, really, Mr Shaw,' said the hostess, 'don't you think this orchestra plays beautifully? These men have been playing together for eleven years.'

'Eleven years?' repeated Shaw. 'Haven't we been here longer than that?'

Shaw refusing to celebrate the 1917 Russian Revolution:

I shan't be in Town on Saturday, and couldn't stand it anyway. It was bad enough to look at England and France licking the boots of that execrable tyranny, but to see them now using the taste of the blacking to stimulate their saliva to spit at it when it is down at last, in spite of their support, makes me run away and hold my tongue lest I should be provoked to useless recrimination.

Shaw refusing to take part in the opening of a Brighton pageant:

. . . You must let me off; the only pageant I expect to attend henceforth is my funeral.

'Fiddlesticks,' he replied when invited to open a new Labour hall. 'Who ever heard of a Labour hall in Bournemouth. You might as well start a branch of the Primrose League in Moscow.'

'No,' said Shaw to Dr Hunter of Dumfries, who had offered to show him the house where Robert Burns died. 'I won't visit it. Any house could kill a poet.'

Shaw refusing to accept New South Wales high-jumper Jack Metcalfe's invitation to attend an amateur sports meeting at Auckland during his New Zealand visit:

> Amateur sport has caused more international ill-feeling than any movement I have known. Should I attend and meet Metcalfe I would certainly dissuade him from continuing with the useless event of clearing 6 ft. 6 in. Why doesnt he use a ladder? It's far easier.

In 1931 G.B.S. refused a motor-cycling grandmother's challenge to a race. Shaw's characteristic reply to Mrs Clara Brown of Leamington was, 'All Mr. Shaw has to say is that he's now a retired champion.' Shaw rode his motorcycle (his second), an Allday's Patent Two Stroke 'Allon', until he was past seventy.

Any mention of schools filled G.B.S. with dread. Thus, when Rugby invited him to see a cut version of his play, *Captain Brassbound's Conversion*, he retorted:

> To tell an author about an unauthorised performance, on a card headed with the emblem of piracy, is audacious. To allow him to witness a mutilated version of his play is to invite murder. I have sent on your invitation card to Mr. Galsworthy (I presume the card intended for me was sent to him) and shall endeavour to forget a transaction which has so many deplorable aspects . . .

When the daughter of an old friend of Shaw's was getting married, he sent one of his plays as a wedding present. It was only when the bride was reading the play, and had nearly reached the end, that she found a cheque for £50 between the pages. The book's inscription was Shavian, for, following the name of the recipient, were the words: 'On the occasion of her first marriage.'

Shortly after her wedding to Shaw's friend, Charles Graves, Miss Peggy Leigh accused the dramatist of stealing her limelight. 'There would have been nothing unusual about our wedding,' she told the *Daily News*, 'if Bernard Shaw had not written a comparatively long letter refusing an invitation to the marriage on the grounds that he had not the proper clothes "on purpose". He enclosed, however, a cheque for fifteen pounds sterling, and requested my husband to buy the correct outfit for a wedding . . .'

> My dear Charles,
>
> My attendance at your wedding, or anybody's wedding, is out of the question. I have within the last week or so stoutly absented myself from similar ceremonies of such pressing importance that if I made an exception in your case I could never look some of my best friends in the face again.
>
> Besides, I have not the proper clothes – on purpose.
>
> I have ascertained that a correct outfit at my tailor's would cost me 15 guineas; and it would be of no use to me subsequently, as I never dress correctly in daylight. But it would be of considerable use to you, as you earn your living by going into society. Therefore, as I suppose I ought to give you a wedding present, it is clear that the sensible solution of our problem is to give you the suit in which I should have graced your nuptials if I were a normal person.
>
> You will therefore hand the enclosed cheque to your tailor and order him to do the best he can for you to that amount. And if there is a list of presents see to it that I am entered as 'Bernard Shaw: suit of clothes.' If there is an exhibition of presents the tailor will lend you a dummy.
>
> I celebrate the passing of your youth and irresponsibility with a melancholy shake hands. I am sorry for Peggy; but you can assure her that any other man would be an equal disappointment after a week or so.
>
> As for you, it is too late to run away now. You are for it, Charles.

Shaw, in February 1930, to the Chairman of the Camargo Society for the Production of Ballets, refusing membership:

> These people are idiots in business. My joining their society will, my own subscription apart, make not one farthing difference in their takings. Tell them to kick out all their press agents and publicity experts, amateur and professional, and stick to their job as Serge Diaghilev did. He succeeded in delivering the goods not by

celebrity-hunting and post-prandial speeches. I cannot do anything for them. I neither dance nor compose nor play ballets, and I have sense enough to keep out of the way under such circumstances. The notion that a dinner can act as the send-off to a ballet season, unless they can make the Lord Mayor drink enough to dance a hornpipe on the table, is beyond my patience. Intimate the same as violently as you can.

—Ever.
G.B.S.

But for once, Shaw was to change his mind. Having produced a number of ballets in London and Oxford, the Camargo Society gained the praise of both English and Continental critics. A still greater accolade was to follow when, in November 1931, they won what few others did, a Shaw subscription.

MEMBERSHIP APPLICATION FOR THE BRITISH INTERPLANETARY SOCIETY (1947),
COMPLETED BY SHAW, WHO BECAME ITS OLDEST MEMBER. FOR PERSONAL
REFERENCES HE LISTED THE SPACE ENTHUSIAST AND SCIENCE FICTION WRITER,
ARTHUR C. CLARKE. TO THE REQUEST FOR CATEGORY OF MEMBERSHIP, THE
93-YEAR-OLD SHAW REPLIED, 'LIFE'

Shaw, refusing an invitation to be put forward as a 1917 Parliamentary candidate for Jarrow:

> . . . I have never been in Jarrow in my life, thank God; and I shall never spend five minutes there if I can possibly spend them anywhere else. I regard anyone who would as a born

fool. Far from being representative of Jarrow, I doubt
whether there is a single voter on the register, or entitled to
come on the new register, with whom I agree on any subject
that is likely to occupy the next House of Commons . . .

I can suggest only one advantage in putting me up; and
that is that the entire press would work so hard to procure
my defeat that there would be no room left in its columns for
attacks on Labor in general. And my chief use in the House
if I got in would be to secure the passage of any bill by
simply opposing it. The British are a remarkable race, but
not quite educated enough yet to be represented by

Yours faithfully

Shaw, refusing the West Edinburgh Labour Party's 1922 invitation to
stand as their Parliamentary candidate: 'Why,' asked Shaw:

. . . should I plead with the citizens of West Edinburgh to
allow me to waste my time at Westminster for a salary on
which I could not live, when I can command a far more
eligible position and much larger emoluments as a leading
member of my profession?

If the Labour Party – or any other party – will guarantee
me an unopposed election and a salary of £4,000 a year with
a handsome pension I may at least consider the proposition
that I should narrow my audiences from civilised mankind to
the handful of bewildered commercial gentlemen at
Westminster who are now earnestly ruining Europe as the
stupidest way of ruining their own country.

But my answer would probably be the same – it would be
easier and pleasanter to drown myself.

'I am not sufficient of a nonentity to accept nomination' cabled Shaw
declining to run for an honorary university post.

'Think you best of nonentities,' the students countered.

Back came: 'NO—SHAW'

The students sent a second telegram, pointing out that they were
surprised at him wasting the opportunity to use seven words in the prepaid
reply and asking for a remittance of balance. Shaw then posted back the
prepaid form unused and without comment.

The students wired again:

CONSIDER YOU ARE WEAKENING, AS YOU STAMPED
THE ENVELOPE. PLEASE RECONSIDER YOUR
DECISION, AS FINAL CHOICE LIES BETWEEN YOU
AND SHIRLEY TEMPLE.

On being enlightened as to Shirley Temple's identity, Shaw commented, 'If that's their idea of a joke I do not see it. Although it is what one would expect.' Disgusted, he ignored the students' final cable.

Shaw, recuperating from an infected foot which had incapacitated him for nearly a year, was unable to attend the March 17th, 1899 St Pancras public meeting being held to discuss the parish's insanitary conditions. He refused on the grounds that the state of his health after residing for eighteen years in St Pancras did not permit his attendance.

Over the years a number of societies attracted Shaw's support, including the Smell Society, of which he was an 'ordinary member' (H. G. Wells was on the Council). At the age of ninety-three he joined the Severn Wild Fowl Trust with its sanctuary for more than a hundred species.

The 1949 fellowship of the Institute of Journalists was one of the last honours offered – and accepted by – Shaw, who replied that at 93½ he would be pleased to accept the appointment – providing it did not entail any extra duties.

THIS SIDE OF CARD IS FOR ADDRESS

Shortly before his death in 1950, Marie Stopes invited Shaw to become President of the Poetry Society. In return she received what was to be the last of the many postcards he had fired at her since the days of World War I. The handwriting, although shaky, clearly read:

A poetry Society that can find no more up-to-date President
than an old fogey of 93 is no place for me, nor for you either.

Bernard Shaw, who never gave his name ornamentally to a committee, treated every meeting 'as a matter of life and death'. 'Dear Sir,' he wrote in response to a Literary Guild's request that he be its vice-president, 'I do not vice-preside.'

Similarly to Miss Mamie Sullivan, 14 September, 1908:

> I dont take the chair for people:
> they take the chair for me. I am for
> use, not for ornament.

In June 1928 American Daniel Archer invited Shaw to become the honorary president of his proposed organization, *The Shavian Society, An Asylum for the Sane.* 'In reply to your letter of the 5th June,' Shaw's secretary Blanche Patch wrote to Archer, 'Mr. Bernard Shaw desires me to say that an asylum for the sane would be empty in America.'

Several newspapers announced the fact that during Shaw's June 1930 stay at Buxton, he was in the habit of walking through the streets wearing shorts, the costume adopted by ramblers all over Lancashire, Derbyshire and Cheshire. A magazine which catered for rambling clubs, scenting an important new recruit to the movement, wrote asking if his preference might be taken as an indication of his interest in rambling, and extended a cordial invitation to him to join their ranks. 'I have never worn shorts in my life,' Shaw responded on a postcard, 'Some one has taken advantage of your wearing them to pull your leg. G.B.S.'

In 1879 Shaw joined a debating club whose subjects of interest included evolution and atheism, their gods being John Stuart Mill, Charles Darwin, Herbert Spencer, Aldous Huxley, Thomas Malthus and Robert Ingersoll. It was during one of their debates, held at the Women's Protective and Provident League in Great Queen Street, London, that he first plunged

IF SHAW WERE TO
WEAR SHORTS

into controversy. After his first nerve-racked and self-conscious speech he
was resolved never to miss a meeting nor an opportunity to speak, however
much he might suffer in the process. He likened himself to 'an officer
afflicted with cowardice, who takes every opportunity of going under fire to
get over it and learn his business.' 'A tall, lean, icy man,' according to the
Workman's Times, 'white faced, with hard, clear, fleshless voice, restless
grey-blue eyes, neatly-parted fair hair, big feet, and a reddish, untamed
beard.' Soon 'hooked' on public speaking, he joined every debating group
and argumentative circle to which he could get an introduction. He
attended public meetings and lectures, of which there were then dozens
every Sunday, and always spoke in the debate. This casual public debating
gained evangelistic purpose, when, after hearing Henry George speak, he
became a desperately earnest propagandist for socialism. As his fame as a
socialist orator spread, he was himself much sought after. His open-air
speeches, long and short, were delivered in both fair and foul conditions.
On one occasion he spoke for no less than four hours at Trafford Bridge,
Manchester, and on another, in the pouring rain at Hyde Park where:

. . . I did achieve something. I delivered the best speech that I have ever made.

It was raining cats and dogs; and my audience consisted of four shrouded and dripping policemen.

My chairman was occupied in trying to hold an umbrella approximately over my head.

I set myself to convert those four policemen. And I believe that I succeeded . . .

To Fabian colleague H. T. Muggeridge, August 31st, 1900:

You are in a devil of a hurry for an answer. I only got your letter six weeks ago . . . Six years is my usual time for answering letters – especially for lectures . . .

To the philosopher and writer Hon. Bertrand Russell:

. . . I must warn you, however, that though, when I speak, the hall is generally full, and the meeting is apparently very successful, the people who run after and applaud me are just as likely to vote for the enemy, or not vote at all, on polling day. I addressed 13 gorgeous meetings at the last election; but not one of my candidates got in.

Although in his lifetime Shaw delivered many thousands of lectures, he never received a payment; that way he secured the freedom to say what he wanted and a safeguard against being identified as a hired agitator. Once, when asked to speak at a north England women's club, he was offered the usual honorarium – but with a stipulation. 'You will not talk on politics or religion, or say anything that will hurt people's feelings.' Shaw remembered later that he wrote back that politics and religion were the only things he was interested in; that he always talked about them; that he always hurt some people's feelings; and that he never lectured for money. Delighted, the Women's Club then replied that he might say anything he darned please on those terms.

Addressing a socialist meeting in London, Shaw spoke bitterly about the unequal distribution of wealth:

> 'As I came into the hall I noticed a Rolls-Royce which cost over £2,000. Is it right,' he asked, 'that one man should be allowed such money? Go and look at it yourself and ponder over the slums of England and how much better this wealth could be spent making the lives of the poor possible and profitable.'
>
> At this, some members of the audience moved to leave, with the light of destruction in their eyes.
>
> 'Ah,' said Shaw, 'I sympathise with you, but before you smash that car I must tell you that it belongs to me.'

American judge Henry Neil related an experience when appearing on the same platform with Shaw: 'Before a great audience in London, I advocated Mothers' Pensions. I spoke for three quarters of an hour. The audience was close to tears when I had finished. George Bernard Shaw arose. "And I too had a mother," he said.'

Shaw's audience, however, was less pleased when he reduced himself to silence during a crowded meeting at the Lyceum Theatre in connection with the National Shakespeare Memorial movement. He was preceded on the platform by Labour spokesman Will Steadman, who spoke at too great a length for many, impatient to hear Shaw, next on the list of speakers. This impatience was expressed by the stamping of the feet and loud mutterings. Mr Steadman, realizing what was happening, flushed and quickly sat down in some confusion. Shaw rose and when the cheering had subsided, said: 'Mr. Chairman, after the excellent speech of my friend Steadman there is no need for me to utter another word.' And down he sat, having administered a pretty snub to the audience, which had been drawn together chiefly to hear him.

He refused in 1940 to be one of the speakers in Luton's War Weapons Week:

IMPOSSIBLE. I am 84½. You don't need an ancient spectre whose artificial teeth fall out every time he tries to pronounce the letter B.

Despite Shaw's highly publicized refusals to accept invitations, they continued to flood in. One of the last, a few months before his death, was particularly audacious:

LONDON SOCIETY OF ASSOCIATION REFEREES
12th July 1946

Dear Mr. Shaw,
. . . Could we have the pleasure of your company at our meeting on Friday, the 23rd August at our Headquarters, the Feathers Hotel, Westminster, at 7 p.m. Our Society would very much like to have a few words from you on this occasion and we feel sure you would interest the sportsmen of London.
    Please do come along, even if only for half-an-hour and I can assure you a very hearty welcome.

'LIKE ALL POETS I HAVE A PASSION FOR PUGILISM'

Shaw continued to make frequent informal speeches into his eighties and nineties, and by the time of his death had addressed more than two thousand audiences.

The secretary of a debating club in Port Talbot, South Wales, invited Shaw during World War II to address his society.

Shaw replied with a query: 'Does Port Talbot know I'm 86?'

Undaunted, the secretary wrote again:

'Your body may be 86 but your brain is still 46.'

'My brain,' an irate Shaw countered, 'will gladly come to Port Talbot. My body will see you damned first.'

From Shaw's secretary to the Hull annual conference of crematorium authorities, 1926:

> Mr Bernard Shaw has asked me to say that it is more impossible for him to accept the invitation this year than last year, as he had a narrow escape this year from being cremated himself, and must for the present go very slowly in the matter of public speaking.

Shaw, declining to lecture:

> I am fully conscious of the
> honor done me by the Philosophical
> Institution of Edinburgh in asking me
> to lecture; but the condition that my
> subject should be non-controversial makes
> it impossible for me to accept the
> invitation.
>   I never speak in public except on
> violently controversial subjects in a
> violently controversial way.

Despite Shaw's oft-repeated refusal to talk to women's societies (he held that the vote would never be won by speeches made by men on behalf of women), requests flooded in:

> Dear Mr Bernard Shaw
>   On Wednesday next
> at 8p.m. in Bow Baths a
> meeting is to be held at which
> Sir Francis Vane is going to
> launch the Training Corps by
> which we mean to fit our
> people in East London to

deal effectively with the
government and the police . . .
    I write to ask whether
you will speak at that
meeting . . . The Baths is quite
a big place and I can
promise that you shall not
be interrupted and that
the people will wait till
you have finished to
applaud. Also I may
tell you that they are
not likely to laugh in the
wrong place . . .

                Faithfully yours
                E. Sylvia Pankhurst

Shaw showed great courtesy in attending the lectures of others:

                    St. Dominic's Priory
                    London, NW5
                    5th October 1931

Dear Mr. Shaw
    A priest's week-end is usually so crowded with work that
he has rarely time even for the necessities of gratitude.
    But I must not let another day pass without paying, in
weakened sterling, my debt of thanks.
    I cannot say how deeply you touched the lecturer of
Friday night by your presence at his lecture. Had you said
no word your presence would have said volumes . . .
    Every circumstance of your coming added to its
graciousness. I cannot forget how you came to an unknown
person – and at short notice. I am told you even advanced
the hour of your evening meal – and that at an age when a
daily routine seems a first duty.
    Especially remembered will be your words with their clear
enunciation of principle; & their final touch of insight into
the heart of a Friar.

Let me offer you a friar's thanks in the old formula: May God reward you!

Believe me. Dear Mr. Shaw

Yours very gratefully
Fr. Vincent McNabb O.P.

As the years advanced, those who wanted G.B.S. to go to them received a special pink postcard warning them that:

Mr Bernard Shaw has long since been obliged by advancing years to retire from his committees and his personal activities on the platform. He therefore begs secretaries of societies to strike his name from their lists of available speakers . . .

When Shaw sent this printed postcard refusal to the Rev. H. S. McClelland, president of the Glasgow Trinity Literary Society, his secretary added a personal note:

Mr. Shaw is inexorable and he advises you to keep the forty guineas you offer for some young man who needs them.

McClelland, annoyed at receiving his tenth Shaw refusal in as many years, replied immediately, expressing his displeasure in no uncertain terms:

> I have received your curt reply to my request that you should address our society, which has already welcomed to its platform Chesterton, Inge, Lodge, Birrell, Zangwill, Gosse, Buchan, Henson, Barnes, Huxley, Masefield, Walpole, and at least fifty of the most famous novelists, scientists, philosophers, and politicians of our day.
>
> You had a perfect right, of course, to say you could not find time to come, though I find that statement hard to believe from a man who evidently finds plenty of time to bask for hours, almost naked, on a raft, on the sunny seas of the Riviera, and can spend whole evenings with a famous Yankee pugilist [Gene Tunney] who seeks to worship at the Shavian shrine.
>
> What you had no right to do was to accompany your refusal with a gratuitous and typically insolent piece of advice to our secretary to keep his guineas for a younger man who needed them more.
>
> If you had been asked to come for no fee, as probably some societies have asked you, there might be some reason for your rudeness. As it was – for you were offered nearly £50 – there was none.
>
> It is quite evident you are not in need of guineas. What you are in need of is the grace of common courtesy.
>
> Barrie and Bennett, Kipling and Galsworthy, Wallace and Wells, were asked to address our society, even as you were asked. Up to the present they have not been able to come to us, though Edgar Wallace has promised to come on his return from America. But the replies of the men, each of them of international reputation, show me what your answer utterly failed to reveal – that it is possible to be both a genius and a gentleman.

Shaw, too, felt moved to reply; but not, one imagines, as the Reverend might have wished!

> Hoots, toots, mon. Dinna' tak offence whaur nane is meant; and gi'e yer siller til the young, a'tel't ye.
>
> G. BERNARD SHAW
>
> P.S. I trust this is worthy of a devoted student of Burns and Walter Scott.

No blushing violet, McClelland tried again, 'Now what about a lecture date for next session? You can have any Monday you please between October and March.' But, Shaw was not to be caught, and Clydeside had to make do with Edgar Wallace!

Shaw, the *News Chronicle* claimed, put on an 'exhibition of bad taste' from time to time for the benefit of Americans. 'Why should anyone who is in London want to go to America,' Shaw asked. '. . . I do not want to see the Statue of Liberty . . . I am a master of comic irony. But even my appetite for irony does not go as far as that!'

Shaw was once asked by an American impresario to go on a lecture tour in the United States. 'There are,' the impresario assured him, 'only two great lecture attractions remaining to be exploited in the United States. You are one of them.' 'And who is the other?' Mr Shaw asked. 'The German Emperor,' replied the impresario. 'Then,' said Mr Shaw, 'I'll go on this lecturing tour you suggest on one condition.' 'And that is?' asked the impresario eagerly. 'That I appear on the same platform with His Majesty!' replied Mr Shaw firmly.

When Anthony Hope, on behalf of Major Pond (who ran lecture tours in America), asked Shaw early in the century to undertake an American tour, G.B.S. replied:

> I can't face America: I should be mobbed to death. For some years past I have received proposal after proposal for a lecturing tour. Every conceivable kind of pressure has been brought to bear, the highest point being £300 per lecture, a private fee of £500 from a leader of New York Society on condition that the first words that I breathed with American air should be uttered in her drawing-room, and a liner or an American battleship all to myself for the journey out. As I resisted all this there is really no use in wasting Pond's time by extracting proposals from him which I don't really mean to accept, though I generally let people make them because I like to know my market value as a matter of business and personal vanity.

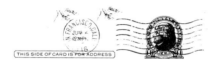

To keep the pressure up, the New York chapter of the Drama League of America sent Shaw an invitation signed by distinguished men of letters and of the theatre. Declining politely, Shaw continued at length in his characteristic fashion:

> Every year the papers announce in desperation that I am actually coming; and every citizen of the United States writes me a cordial private invitation to stay at his house . . . I cannot help asking myself whether it is not now too late. I could have come when I was young and beautiful. I could have come when I was mature and capable. I did not. I am now elderly and doddering. Could I live up to my reputation? Have I any right to bring my white hairs and my crowsfeet to blast the illusions of the young American women who send me my photographs of thirty years ago to be autographed, and to address American audiences with a fictitious clearness of articulation that is due wholly to my dentist? If I were a modest man I should not think of such things. Being notoriously an extremely vain one, they daunt me. Authors, unlike good little children, should be heard, not seen. I shall leave America its ideal unshattered . . .

SHAW TO VISIT AMERICA

Mr Bernard Shaw is going to the
United States of America – but for only
a few minutes.

He said yesterday: 'Probably the
United States will be greatly excited,
but there is nothing for them to get
excited about.

'I am going on a cruise, and part of
the time we shall be in the neighbourhood
of the United States. When we are, I
may land – but only for five or six
minutes.

'But there is no need for America's
millions to come racing to the favoured
spots.'

News Chronicle, *7 November 1932*

Shaw's only visit to the United States took place in 1933. He landed at San Francisco, went by aeroplane to stay with William Randolph Hearst, re-embarked at Los Angeles, sailed down the Pacific coast to Panama and up the Atlantic coast to New York, where he spent a single day and addressed a large audience at the Metropolitan Opera House in the evening before returning to the ship. The lecture agents still had not lured him, and he never came back.

Religion

'I am a socialist because I have learnt . . . that freedom without law is impossible; and I have become a religious agitator because I have observed that men without religion have no courage.'

Shaw

Take a vote as to whether I am a good man or not. Some people will tell you that my goodness is almost beyond that of any other living person. They will even tell you that I am the only hope of religion in this country. You will not have to go very far to find persons who are of exactly the contrary opinion.

The Case For Equality

Dear George

I enclose a little
medal which I beg
you to wear
and believe that
I wish to be
your sincere friend

     E. A. Collier
unless you <u>wear</u> the
medal send it back
to me . . .

On March 21, 1878, the 22-year-old Shaw noted the receipt of one of his earliest gifts, a medal of the Virgin Mary. His benefactor is thought to have been Mrs Collier, one of several London hostesses who sought to befriend the awkward, lonely young Shaw in his early London years. At the time of her letter he noted: 'Received on the 21st March 1878, with a medal of the Virgin Mary enclosed. Agreed to wear same for 6 mos & discarded it accordingly 21/9/78.' The tiny medal, affixed to a black cord, survives in the British Library archives, Shaw having preserved it all his life.

When in 1925 Shaw touched upon religion during a lecture to business girls at a London luncheon club, a nervous lady on the committee hardly knew which way to turn, especially when she noted the expression on the face of one of her favourite protégées. When it was over, she went up to the girl, and said, 'I hope you were not shocked by what Mr Shaw said about religion.' 'Shocked!' cried the girl. 'Good heavens! the dear old gentleman's been simply *too Victorian* for words.'

One 1947 philosophy major at the University of Michigan was troubled by a 'God-Problem'. He wrote to Shaw that 'After four years of Plato, Aristotle, Kant, Leibnitz, Schopenhauer, Bergsen, Freud, Wagner, Strauss, Beethoven, Sappho, Homer, Brooke, Mill, etc, I am as much confused as ever. Perhaps this is because I have had no word of assurance from Bernard Shaw . . .'

Shaw's 1947 sale by auction of a Breeches Bible evoked sharp words from Mr Etienne Dupuch, editor of the *Nassau Tribune* in the Bahamas:

. . . time will catch up on the old goat. All his life Shaw has
played with fire – he will miss the rope here – but in the end
he is bound to catch hell. And we mean that literally.

Shaw's flyleaf remarks which so inflamed Dupuch were:

This ugly family Bible, with its register of births and deaths
scrawled all through it as well as at the end, is what is called
a Breeches Bible. The leaves are numbered, not the pages.
The word breeches (instead of aprons) is on the recto page
of leaf 2. There also are the thumb marks shewing that this
page was looked at oftener than the book was read . . .
  Except as a curiosity the book, as a material object, is a
most undesirable possession. The binding is heavy,
common, and graceless. The printing is of the worst period.
To anyone who has seen a page from the press of Jensen or
William Morris it is heathenish.
  I must get rid of it. I really cannot bear it in my house.

G. Bernard Shaw

Its value increased by Shaw's inscription, the Bible was sold to a Cambridge
bookseller for £31. Shaw, untroubled by Dupuch's attack, countered:

Ask this foolish American, who thinks I should be hanged
for selling an ugly Bible, what should be done to the Bible
Society, which sells thousands of much handsomer ones
every day. The silly fellow need not be anxious about me: I
have half a dozen Bibles left and never travel without one.

In 1947, 22-year-old Albert Stanford, a student at the Piedmond Bible
Institute in North Carolina, wrote to Shaw when he became worried over
the state of the playwright's soul, after reading that Shaw had said he
wished to die in peace, and later that he had sold his wife's Bible because he
found it 'ugly'. In his letter the young man advised Shaw to 'stop running
from God and the Bible' and that the only way to die in peace was to die 'in
the Prince of Peace, the Lord Jesus Christ.' In reply Shaw assured Mr
Stanford that he had plenty of Bibles left. 'The Bible,' he said:

is not a book but a literature and, like all literature, it
contains not only wise doctrine and inspired poetry, drama,

and edifying fiction but is mischievous and superstitious. What is more, there are five gods in the Bible and there are many Bibles in the world, ancient and modern. I have written part of the latest. Until the Kingdom of Heaven is within you, you will search the Scriptures in vain . . . I do not usually answer the people who write nonsense to me about my doing what the Bible Society does a thousand times a day . . . The sympathy and sincerity of your letter touched me.

Elsewhere, an unexpected tribute to the Bible Society bobbed up in Shaw's reply to a request for his advice on radium purchases for hospitals. He advised the correspondent to buy a pound or two, but to do it out of sound investment income, not capital. Radium treatment, he hastened to point out, was not discovered by 'the Research people' whose activities had had

the effect of distracting attention and diverting funds from fruitful and essentially noble work in physics to useless enquiries and the pseudo-bacteriology which assumes that God made typhoid and tetanus bacilli, and duly let them loose in the Garden of Eden to be named by Adam along with the other animals. The silly people don't even know their own silly business. I assure you the Bible Society is a far worthier market for spare cash than the Research Societies. Bible science, such as it is, is sounder than the science of Pasteur and Lister, and is now much less blindly believed in . . .

To the 1926 symposium query 'Have We Lost Faith?', Shaw exclaimed, 'Certainly not, but we have transferred it from God to the General Medical Council.'

Shaw's later heresies, he told a Devon man who was conducting an argument with him about the Resurrection, would have made him liable to prosecution as an apostate were it not for the fortunate circumstance that, though he was duly baptized as a member of the Episcopal Church of Ireland, he had never been confirmed, and the responsible parties were his godparents, long since dead.

After Shaw addressed a Hampstead meeting, a nervous and forbidding clergyman rose in response to the usual query, 'Any questions?' 'Are you a Christian?' he asked. G.B.S. rose, and, smiling blandly, replied: 'Yes, but I often feel very lonely.'

Over the years Shaw engaged in a number of correspondences on religious themes. One such exchange took place in 1937 between Shaw and the Rev. A. B. Morley of Theale, Berkshire. The correspondence began in July when Morley wrote countering Shaw's 'charges against the Faith'. Shaw's reply was sufficient to encourage Morley to write again – at greater length. Question followed question.

10th October 1933

Dear Mr. Shaw,

I thank you for the return of my sermon.

Should I be putting you to too much trouble if I asked you to answer the following quite briefly?

1) Do you think Bunyan, Dante & Milton & others who tried to present truth through visions & dreams were drug addicts?

2) Do you still think that Roman Catholics believe in the parthenogenetic birth of Mary & all her ancestors back to Eve? & where did you hear this?

Yours sincerely,
Arthur B. Morley

12th Oct. 1933

Dear Mr. Morley,

1. There is not the slightest trace in the works of Dante, Bunyan or Milton of the illusion as to time and space which betrays the drug addict, for whom ten thousand years pass in ten seconds and the whole earth and the heavens are visible at a glance. Read De Quincey's Confessions of An English Opium Eater and you will see the difference at once.

2. No; but they ought to. It has not occurred to most of them that the logic that leads to the immaculate conception of Mary leads to the immaculate conception of all her progenitors from the beginning of the world. This reductio

ad absurdum comes, I believe, not from Rome, but from
Belfast. But it is perfectly sound – logically.

Not satisfied, Morley pressed Shaw to continue the argument. However,
G.B.S. had had enough and proved unwilling to quarrel further, writing to
the then bachelor vicar:

19th October 1937

Dear Mr. Morley
. . . Your sermons about the Book of Revelations will do very
well for Jack the Giant Killer if it is ever proposed to add
that tale to the canon. I am under no such obligation. I know
delirium tremens when I meet it; but my diagnosis does not
imply that its ravings have no reference to actual facts and
beliefs known to the patient.

   You must now definitely drop it. You are molesting me
with a view to my salvation, I presume, and thereby leading
yourself into temptation, as your faith is in greater danger
than mine. And I have to consider your wife and family if
you wont consider them yourself. You are young enough to
like arguing: I am not, though I could probably argue your
head off if I sat down to that unamiable and unChristian
game. No more, therefore.

One then unknown young man to whom Shaw sent a profoundly challeng-
ing message was the Indian, Amiya Chakravarty, who later – after teaching
at Calcutta University – was to become Professor of Comparative Oriental
Religion and Literature at Boston University. Shaw's letter, Chakravarty
informed Dan H. Laurence in May 1964, 'is associated with a great event in
my life – I had just lost my own brother in a terrible catastrophe . . .'

Dear Sir
   Did you ever read the autobiography of John Stuart Mill?
Or John Bunyan's Grace Abounding? If ever you do you will
find that it is not unusual for young men to fall for a time
into 'a terrible state of mind' in which they describe
themselves as 'unhappy creatures of God'. It is a sort of
adolescent melancholia: one grows out of it; and it does not

recur. While it lasts you must put up with it as best you can . . .

You ask yourself why God made you; and your answer is that he made you that he might amuse himself by tormenting you. Are you then so very amusing – or very interesting – that you are a sufficient amusement and occupation for God?

He must certainly have made you for no other purpose than as an instrument to help him in making his will prevail. No doubt you are a disappointment to him, as you pity yourself and blame him instead of helping him. But then he is used to disappointments. When he made the cobra, he thought it would redeem the world for him; but it failed, and he had to make the mongoose to kill it. And unless you take up the fight against evil, he will certainly make something higher than man to kill you.

It is curious that an Indian should have come to the remotest west to be taught so simple a thing as this.

It was not at all unusual to find 'Dear Mr Shaw' letters – especially towards the end of his life – questioning his religious position, and from time to time it was suggested that he would be the truly perfect man, if only he would become a Christian, a Roman Catholic, etc. 'I receive letters from Belfast Protestants,' Shaw commented in 1925 upon being informed that a Rome newspaper had announced that he was about to become a Catholic, 'congratulating me on having exposed the Scarlet Woman, and on having shown up the Inquisition. Roman Catholics also congratulate me on my attitude, and say that I should join the Roman Catholic Church because I appear already to be a Roman Catholic. On the whole I am highly gratified with the position that I occupy, and think I can do nothing better than sit tight.'

To an enquiry in his last year as to whether a rumour that he was to be received into the Roman Catholic Church were true, Shaw exploded: 'Tell *him* there is not *room* in *Rome* for *two* Popes!'

Even a Benedictine monk (one who had never read Shaw's works), the Rev. J. J. Murty of a Northumberland parish, tried to 'convert' Shaw:

ST. WILFRIDS'
Blyth, Northumberland
26th July 1946

Dear Mr Shaw,
   ... I have always taken
a friendly interest in you. You
have always been a bit of a
comedian. I havent read any
of your works but from what
I can gather your flippancy has
extended itself even to the Almighty.
In your case I should put this
down to 'invincible ignorance'.
Fortunately this does not carry
with it any serious responsibility
or guilt.
Have you any rational convictions
on the future life?
I am a catholic Priest. I would
gladly put my services at your
disposal & place before you the
only rational solution of the
reason for the existence of this
world that has ever been made
viz – the catholic one . . .

At least one obscure Irishwoman also wished for his conversion:

Ard Beinean
Blackrock, Dundalk
August 8th 1946

Dear Mr. Shaw,
   I have waited till the Captains
and the Kings depart to offer to you the homage
and prayers of a very obscure Irishwoman.
   . . . If your English secretary is tempted to put
it in the waste paper basket, maybe, you'd
let your Irish servant read it instead.
   Countless Irish people are, while
wishing you *ad multos annos*, praying
that you may become a Catholic, and join the
great company of Joan, Aquinas, Francis of Assisi,
Francis de Sales, Patrick, Columcille, Chesterton

and the generations of your own fellow countrymen
and women among whom you would surely be at home.
. . . The Redeemer took the Good Thief to Paradise
with him, and, indeed, he will take you, – I had
almost said whether you like it or not – for you
gave back more than ever you took . . .

Mary MacCarvill

And from Cheltenham came the following provocative letter:

July 31st 1946

Probably no human in modern times has done so much as
yourself to undermine traditional Christianity – I mean the
simple faith in God and the Bible held by millions of
trusting humans in recent centuries. Your conceptions of
religion and philosophy permeate all modern thought – your
influence is immeasurable, that is surely indicated in the
consensus of tribute you have received from the world's
journalists in connection with your 90th birthday.

Will you tell me – in whatever way you like – whether you
ever doubt your own judgment of this world: whether the
thought ever crosses your mind that you may possibly be
completely wrong, and the traditional Christians right, in
their simple faith in the Bible?

Is there no possibility that they are right?

Your 'Life Force' – even if you are right in your
conception of it, may there not be an over-riding truth, that
it is indeed, in its possession of you, a demoniac possibility?
Supposing that all you believe is true, and there is just this
one weakness in your belief – that the God you believe in,
the Creator of Superman, is not the Highest God, but an
Odylic Force (expressed, for instance in Psychic
Phenomena) which is malevolent? Where are you, if this
should happen to be the truth?
yours sincerely,

Arthur Constance

There were others, however, who were less gentle in their treatment
of the suspected heretic, strongly evangelical in their desire to 'save' him.

My dear George Bernard Shaw
. . . You want to do good in the world and not evil. That I
take for granted. You have begun at the wrong end and you

are going about it the wrong way. The great man is reverent.
You are irreverent and therefore not a great man . . . As I
knelt in my study just now and asked this Mighty Counsellor
to give me the spirit of Wisdom and understanding that I
might write His message to you – brother man – a knock
came to the door and when I unlocked it my eldest boy came
in and said to me – 'Have you that book of Bernard Shaw's?'
alluding to 'The Irrational Knot' which I got out of The
Hampstead Library. I said 'Yes. there it is – I haven't read it
myself yet but <u>don't take too much notice of it. Bernard
Shaw is not a good guide for a young man.</u>' Why should I
have to say that when you <u>want</u> to be a good guide . . . Start
again, old chap, and start on your knees. Ask for wisdom &
the power to see things from Christ's point of view and you
will be <u>inspired:</u> You may not be understood. <u>That</u> doesn't
matter. Nor do you care. But. when H E asks you how you
used the Prophet's gift which you have in part – even now,
you can look into His face and say – 'When I was down on
that little earth I saw things going all wrong. I tried hard to
set them right. Men praised and men blamed me & by and
by I looked back the way I had come, and I saw – where I
had been a false prophet and **You** were watching me all the
while. And one morning you put it into the heart of a
brotherman who also saw the world pretty much as I saw it,
to write me a letter from his very soul – and he wrote it'

I am, my dear George Bernard Shaw
Your friend & brother
John Henry Hill

Twenty years later Shaw was still causing controversy. The Co. Wexford
Bee-Keepers Association even proposed that his name should be removed
from its membership list in the light of his 'blasphemous statements
concerning Christ and His Apostles' in his book, *The Adventures of the Black
Girl in Her Search for God.*

The barrage of attacks on Shaw's religious views continued well into his
nineties; letters from 'well-wishers' asking 'very earnestly where I will
spend Eternity.'

BERNARDO DE SHAW – A CANTERBURY PILGRIM OF TO-DAY

Dear Mr Shaw,
    In your letter of the 25th ultimo to
Dr Hernon (Dublin's City Manager) there
is one sentence which must give you food for
thought . . . 'Suppose, I die to-day
or to-morrow . . . ?' Well, old
man, <u>you will die to-day or to-</u>
<u>morrow!</u> What do you think
will happen to you after you
die? What will God say
to You? What will you say
to God?

But:

Peasmarsh, Nr. Rye

. . . may I say that I feel I owe to you more of mental enlightenment and stimulation than I have gained from any other writer, living or dead.

The Rev. L. E. Roberts
Vicar of Peasmarsh, Sussex

Many years earlier, on April 26th, 1924, Shaw had received another fan letter, from a prelate, Lord Tredegar, offering to serve as a Papal emissary on his behalf.

My dear Mr. Bernard Shaw,
. . . I have the honour to be Private Chamberlain to the Holy Father and to be in the confidence of Vatican officials. I live nine months out of the year in Rome.

I went to see your play, St. Joan, which I thought magnificent and, if I may be allowed to say so, one of your greatest works of which I am an admirer. But it struck me that some Catholics would not view it in the same light as myself. I am fully aware that the opinions of Catholics on the matter can be of not the slightest importance to you and that it can make no difference whether persons of my religion are interested in the work or not. But it seems to me a pity that some interfering and over-zealous person may go and represent your play to the Vatican as one unfit for Catholics to read or to visit; such things are done unfortunately. From my own point of view I have no doubt that it will make many converts to the Faith because of the fair way you have treated a matter which has so often been misrepresented.

Your fairness to the clerics and to the clerical court has opened and will open the eyes of a large number of people who expected you to make them ridiculous, or at best, imbeciles.

What I should very much like to do would be to ask you either for a typewritten or printed copy of your play which I would have conveyed to the Vatican before the end of the month, with a covering letter suggesting that it was exceedingly profitable that such a play should be seen and read by all of our Faith . . .

May I end this letter by apologising for my impertinence in so writing to you, and asking you to forgive the indiscretion as arising from youth and inexperience.

Yours sincerely,
Evan Morgan

As Shaw's ninety-fourth birthday approached, the Rev. G. W. Parkinson, Minister of Doncaster Free Church, informed him that he intended to preach on his works. In reply Shaw sent a signed photograph of himself inscribed, 'As from Devil to Disciple'.

'CONCERNING THAT DISTINGUISHED CHRISTIAN, MR BERNARD SHAW AND THE LIFE-LONG HYPOCRISY OF HIS EFFORTS TO APPEAR AN IMMORAL MAN'

Theatre:
Don't Put Your
Daughter
On The Stage!

'If you have parents who advised you to go on the stage, all I can say is that the sooner you get a new set of parents the better.'

G.B.S. to British Drama League summer school students

CROMWELL ROAD SITE

NATIONAL THEATRE
THE PHILANDERERS OR LOVE'S LABOUR'S LOST

NATIONAL THEATRE
MUCH ADO ABOUT METHUSELAH

NATIONAL THEATRE
HAMLET OR HEART-BREAK CASTLE

NATIONAL THEATRE
THE MERCHANT OF VENICE

NATIONAL THEATRE
OTHELLO OR HOW HE LIED TO HER HUSBAND

NATIONAL THEATRE
YOU NEVER CAN LIKE IT

A NATIONAL THEATRE?

"TO BUILD OR NOT TO BUILD, THAT IS THE QUESTION."

To Leslie J. Brown of Fulham:

2nd February 1905

People who ostracize theatres and music halls are neither
Christians nor pagans: they are idiots. A child who has never
seen a pantomime, or an adult who has never seen a play, is
a public danger. People who are unacquainted with the
masterpieces of dramatic literature and music are heathens,
no matter what sect they belong to. Those who bring up
children in such ignorance are every whit as culpable as
those who forbid their children to enter a cathedral or to
open the Bible. There is danger in the theatre just as there is
in the church; but parents who think it wrong to send their
children into the theatre after thinking it right to bring them
into the world are beyond reason.

G. Bernard Shaw

Shaw claimed that once he became famous he received three marriage
proposals a week from young women who had read or seen his plays.

Even at ninety I am not free of their attentions. Sensual
actresses fling their arms round me and hug me because
they want me to let them play St. Joan and Candida. They
know that it is the shallow side in me that is the most
sensitive; they send me idiotic ties and chocolates because
they want to play Cleopatra. I have my hands full in keeping
them at bay . . .

After a film star insisted on sitting on Shaw's lap and kissing him, he
commented:

This lady asked me what she could do to make me happy. I
asked her to pray for me. She said that she had never prayed
in her life.
And then she asked me to let her play St. Joan.

This impromptu 'audition' failed, however, to impress Shaw. 'She would
never do for St Joan,' he said, 'because she is far too pretty. My St Joan must
be as beautiful as a farm wagon . . .'
Shaw, frequently approached by young people determined to go on
the stage, always directed them to RADA (the Royal Academy of Dramatic
Art) as he knew that after a stiff entrance test, the Academy gave an
indispensable sound training. The RADA (Gower Street) building was
put up in 1931 from a fund which G.B.S. himself had opened with a £5,000

donation. A very active member of the Academy's Council, Shaw personally rehearsed the students for its public shows.

As early as 1897 Shaw was trying to ward off aspiring actresses who sought his support. 'If,' he wrote to Sally Fairchild, an American friend of Ellen Terry:

> you send any 'nice, pretty, ambitious little girl who is an
> actress' to me, you will not survive our next meeting. I know
> those females. They come to me once a fortnight, on an
> average – sometimes once a week. They have all had four
> years experience; they all have faith in their determination
> and honesty; they all mean to make a chance for themselves
> by grit and ability; they all know the difficulties and
> objections, and have weighed and considered them all; they
> are all smart and pretty and clever; they are all willing to play
> the smallest part; and they all believe that the lead in my
> next play would be about the chance they are waiting for. I
> tell them all that they are not wanted. I tell them to spend
> their money in going to see all the acting they can in London
> & the European capitals, and then to hurry back to America
> or anywhere else where they can get an engagement. I warn
> them that if they stay here they will languish in lodgings
> wearing out their hearts and clothes until they realise at last
> that their chances & their youth & their four years
> experience and their hope & courage are gone, and their
> money too. Then they write me extremely sarcastic letters;
> and relieve their feelings by circulating mendacious
> accounts of my conduct in the American papers. I now get
> mad over their applications, and brutally repulse their letters
> requesting me to name an hour at which they can call on me.
> But it's of no use: they waylay me at the theatre, and get
> handed over to me by other people who are too goodnatured
> to tell them the truth. So don't encourage such expeditions
> and aspirations – above all, don't send the victims to me . . .

In April 1917 Shaw took great pains to assure one Wimbledon father, troubled by his daughter's theatrical ambitions, that the stage was not the den of iniquity he feared.

> Dear Sir,
>   I think you are perhaps exaggerating the risks of the
> theatrical profession. It is true that no sensible person ever
> advises a young man or woman to go on the stage, or indeed
> to adopt any of the artistic professions: we who are in them

always say 'sweep a crossing first'. I have told many young women that if they go on the stage they must do so against the advice of everybody who cares for them – that nothing but irresistible vocation justifies such a step. But if the irresistible vocation is there, whether it be real or delusive, and the postulant is determined, then it is far better for all the friends and relatives to accept the situation and make the best of it.

And once it is so accepted, there is a good deal to be said for it. The stage is the only profession in which women are on equal terms with men, and cannot have their work taken from them. They can attain the highest places. Mrs Siddons is as famous as Garrick and was probably more highly paid. In England the presumption that an actress is unchaste, which still lingers on the continent (where it applies to all artists and even to men of letters) has died out: actresses are received freely in general society, and many just as well as other women of their class: indeed very often better, as they have more opportunities, and have had to study the art of making the best of themselves personally . . .

I must add that a woman may pass her life on the stage, and remain as good a Catholic, and as innocent and genuinely respectable a woman, as if she had spent it in an Irish convent. Very few working women can protect themselves as effectually as an actress can, if she wants to. And if she does not want to, there is no profession in which she suffers less; for if an actress has good manners and is professionally capable and industrious and pleasant to work with, nobody troubles about her love affairs, if she has any. There are no 'ruined' women on the stage. The virtuous woman says no, and the woman of gallantry says yes; and that is nobody's business but their own . . .

You must understand, of course, that the theatre is a little world in itself and that there are disreputable quarters in it just as there are anywhere else. There are rowdy travelling companions and rowdy theatres, where the conversation behind the scenes is foul, and the women are prostitutes using the stage as an advertisement, thereby enabling themselves to do with salaries on which no respectable woman could live; but there are such places and such people in all businesses which employ women . . . But it is as well that your daughter should know that they do exist and that it is therefore as necessary for an actress to be on her guard against accepting an engagement in a disreputable company as for a waitress to be on her guard against hotels which are really brothels . . .

The severest strain on an actress's character arises from the fact that her income is so extremely irregular. For months at a time she earns the means of living extravagantly: for months she has absolutely nothing. The temptation to run into debt and live within her salary rather than within her income is obvious . . .

To strength of mind must be added a considerable strength of body. The life is sometimes very hard; and touring requires the constitution of a horse, as draughty stages and insanitary dressing rooms with endless stairs to them, and waiting about at rehearsals in cold weather often produces a total of hardship that would kill many sailors . . .

Being true to Shaw cost talented amateur actress, Antoinette Newell, her 1943 elocution prize at Australia's chief centre of dramatic art – the Ballarat Eisteddfod. There was no doubt she had won it. Adjudicator Victor Trotman told her so in a written comment. But, he added, she was only getting the third prize.

Asked why, he said: 'As Eliza Doolittle, in Shaw's *Pygmalion*, she stuck too closely to the text. She said, 'Not - - - - - - likely.' That lost her the first prize.

'All right,' he added, 'I know I'm a bit of a wowser [Puritan], but I can't help that.'

'Are you going to appeal against the decision?' Antoinette was asked.
'Not - - - - - - likely,' she said.

Shaw's secretary, Blanche Patch, recalled that during the run of *St Joan*, a succession of young women called at Whitehall Court, each wanting to play the title role.

> . . . One of them, who told us that in her dwelt the spirit of Joan, refused to leave the doorway. She was a rugged young woman, as if from the London School of Economics . . . Yet another aspirant to the part tried to demonstrate the excellence of her elocution by reading to G.B.S. and me the chapter about Jezebel from the Bible. The performance embarrassed us both. But Shaw had a practical sympathy, ready to serve anyone who showed the least promise. On one occasion he took a girl into the church at Ayot and told her to stand up and read from the pulpit while he sat in the back pew to test her voice for carrying power . . .

After a talk with another young claimant, who came by appointment, G.B.S. shook hands with her as she left. When Miss Patch saw her to the door she held out her hand too. The girl shook her head: 'No one else will touch that hand again to-day,' she said.

One Hampshire father thought his daughter ideally suited for the film role
of Joan.

> . . . I have a daughter, Joan
> aged 18 years, whose name we
> chose for her, having in mind,
> the beautiful character, about
> whom I understand, you have
> written your play.
>   Joan has been brought up
> in a country village, educated
> locally, is delightfully simple.
>   She has not received
> any histrionic training, other
> than her performances, in the
> church & school concerts & plays.
>   As her father, I can only add,
> that she is kindly &
> majestic, responsive to all
> matters, that are right & correct,
> critical of faults & weaknesses.
>   At her birth, which was a great
> difficulty, the doctors
> declared, she could not live.
>   Five days after her advent
> a miracle happened.
>   She has progressed slowly,
> as one of God's Children, until
> today, we know that her future
> is secure.
>   I, therefore, will be pleased
> to hear from you, suggesting
> that you would meet her and
> make your own judgement.
>   Perhaps you will observe
> in her the characteristics of
> Liza in 'Pygmalion', before
> her transfiguration!

And then there was the American girl interested only in 'Art for Art's Sake'.

> My dear Mr. Shaw,
>   I am mailing you
> a copy of 'The Media News' with a

picture of Catherine Rieser of 'Hedgerow'.
As Joan of Arc I feel that she is
unsurpassed. Philadelphia critics
have told me that she is the
greatest St Joan, excepting none.
She is a graduate of Shipley School
and Bryn Maur College, where
the dramatic coach Samuel A. King
called her a genius.
A character actress of great ability
I am sure spending years at Hedgerow.
I asked her if she would like to play
St Joan for the Movie. This was
her answer.

   Not for fame or money
but I would like to do it for
Mr. Shaw I think . . .

   She is a selfless person – interested only in
Art for Art's Sake – the movie scouts have been
after her from time to time – but she has had
no interest out of Hedgerow.
I apologize for this intrusion upon your time.

> Very truly yours,
> Helen R. Collins,
> Media,
> Delaware County
> Pennsylvania
> U.S.A.

PS. As an old woman Catherine Rieser is wonderful.

> H.R.C.

Casting proposals, on occasion, got more than a little out of hand.

Dear Mr. Bernard Shaw,
   You are credited in the papers
with having suggested to Sydney Carroll
that Shirley Temple should play
Cleopatra in the Open-Air Theatre. If
this is correct it is quite obvious you
have never seen Shirley Temple.

   We have a very comfortable Private
Theatre here and would be delighted to
show you Shirley Temple's latest film

at any time and day convenient to you . . .
Roy Simmonds,
Twentieth Century-Fox Film Company Ltd.

In 1937, one 14-year-old girl in Western Australia believed herself tailor-made for the role of Cleopatra.

Dear Mr. Shaw

I read in a recent paper of your letter to Shirley Temple, asking her to act as Cleopatra in your play. She is only a little girl of nine, but my age is fourteen, and I am fifteen in September.

Cleopatra was an Egyptian. I have an Egyptian profile, so I suggested to my mother that she wrote to you enclosing my photographs, but she promptly replied that you would be in your dotage if you listened to anything about me. It therefore appears that I must write myself, and tell you how I feel.

You are a clever writer and a man who can give me my opportunity in a lifetime. The screen has always fascinated me and I love its actors. The wonderful inventions and scenery made to make a picture seem more life like, enthrall me, and I am not ashamed to own that in sad parts I cry, and my body positively tingles in exciting parts. When a picture is over I often try to imagine what the personality of an actor or actress whose picture I have seen can be like.

My elocution teacher says I have a good voice and ability. I would love to help you in your new play which must cause you some anxiety. I am taking my Junior Examination this year, but studying bores me, although I must do it or fail, which would be a disaster for no one in the family clan has failed in the Junior Examination yet. I prefer to read or pretend I am a popular actress, with a charming personality and a great deal of ability. I suppose people would laugh if they knew I wrote you this letter, but although it seems hopeless, one never knows ones chance does one? . . .

I hope, Mr Shaw, that you wont angrily throw this school girl's letter away, and settle down to business with a gifted actress with impatient haste. I suppose I am a sentimental screen enthusiast, but please remember, I can't help it. You probably read thousands of letters a day (exaggeration) all well written in clear neat handwriting; all polite and proper. Well I wont pretend to be proper or polite for that matter. In this letter I am writing to you as I would a friend – frankly (sentimental).

Enclosed you will find two photographs of myself, one full-face and the other side-face. They are only snaps but they are all I have unless I go to my mother, who probably wouldn't give me any. I thought you may wish to know what I look like. I am sorry they are not better but I could not afford anymore. Please accept my profound apologies for my boring selfish and personal interests in this letter – but I know you will. Many people in your position would treat this as a joke, probably publish it, but having your experience you will understand. Please excuse my writing, I am not very good at it.

At least one young lady became Candida thanks to Shaw's indirect assistance.

Danvers, Massachusetts
29th July 1946

Sir:

I am writing on behalf of my wife and self to express our appreciation of your indirect assistance in the matter of a recent decision.

We attended last Thursday's fine performance of your 'Candida', presented by Jane Cowl and the North Shore Players.

My wife regrets that she was unable to give her full attention to the third act. As the final curtain fell, it signaled a race with the stork to the Beverly Hospital, conveniently just around the corner.

She, and the baby, Doreen *Candida* Peterson are doing fine.

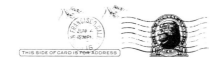

Shaw received the following letter when the papers announced that he was writing a play on Charles II (*In Good King Charles' Golden Days*):

26th December 1938

Dear Mr Shaw
This is Baliol Holloway
speaking – not only to
wish you a Happy New Year
but to remind you that I
am six-foot-one, and have
played a good deal in
Restoration Comedy
and I look the **DEAD
SPIT** of Charles II.
(Why the spit should be dead,
　　　　　　　I dont know)
for I possess those characteristic
marks from nose to mouth
– the outcome of headlong dis-
sipation, generally; but in
my case, the result of a
Puritanical abstemiousness.

And, from one actress *not* wishing to be cast – a most unusual situation:

You <u>are</u> a wonderful man!
It is quite impossible for
an ordinary being like
myself to answer your
letter – you terrify me
with your wonderfulness! . . .
　　I should like to add
<u>please don't give me up</u>
but as I am not face to
face with you I honestly
confess I should be <u>afraid</u>
to try a piece of yours
for I don't believe I could
possibly carry out your
ideas. You take my breath
away always & I always
feel quite limp &
brainless & a fool after
reading anything of

yours. I can't think
how your wife <u>dared</u> to
to marry you. Is she
stupendously clever or
the bravest woman in
the world?
Yours always in awe.

Winifred Emery.

Over the years Shaw treated young actors and actresses with great delicacy. He was particularly kind when Phyllis Neilson-Terry was unsure of her words during a 1930 rehearsal of *Candida*. 'I dare say your words are as good as mine,' he said.

When justified, Shaw could criticize as easily as praise, as Louis Calvert was to discover when his 1905 performance as Undershaft in *Major Barbara* merited the ultimate Shavian insult, 'I will tell your mother of you.' After first describing Calvert as the most infamous amateur ever to disgrace the boards, he proceeded to detail his proposed campaign to improve the quality of the actor's performance:

> . . . I have taken a box for Friday and had a hundredweight
> of cabbages, dead cats, eggs, and gingerbeer bottles stacked
> in it. Every word you fluff, every speech you unact, I will shy
> something at you. Before you go on the stage I will insult
> you until your temper gets the better of your liver. You are
> an imposter, a sluggard, a blockhead, a shirk, a malingerer,
> and the worst actor that ever lived or ever will live. I will
> apologize to the public for engaging you: I will tell your
> mother of you . . . If you do not recover yourself next time, a
> thunderbolt will end you . . .

One of Shaw's humblest theatre critics was the coster who wrote telling him how disappointed he was with *The Apple Cart*. After buying a ticket to the play, he could not find a single reference to apples anywhere.

There were always messages of both the solicited and unsolicited variety. The biting cable was a Shavian speciality. When, in 1920, cuts in the text of *Heartbreak House* were demanded by its director, Emmanuel Reicher, former managing director of Berlin's Volksbuhne Theater, Shaw cabled: 'Abandon play, cancel contract, advance will be returned, writing'. Reicher gave in instantly.

Similarly, when the New York Theatre Guild – about to stage *St. Joan* and worried about suburban theatre-goers missing their last trains home – wrote asking for textual cuts to shorten the play's running time, Shaw cabled laconically:

THE OLD STORY BEGIN AT EIGHT OR RUN LATER
TRAINS AWAIT FINAL REVISION OF PLAY.

When Arnold Daly, American producer of Shaw's *Candida, You Never Can Tell* and *The Man of Destiny*, was burned to death, the New York *World* approached Shaw for comment. His cabled reply shocked the American public:

> IMPOSSIBLE NOT TO BE INTERESTED IN POOR
> DALY'S EXTRAORDINARY DEATH. CASES OF
> SPONTANEOUS COMBUSTION ARE VERY RARE.

After the American actress Cornelia Skinner had appeared in a performance of *Candida*, she received a cable from Shaw, which read: 'Excellent – greatest', to which she replied: 'Undeserving such praise'. Whereupon Shaw wired back: 'Meant the play.' Miss Skinner, one of the few to 'outShaw' Shaw, replied: 'So did I.'

In September 1947 Shaw received the following cable from David Lowe in New York who hoped to be given permission to stage his *Buoyant Billions*:

> THIS CABLE FROM YOUNG PRODUCER
> . . . PUZZLED BY CURIOUS TWIST IN HUMAN
> BEHAVIOR NAMELY WHY ESTABLISHED
> PLAYWRIGHTS SHY FROM NEW BLOOD IN
> THEATRE COULD YOU POSSIBLY REVERSE FIELD
> AND GIVE ME OPPORTUNITY TO PRODUCE WITH
> IMAGINATION AND ZEST YOUR NEW PLAY . . .

To which Shaw's third person reply was immediate:

> SHAW'S NEW PLAY IS NOT AVAILABLE
> UNTIL AFTER ITS PRODUCTION
> AT THE MALVERN FESTIVAL ON THE
> 26TH JULY 1948.
> HE HAS NO OBJECTION TO NEW BLOOD IN THE
> THEATRE. IT IS THE DAILY OCCURRENCE OF IT IN
> EXCESS OF THE NEED THAT MAKES MATTERS
> DIFFICULT FOR BEGINNERS.

THIS SIDE OF CARD IS FOR ADDRESS

After *John Bull's Other Island* was performed at 'the King's Request' on March 11th, 1905, Shaw, who had refused to sanction a command performance, noted on the box office statement, 'Sent me with a cheque for £16-8-3 royalty at 10%, which I returned, not making any charge for the performance.'

Shaw to Messrs. Vedrenne & Barker of the Royal Court Theatre:

Dear Sirs

I learn with regret that the Royal prerogative has been stretched – in direct contravention of the Bill of Rights – to the extent of compelling you to give an unauthorized performance of my play 'John Bull's Other Island'.

Were I to accept any royalties I should be subject to heavy penalties for compounding a felony.

Short of organizing a revolution . . . I have no remedy.

I return your cheque, and hope you may not be held responsible hereafter for an offence committed at the behest of your sovereign.

On occasion a Shaw cable met with a bewildered reception, as in March 1944 when the New York Theatre Guild received the following Shaw message: 'THE ANSWER IS NO; ABSOLUTELY NO'. As the Guild had not communicated with G.B.S. nor addressed any inquiry to him since 1940, it was somewhat puzzled.

On Visitors
&
Would-Be Visitors

Dear Sir,

Is there any possibility of seeing Mr Shaw, better still of hearing him, on Monday or Tuesday morning? My motive is sheer, undiluted interest: – I don't want literary advice, autograph, or any such ulterior gain.

'BERNARD SHAW RECEIVES A SHOCK'
A COMIC EPISODE ENACTED BY PERSONALITIES AT THE MALVERN FESTIVAL
(INCLUDING J. B. PRIESTLEY AND CEDRIC HARDWICKE) AND FILMED BY WEE GEORGIE
WOOD

From Greek Street, Soho, came the following, which, without indication of town or street, was addressed simply to *Sir Bernard Show*.

> Sir.
>
> Please be Kind anaf to see me a Russian Lady. I am your Great admirer. please be Kind to Sper. me fife minits I am Sinsirly yours.
>
> ELENA. BoLgARKOFF.
>
> 56. Greex St w-1. London.

'You have no notion,' Shaw wrote to his cousin, Mrs Meredith, 'of the hosts of people who knock at my door every day: beggars, sightseers, people who claim to be my cousins because my picture in the papers resembles their grandfathers, autograph hunters, interviewers, photographers, all the nuisances on earth. But for Mrs Laden, my invaluable housekeeper, I should spend my life setting the dogs on them . . .'

Of course, there would be such celebrity visitors as Pandit Nehru, Maurice Chevalier, Lilli Palmer, Rex Harrison, Vivien Leigh, Sean O'Casey, Lady Astor, and the Shaws' good friend, Lawrence of Arabia. Once, when he was ninety-two, Shaw broke into a duet with a visitor: no other than Gertrude Lawrence.

> 'Come little girl for a sail with me,
>   Up in my bonny balloon,
> Come little girl for a sail with me,

> Round and round the moon!
> No one to see us behind the clouds:
>   Oh what a place to spoon!
> Up in the sky – ever so high,
>   Sailing in my balloon.'

American humorist and conversationalist, Will Rogers, met his match with Shaw, according to his account of their meeting:

> WILL ROGERS: How do you do, Mr Shaw?
> MR SHAW: I – – – – – – – – – – – – – – – –
> –
> –
> etc, etc, etc, and so on and so on.
> WILL ROGERS: Goodbye Mr Shaw

Similarly, Field Marshal Lord Montgomery found that conversations with Shaw were solo performances. During their meeting in Augustus John's Chelsea studio, Shaw gave Montgomery a racy lecture on tactics, strategy, Napoleon, and the military art in general.

Shaw's secretary, Blanche Patch, would recall later that, right up to the end, there was always somebody who wanted to see Shaw.

> The Soviet story that he was living 'lonely and forgotten
> near London' was one of their stupider myths. He refused
> almost with ferocity, to admit that he was lonely, explaining
> that he had the gift of 'solitariness' . . . He would never give
> an appointment to a tourist who simply wanted to include
> him in a round of sightseeing as if he were the Tower of
> London or the Zoo or Madam Tussaud's.

Even the fortunate few who were invited, were not encouraged to stay long.

> Those who went by car to Hertfordshire, were, at the
> appropriate seasons, advised to come early 'in this light', and
> when G.B.S. felt that he had had enough of them he would
> considerately suggest that they must be getting back as it was
> getting dark, and that they would need to have their car
> lights on; or, more abruptly, he would just pull out his watch
> and remark, 'Well, I must get back to work.' He had no time
> for bores.

When, in 1939, Mrs Henry Luce, the American authoress, came to London to meet the famous people of England, she was fortunate early in her visit to meet Shaw. At the end of the interview she asked him whom else she ought to see in the country. 'That is an unnecessary question,' he replied, 'You have already met incomparably the greatest figure in this land.'

However, the elderly Mr Charles W. Harrison from Ohio was less fortunate. Despite his being born the same day and year as the playwright, G.B.S. wouldn't see him. 'Mr. Shaw could be very cussed and cantankerous sometimes,' commented Mrs Jisbella Lyth, the postmistress at Ayot St Lawrence, recalling the incident later, 'it wasn't meanness, but sheer cussedness and obstinacy. He'd made up his mind – and there was an end to it.' 'Another time,' she continued:

> . . . I remember, a woman was desperately keen to see him
> and just walked right into his garden. She was trespassing
> really, of course, but Shaw didn't turn a hair, or say a harsh
> word to her. She was a complete stranger, but he treated her
> most hospitably and talked with her quite a long time.

Towards the end of Shaw's life an enterprising photographer, Allan Chappelow, managed to slip through the Shavian safeguards to the great man himself. 'You came to photograph ME with only half a roll of film?' exclaimed Shaw. 'Monstrous.'

Even ties of consanguinity were no guarantee against being 'fobbed off', as young George Meredith found out in 1950 when he turned up unannounced at Shaw's Ayot St Lawrence door, only to be turned away by Shaw's reputedly fierce housekeeper, Mrs Laden. The incident was still vivid to him over thirty-five years later:

> I recall the day very well indeed. The bus from London let
> me down some miles from Ayot St. Lawrence. I walked on
> this very hot July day and when I arrived I thought I had
> been expected because my mother had dropped him a line
> about 2 weeks previously to say I would call – as I was
> already in the U.K. on a business trip. Shaw, on receipt of
> this earlier letter had written to my mother explaining 1) the
> difficulty in getting to Ayot and 2) that Sunday was his
> chauffeur's day off and he could not have me driven. I was
> unaware of this letter when I got to Ayot – we did not have a
> telephone at my house – and was very disappointed to be
> told by Mrs Laden that G.B.S. was having his afternoon nap
> & could not be disturbed . . . I'm sure Mrs Laden was
> invaluable to G.B.S. but I must confess I didn't think too
> much of her at that moment!

The firmness of Shaw's secretary in turning away unwanted visitors earned her the nickname of 'Miss Cross Patch'. However, nicknames for Alice Laden, his housekeeper for the last seven years of his life, were more colourful. She became variously known as 'The Pillar of Stone', 'The Vinegar Bottle' and 'The Dragon'. She liked the last title so much she bought a brooch in the form of a green dragon which she wore regularly and would point out with some amusement to those not immediately turned away. 'I looked after Mr Shaw as I would a piece of rare Dresden China,' was how she summarized her attitude to the great man . . . 'When Mr Shaw first offered me the job he said, "I don't want a housekeeper who is a Shaw fan, but one who is a good housekeeper." "Well," I said to him, "I am a rank Tory and I heartily disagree with all socialist views." So Mr Shaw and I knew where we were from the start.'

At least one visitor was allowed to interrupt his morning work routine.

New Delhi
4 September 1948

My Dear Mr Shaw

I do not quite know why I am writing to you, for we are both busy men and I have no desire to add to your work . . .

Forty years ago, when I was 18 and an undergraduate at Cambridge, I heard you address a meeting there. I have not seen you since then, nor have I ever written to you. But, like many of my generation, we have grown up in company with your writings and books. I suppose a part of myself, such as I am today, has been moulded by that reading. I do not know if that would do you any credit.

Because, in a sense, you have been near to me, or rather near to my thoughts, I have often wanted to come in closer touch with you and to meet you. But opportunities have been lacking and then I felt that the best way to meet you was to read what you had written.

Devadas [Gandhi] apparently asked you as to what we should do with Gandhi's assassin. I suppose he will hang and certainly I shall not try to save him from the death penalty, although I have expressed in favour of the abolition of the death penalty in previous years. In the present case there is no alternative. But even now in a normal case, I have grown rather doubtful if it is preferable to death to keep a man in prison for 15 or 20 years.

Life has become so cheap that it does not seem of very much consequence whether a few criminals are put to death or not. Sometimes one wonders whether a sentence to live is not the hardest punishment after all.

I must apologize to you for those of my countrymen who pester you for your views on India. Many of us have not outgrown our old habit of seeking testimonials from others. Perhaps that is due to a certain lack of faith in ourselves. Events have shaken us rather badly and the future does not appear to be as bright as we imagined it would be.

There is a chance of my going to England for two or three weeks in October next. I would love to pay you a visit, but certainly not if this means any interference with your daily routine. I would not come to trouble you with any questions. There are too many questions which fill the mind and for which there appear to be no adequate answers, or if the answers are there, somehow they cannot be implemented because of the human beings that should implement them. If I have the privilege to meet you for a while, it will be to treasure a memory which will make me a little richer than I am.

> Yours Sincerely
> Jawaharlal Nehru
> PRIME MINISTER
> INDIA

However, it was not until Pandit Nehru came again in the spring of 1949 for the Conference of Premiers, that his desired visit finally took place. Like the Walrus and the Carpenter, they 'talked of many things', from India's religions to how many mangoes one might wisely eat, a basket of which the Indian leader thoughtfully left behind, after explaining how they ought to be eaten.

One would-be visitor whose audacity won the day was John Lucas, in recent years chief sub-editor and writer in the Features Department of the *Sunday Telegraph*. In February 1945, a month away from call-up, the seventeen-year-old Lucas cycled to Shaw's Corner, hoping for a chance meeting wth G.B.S. 'My younger brother was scornful,' he recalls:

> . . . We had come about 10 miles to George Bernard Shaw's house, and now, at the last moment, I was jibbing. We leaned our bikes against the fence. 'You're windy,' he said. I took off my cycle clips and tiptoed up the gravel drive to the tradesmen's entrance.
> I had cycled to the house at Ayot St. Lawrence that

February day in 1945 simply to seek his advice about
entering journalism. It didnt seem a bad idea: after all, he
had made a pretty fair stab at it himself. Also, my father had
promised me £2 if Shaw spoke to me.

I explained this to Mrs. Laden, Shaw's housekeeper, who
went into the garden, where Shaw was showing off his roses
to, as I recall, Gabriel Pascal, producer of the film 'Caesar
and Cleopatra'. Up the garden stomped Shaw, a bearded
hairpin of a man, like Santa Claus on hunger strike;
knickerbockered and irritated.

Shaw: Are you the young man who has had a bet about me?
Lucas: Not a **bet** . . .
Shaw: So now you've seen the animal, you might as well go
        home.

Crestfallen, I went back to my brother and then told Mrs.
Laden, who was sympathetic and asked us inside. 'It's his
sense of humour,' she said. 'He's like that, you know. You
get used to it. Have some tea and treacle tart.' A few days
later I wrote to Shaw, explaining, and he sent me a card
back, enclosing a newspaper advertisement for the London
School of Journalism. On the card was written:

Teaching youngsters their A.B.C is not my job. If you
cannot teach yourself as I had to, you must go to school. I
know nothing about this one except what it says about itself.
You had better buy The Writers' and Artists' Year Book and
read it from cover to cover, advertisements and all. And you
will need Whitaker's Almanack. Who's Who, and Enc. Brit.
are expensive: you can resort to the public library.
                                                    G.B.S.

Many young people wished to visit the 'great man' at home.

                                        Ascot, Berks.
                                        31st August 1946

Dear Mr Shaw,
    You don't know me from
Adam. Why should you? I am just
one human insect amongst countless
millions. You may not read this
letter; then again you may. I hope
you do. If you do, you may
regard me as a fool – but then I
probably am. It may even be the

impetuosity of youth that brings me to
write to you. I am twenty-one
and comrades of the Bracknell local
Labour Party – of which I am the
Chairman – dub me impetuous.

Perhaps it is because I am
young and foolish and because you
are old and wise that I want to
meet you.

Would you invite me to tea one
day? (I can bring my own food!)

I hope this letter will not
annoy you too much.

Yours truly
A. Barnett

From two would-be visitors:

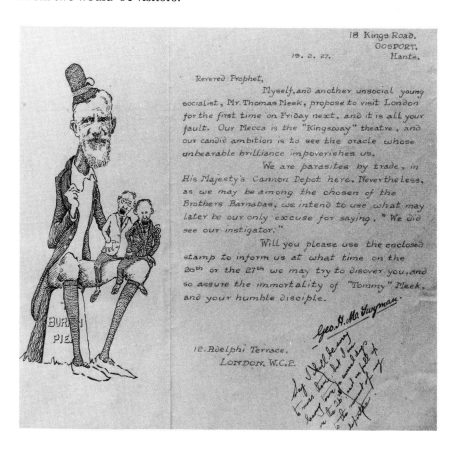

Ironically, Roland Wolpert, an American soldier who interviewed Shaw while on furlough in England would afterwards find himself plagued by the press. The interviewer would become the interviewee after the Associated Press picked up the report of his Shaw meeting, printed in the camp newspaper he edited. Ten months after their meeting, he wrote to Shaw:

> It is doubtless old stuff to you, but your name is like magic.
> In fact, for a while it was becoming quite annoying.
> Wherever I went, I was the man who interviewed Shaw. It
> was as if nothing else I had ever done mattered. A theatrical
> group in Paris asked me to give a lecture on you. A relative
> of Mark Twain who's writing a book about you, wrote to me
> for some anecdotes. People who seem to have made a life
> study of you, buttonhole me and want to know about every
> second I spent with you. It's beginning to wear off now and
> I'm glad. I felt like a parasite . . .

His brief meeting with Shaw would have a lasting effect on Wolpert, leading to a change of career plans.

> . . . It's funny, but thanks largely to you I'm in a position to
> get a good newspaper, and largely because of you I've
> refused one. In fact, because of you, I've decided not to go
> back to school for a degree that would be meaningless. I
> don't know where it will lead, and I don't care. If I ever write
> four books though, I plan to dedicate the fourth to you . . .
> When I left you in September I said, 'God bless you. I'll
> send my children to see you.' I hope my children (if I ever
> have any) will someday see you. I wish all young people
> could see you. Not 'the old animal' you describe yourself as,
> but as the symbol of eternal youth and wisdom that is you. It
> would give them something to remember always.

Not even dogs were immune to Shavian charms:

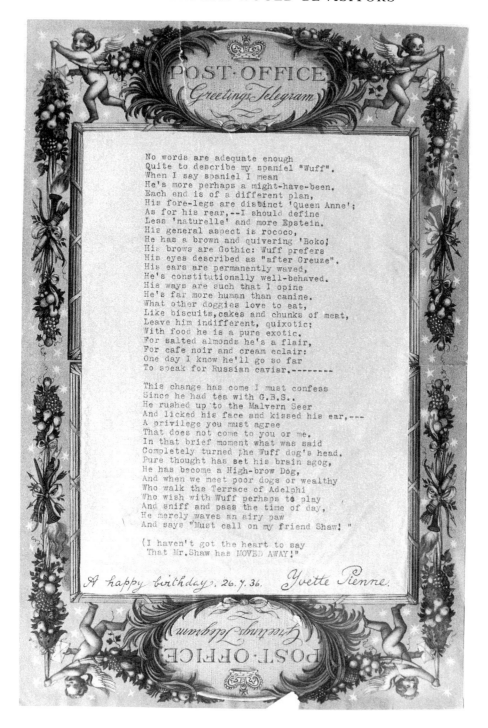

POST·OFFICE
Greetings Telegram

No words are adequate enough
Quite to describe my spaniel "Wuff".
When I say spaniel I mean
He's more perhaps a might-have-been.
Each end is of a different plan,
His fore-legs are distinct 'Queen Anne';
As for his rear,--I should define
Less 'naturelle' and more Epstein.
His general aspect is rococo,
He has a brown and quivering 'Boko,'
His brows are Gothic: Wuff prefers
His eyes described as "after Greuze".
His ears are permanently waved,
He's constitutionally well-behaved.
His ways are such that I opine
He's far more human than canine.
What other doggies love to eat,
Like biscuits, cakes and chunks of meat,
Leave him indifferent, quixotic;
With food he is a pure exotic.
For salted almonds he's a flair,
For cafe noir and cream eclair:
One day I know he'll go so far
To speak for Russian caviar.--------

This change has come I must confess
Since he had tea with G.B.S..
He rushed up to the Malvern Seer
And licked his face and kissed his ear,---
A privilege you must agree
That does not come to you or me.
In that brief moment what was said
Completely turned the Wuff dog's head.
Pure thought has set his brain agog,
He has become a High-brow Dog,
And when we meet poor dogs or wealthy
Who walk the Terrace of Adelphi
Who wish with Wuff perhaps to play
And sniff and pass the time of day,
He merely waves an airy paw
And says "Must call on my friend Shaw! "

(I haven't got the heart to say
That Mr.Shaw has MOVED AWAY!"

A happy birthday. 26.7.36.   Yvette Pienne.

Shaw had a miniature wicket gate separating his top flat in Adelphi Terrace, London, from the outer world. He is alleged to have said that delicacy prevented interviewers from stepping over it . . . When chaffed about his iron 'fortification', Shaw replied, 'Yes it does look rather like a private madhouse, doesn't it?'

Some would-be visitors wouldn't take *NO* for an answer. There was the case of the climbing American, Leon de Swarte, who on arrival in London demanded an appointment with Shaw, ostensibly to discuss journalism. When Shaw refused, de Swarte began writing a series of ridiculous letters, some of which he repeated in the personal column of *The Times*. 'Would Shumble meet Swumble for a wumble and a good tumble?' was one which G.B.S.'s secretary translated as 'Would Shaw meet Swarte for a walk and a good talk?' Although Shaw ignored this nonsense, the matter did not end there, for shortly afterwards a strange package arrived in the post. Shaw's secretary, Blanche Patch, later recalled the incident:

... Then, one Saturday morning, when the Shaws were out of town, I opened a package containing twenty £1 notes and a letter from de Swarte thanking G.B.S. for the operation which he had 'so successfully performed' on him. At this I wrote to Shaw suggesting that the affair was becoming something more than a silly joke. Shaw was as succinct as always. Would I take the numbers of the notes; put them in an envelope; go round with them to Scotland Yard; explain that the reference to an operation was unintelligible, but that I recognised the handwriting as that of a man who sometimes wrote crazy letters; and say that he ought to be looked after? 'How nice,' they remarked at the Yard, 'to get a big sum of money like that on a Saturday morning!' ...

The detective flattered himself when he had run de Swarte to earth that he had talked him into good behaviour; but he was soon at it once more, this time inviting Shaw to meet him by the Marble Arch. The plain-clothes man who went there in Shaw's place was again congratulating himself that he had stopped the fellow's nonsense when de Swarte turned up at Shaw's Adelphi Terrace flat. Informed that Shaw was not at home, he went away. However, he was soon back, climbing over the iron gate 'fortification', demanding to be shown every room to prove that Shaw was not in the flat. While the housekeeper remonstrated with de Swarte, another member of the household telephoned Scotland Yard. Captured, the persistent – and unwanted – visitor was taken to Brixton Prison where he was kept for six weeks as an alien without a passport, for, having wished to be taken as an Englishman, he had destroyed his own. He was later shipped off to the United States and Shaw never heard of him again.

There were those who wanted to present their scientific 'discoveries' to Shaw. There was the Italian engineer who wanted to discuss his experiments dealing with the transmission of thought and with hypnotism and suggestion, and the Englishman who claimed to have proven both in physics and in Logic, and in conjunction with classical mathematics (Newton and Einstein), that the Earth's motion was 'the cause of Mind, and as well of all institutional structure and function'. There was also the woman who claimed to have discovered a means of circulating air in water to consolidate it as solid material. But she wanted *Shaw* to do the visiting!

... If therefore, you will promise not to make known the secret to any person without my sanction I shall be obliged if you will call on me that I may show you how I can cause distilled water to consolidate into a stone which I can prove will not dissolve in the flame of a candle. My object is that you will if satisfied with my experiment call together a few

socialistic scientists and let them give their verdict on my
work. Then if it means money over and above my needs I
am willing that (beyond a tenth which must go to a special
cause) it should be used for the purpose of furthering the
object of socialism . . .

Similarly, there were those like American Thomas Mooney who had no
choice but to ask Shaw to pay him a visit. A prisoner on Death Row,
Thomas Mooney was the centre of controversy for over a quarter of a
century. A stormy radical leader and agitator, he was sentenced in 1917 to
be hanged for murder for dynamiting a Preparedness Day parade at San
Francisco. The sentence was later commuted to life imprisonment, when
evidence was produced to show that false testimony had been given at his
trial. For many Labour groups his case became a symbol of 'class persecution', and Mooney, who had always professed his innocence, refused to
accept anything short of complete vindication. Pardoned in 1939 after
twenty-two years in prison, he died three years later after a long illness. The
Mooney controversy involved five Governors of California, President
Woodrow Wilson, the Supreme Courts of California and the United
States, and – Bernard Shaw.

When, in February 1933, Mooney heard that the Shaws would dock
at San Francisco during their *Empress of Britain* world cruise, he invited the
dramatist to visit him at San Quentin.

> California State Prison,
> San Quentin, Calif.,
> February 16, 1933.

George Bernard Shaw,
R.M.S. 'Empress of Britain',
c/o Postmaster, Yokohama, Japan

Dear Geroge Bernard Shaw:
. . . For many years I have been hoping against hope that
some day my case would be called to your attention and that
you would add your voice to those who have taken a stand on
my behalf. I have even permitted myself to dream of the day
when I might see you in person. As my opportunities for
visiting are somewhat limited, it is obvious that this vision
would only be consummated by your coming to see me . . .

   Is it too much to ask you, who have received the plaudits
of a grateful and admiring world, to utilize part of your time
while in San Francisco to visit one who has spent 17 years of
his life in the penitentiary? San Quentin Prison is one hour's
ride from San Francisco. At this time when my attorneys are
taking action to have me tried on an old indictment pending

for 17 years, if you would take a stand on my behalf by visiting me at San Quentin, my case would be dramatized on a world-wide scale and your help might bring the added weight to swing the scales in my favor . . .

I think as a matter of human interest you might like to know a little about the place from which I am writing this letter. It is being sent from Cell 155 in the 'old' prison. This cell is exactly what it first impressed me as when I walked into it under sentence of death – a tomb. It is 8 feet long, 4 feet wide and 7 feet deep in the center. The roof is arched like an old covered wagon. The walls of stone are 2 feet thick. There is a solid steel door with a double 1½ inch bolt of steel with steel straps attached, which are locked with another lock and there is still another lock (in all, four locks are on this solid door). The door has a small wicket in it – the only opening from which I can look out at the world. This wicket is 2 × 8 inches. In this small cell that was never large enough even for one are now housed two human beings on account of the crowded conditions of the prison.

There are over 5,000 prisoners inside the walls of San Quentin. There are men of all ages and all types, from wild-eyed adolescents to crinkled doddards. All day long I see them in the yard; a few mumble and hum; a very few walk agitatedly up and down; but the great majority are apathetic with a hopeless, horrible apathy which changes only by a glance to swift animal suspicion and fear as the guards come into sight. The place is clean. It is, in fact, too almost obviously scrubbed. No doubt it represents a vast improvement over the institutions of a few years ago. And yet it is indescribably inhuman, fetid despite its cleanliness, sordid with an overwhelming sordidness that goes beyond any physical, tangible thing. . . . There is something about prison life that never can be described. It is the force, the vividness, of one's sentiments. A monastery will do that too, but in the unholy claustration of a jail one is drawn back wholly upon oneself, for God and Faith are not there. The people outside disperse their affections; we hoard ours. What they let slip, what they forget in the movement and changes of free life, we hold on to, amplify, exaggerate into a monstrous growth of memories. They can look with a smile at the troubles and pains of the past, but we can't. Our pains keep on gnawing at our hearts. Old desires, old deceptions, old dreams assail us in the dead stillness of our present when nothing moves except the irrecoverable minutes of our life. I hope you will pardon this lengthy letter. I have poured out my soul, feeling that it would strike a responsive chord in one who has for so many years fought injustice and oppression. I hope you will come to visit me at San Quentin and that you will make a statement about my case after you reach San Francisco.

Yours sincerely,
Tom Mooney 31921

On his arrival at San Francisco, Shaw declined 'as a visitor' to comment on the merits of the Mooney case, expressing, however, his hatred of imprisonment:

> . . . I cannot pretend that I am not shocked at having any person put into a vault for 16 or 17 years . . . Unfortunately the Mooney case has been made an instrument of attack upon the government and the constitution and Mr. Mooney has been made a political martyr. I would like to see the case treated as simply from a humanitarian angle. I would be afraid to go to see him because it might do him more harm than good . . . It would be a great relief to my feelings if the Governor would pardon him.

Several days later, from his host William Randolph Hearst's palatial ranch at San Simeon, Shaw replied personally to Mooney:

CASA DEL MAR

SAN SIMEON, CAL.

Dear Mr. Mooney

You have combined two of the worst pieces of luck that can happen to a man in a civilized country.

All civilized countries now have an elaborate theory of criminal law. If when a crime is committed something cruel is done to somebody and the public can be persuaded that this unfortunate somebody is the person who committed it, then the rest of the community will be 'deterred' from committing similar crimes by the fear of suffering similar cruelty. All our judges and juries (except those who are naively vindicative) cling to this theory to justify the atrocities in which they take part every day.

The advantage of the theory is that it does not matter in the least whether the person who is hanged or flogged or imprisoned is the real culprit or not. The deterrent effect is precisely the same in either case.

The disadvantage is that if the guilty party cannot be found, the police have a very strong incentive to substitute an innocent one and to persuade themselves that the substitution is a genuine detection. And the judge and jury have the same incentive to support the operation. Even those who are not quite self-deluded or imposed on say 'It is expedient that one person die for the people'.

Consequently the fact that though ten people were killed by a bomb and a victim was sacrificed 'pour encourager les autres' it by no means follows that the selected victim – yourself – ever saw that bomb. But you would have the satisfaction of believing that your fate had put a stop to bombing were it not that many more bombs have been thrown since your conviction than in the same number of years before it. That is your first stroke of bad luck.

The second is that your friends have boosted you as the champion and martyr of the Proletarian Revolution. Consequently your release would be the greatest misfortune that could happen to them. What use is a martyr when he no longer suffers? Also your release would be a political defeat for the dominant capitalist classes, for the police, and for the courts. The door that was locked on you is thus double-locked by your friends and triple-locked by your opponents.

Now I have no interest in the theory of deterrence. And I do not consider it humane to use you as a stick to beat Capitalism. My sole concern with you is to get you out of prison. If somebody would bomb the Mooney Defence Committee out of existence – if it were made a crime to mention your name in the papers – if only you could be allowed to take your true present position as an amiable elderly gentleman whose career as a Labor pioneer was cut short many years ago by a verdict vaguely remembered as having been much questioned at the time, and whose imprisonment has gone to a length which is now out-of-date and shocking, then perhaps the remonstrances I have made in response to Press inquiries might have some effect. I still have some hope that they may be listened to in spite of everything.

I very greatly regret that my short stay on the west coast, and my fear of associating you with my own political views, which are much more extreme than yours, have prevented me from paying you a visit which would have been personally most interesting to me and would have varied prison routine to you for a moment.

Wishing you a speedy release, I remain, dear Mr. Mooney,

Faithfully yours,
G. BERNARD SHAW –

Bernard Shaw on Capital Punishment

In reply to many enquiries as to his views on this subject Bernard Shaw has made the following statement.

There are three questions at issue. 1. Is punishment a necessary or desirable institution? 2. Is the killing of human beings a necessary practice? 3. If it is, what is the best method of execution?

1. Punishment should be completely discarded on the simple ground that two blacks do not make a white.

2. If we find a hungry tiger at large or a cobra in the garden, we do not punish it. We kill it because, if we do not, it will kill us. Fleas, lice, locusts, white ants, anophele mosquitos, Australian rabbits, must be exterminated, not punished. Precisely the same necessity arises in the case of incorrigibly dangerous or mischievous human beings, including enemy soldiers.

3. The kindest method so far known is to let criminals go to bed and to sleep as usual, and then turn on an odorless gas to prevent them ever waking. Enemy soldiers we have to kill how we can.

REMARKS TO BEAR IN MIND

If criminals can be reformed, reform them: that is all.

Many persons: for instance, children, soldiers, and well-behaved prisoners, are useful citizens under tutelage, with their food, clothes, and lodging found for them. Set free, they are unable to take care of themselves, and are presently in the dock for some offence, grave or petty. They should be kept under kindly tutelage, guided and provided for as children are, but otherwise living normal and respected lives.

The established theory of punishment is that it is deterrent. The insuperable objection to this is that it makes it the first business of the detective police when a crime is committed to make sure that somebody is punished, guilty or innocent, hanging the wrong man being as deterrent as hanging the right one. All police cases are therefore under suspicion of being 'frame-ups'.

Death sentences are often objected to as being irrevocable. So are all sentences when they are executed. A day of imprisonment is as irrevocable as twenty years.

Most objectors to capital punishment are actuated only by dread of death as such. They sign petitions for the reprieve of every murderer, however villainous; but when the Home Secretary changes the sentence to one of life imprisonment, a horribly cruel alternative, they are quite satisfied, and forget all about it.

Executions should be kindly and apologetic. The knout, the cat, the gallows, the axe, the stake, the wheel, the guillotine, the garotte, the electric chair, are all psychologically mischievous, provoking imitations of them by hysterical adolescents, and making the tenderhearted sympathize with the criminal. Killing should never be made a sport or a spectacle. But it must be done. There is nobody on earth who will not kill a flea; and only vegetarians will not kill for food. Mr. Shaw is a vegetarian.

Revenge and retaliation are very natural to us; but they are absolutely ruled out by Christian Civilization.

AYOT SAINT LAWRENCE, WELWYN, HERTS.

Shaw

&

War

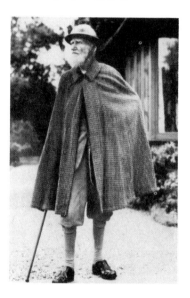

I have never written a line to start a war ... War is more distressing for me than for the Jingos because I feel the losses on both sides, whereas they seem to feel they have made a good bargain when the slaughter of one Englishman is followed by the slaughter of two Germans or Italians. I can never forget that the loss to Europe, and consequently to us all as Europeans, is the same whether the slaughtered man's name is John or Fritz or Beppo ...

Everybody's Political What's What

In 1916 a thirteen-year-old Brooklyn schoolgirl, Cecilia Zilbermann, protested against the raising of funds from American schoolchildren to build a battleship, insisting that the money would be better spent in improving the conditions under which children laboured in factories. Her protest letter, adopted by the National Child Labour Committee, was distributed as campaign literature, a copy of which Miss Zilbermann sent to Shaw, who sent her a postcard reply.

> The point about the factory children is very well taken, but
> at present I think you had better have both a fleet and a
> factory act. There are too many rogues about for
> honest men (such as they are) to be quite safe without
> weapons.
>
> G. BERNARD SHAW.

Shaw, a pragmatist, did not hold with half-measures. He insisted that if a war were to be fought, one must go all out to win. You were either at war or peace; there could be no in between. When words failed to prevent war, and war became a reality, it was useless to try and fight with kid gloves. He forbade all overseas productions of his own play, *The Devil's Disciple*, as long as the war lasted, not wanting a play about English military stupidity and other stupidities during the American Revolution to be turned into 'an attempt to exploit anti-English feelings'. Few of his critics – or, for that matter, his admirers – knew of his generous support for the British war effort. As he wrote to Augustin Hamon, December 3rd, 1925:

> I contributed £20,000 to the War Loan Patriotism at 5%.
> Why does this surprise you? I had no illusions about the war.
> I hated it intensely; and I hate it still. But when the first shot
> is fired the case is taken out of the sphere of political justice
> into that of killing or being killed. If a man attacks me with
> the intention of killing me, he may have received plenty of
> provocation and may deserve to win; but I am none the less
> obliged to defend myself for all I am worth. And in such
> emergencies a man must stand by his neighbors, no matter
> how stupid or how much in the wrong they may have been.

After putting all the money he could into the War Loan, Shaw gave up his work to study the war situation, after which he published his controversial *Common Sense About the War*. This led to widescale attack:

> I was considered as monstrous as Tolstoy, after the
> publication of my *Common Sense About the War*. I was, as a
> matter of fact, excommunicated from every tennis club,

every golf club and even from the Butchers' Guild; in short, from every religious order. I had to stop doing all the things I never wanted to do and never did.

Shaw was even expelled from the Dramatists' Club. As its Honorary Secretary wrote to him on October 27th, 1915:

> My Dear Shaw –
>   I regret to say that at today's meeting of the Club I was instructed (as the secretary) to write to you to inform you that several members of the Club have intimated that they refrain from attending the meetings as they do not wish to meet you, owing to your attitude in regard to the war. In these circumstances the members present presumed that you will prefer that the usual notice of the meetings shall not be sent to you for the present.
>
> Sincerely yours,
H. M. Paull

The Hon. Secretary should have known better. His letter was like a red flag to a bull, and Shaw's reponse was immediate.

> My dear Paull
>   The members present did me a great injustice. I enjoy meeting them very much; and I have not the slightest intention of depriving myself of the pleasure of lunching with them for the sake of those members whose absence from our meetings during the year did not seem to me to have any political significance, as it was equally conspicuous before August 1914. So please send me my notices just as usual, and accept my five shillings (enclosed) without any misgivings . . .

Shaw then merrily proceeded to outline the correct procedure for his own expulsion.

Barely two weeks after the publication of *Common Sense About the War*, Shaw felt compelled to write to the Labour paper, the *Daily Citizen*, about the many anonymous letters he had received. 'May I appeal to their authors,' he asked, 'to bear in mind in future that young ladies are now very largely employed as secretaries to public men, and that letters that are not suitable for their perusal should be marked "Obscene" on the envelopes.' He was particularly amused by one abusive letter which accused him of pro-Germanism, as it began with an illiterately Germanic misspelling: 'You son of a bitsch . . .'

As a result of his war writings Shaw was cut dead by former friends and his works removed from libraries and bookshops. While the Prime Minister said privately he ought to be shot, *New Statesman* colleague J. C. Squire more publicly recommended he be tarred and feathered. Socialist colleague Robert Blatchford, describing *Common Sense About the War* as 'insensate malice and dirty innuendo', demanded a public enquiry into Shaw's apparently 'unpatriotic' position. To Theodore Roosevelt he was the 'blue-rumped ape – Bernard Shaw'.

Inundated by letters, Shaw responded individually only to his critics, of which about 6% were 'hostile – mostly unprintable', he informed Lady Ottoline Morrell on February 11th 1915. Friendly correspondents had to be content with a printed postcard, with a holograph note or postscript.

I have received so many letters upon *Common Sense About the War* that I have had to give up all hope of dealing with them separately. Even the very kind and entirely reassuring letters elicited by my protest in the *Daily Citizen* must go unanswered. Many branches of the Independent Labor Party and other Liberal and Socialist organizations have passed resolutions which have been of the timeliest service to me publicly, and which have given me sincere personal gratification. In the hope of being able to write a separate letter in every case I have deferred my acknowledgements until it has become plain that I must make them in this fashion or not at all. It is the best I can do; and I rely on the same kindness that prompted the letters and resolutions to accept my thanks in this indiscriminate but very earnest form.

G. Bernard Shaw

From a 'friendly correspondent':

H.M. Embassy
Petrograd
19 March 1915

Dear SIR
Forgive me for troubling a busy
man at this juncture, but I have

just received the 'Nation' of 6th March
and read your letter therein.
    I thank you from my heart
for letting in this breath of
fresh and wholesome air to the
murky and dirty atmosphere
that our unthinking patriots
and utterly and unspeakable
vile press of the baser sort
(apparently-alas-with the more
or less tacit approval of
those in authority) have between
them succeeded in creating.
    If it were not for some
of the other effects, one wd be
sometimes almost tempted to
hope that we shall be beaten,
for it wd seem that only
by humiliation and loss
can we be taught a
sense of decency and good manners
which perhaps after all is
of more real worth to a nation
than that abominable and
dangerous quality known as
'prestige'.
            Believe me, Sir,
                with sincere admiration,
                     very truly yours,
                    Harold Grenfell
                    Commander RN

Playwright Henry Arthur Jones was rather less friendly, penning in an open letter to Shaw:

The Hag Sedition was your mother and Perversity begot you. Mischief was your midwife and Misrule your muse, and Unreason brought you up at her feet – no other ancestry and rearing had you, you 'freakish homunculus', germinated outside of lawful procreation . . .

Elsewhere, while less splenetic, he was no less damning.

1st November 1915

My dear Shaw,

... Whether you know it or not, you are one of our country's worst enemies. And you are an enemy within our walls. One of the leading American papers in commenting on your pamphlets said if you had written it in Germany on behalf of her enemies you would have been shot. I cannot think you are so shortsighted as not to have forseen that you were furnishing Germany with a powerful weapon to attack England, that you were offering her evidence that our cause was unjust, that we were to blame for this war ...

If you do not allow our cause is just do you wonder that every Englishman is against you? Do you wonder that you are generally regarded as a man who for the sake of showing his agility kicked and defamed his mother when she was on a sick bed? You will say that England is not your mother – well then put it that Englishmen regard you as a man that kicked and defamed their mother when she was on a sick bed. This is not intolerance; it is mere natural human feeling – always so hard for you to understand. But it is the primal instincts and emotions that govern men in days like these and you should not be surprised that in the agony and bloody sweat of fighting for our life we have no patience with a man who tries to trip us up – and with us the mercies and humanities of European civilization.

'Most people,' commented Shaw, 'are convinced that when I am alone I stand on my head and write with my toes. It does not occur to them that it is the world that is upside down. Because I prefer to see things as they are, they regard me as a crank.'

One outraged citizen on reading that Shaw had been at the Front, criticized the War Office for sending him out. Two weeks later the complainant received the following reply:

War Office, Whitehall S.W.
24 March 1917

Dear Sir,

I am directed to acknowledge the receipt of your letter of the 6th March 1917, and to inform you that the case has been investigated, and that nothing is known against this officer.

I am, Sir, your obedient servant
E. W. Engleheart, S.C.
(For Lieutenant-General,
Military Secretary).

CESARE (AMERICAN) IN THE NEW YORK *SUN*: 'G. DON QUIXOTE SHAW' 'HIS
TRENCHANT QUILL WHICH PENNED ''COMMON SENSE ABOUT THE WAR'' TOWERING
ALOFT LIKE A MIGHTY LANCE – THE SHAW, WHO UNFLINCHINGLY PRIDED HIMSELF
UPON HIS IRISH CAPACITY FOR CRITICIZING ENGLAND WITH SOMETHING OF THE
DETACHMENT OF THE FOREIGNER, AND PERHAPS WITH A CERTAIN SLIGHTLY
MALICIOUS TASTE FOR TAKING THE CONCEIT OUT OF HER'

It was at his wife Charlotte's insistence that Shaw finally accepted Sir
Douglas Haig's invitation to visit the Front and write about it. G.B.S, she
felt, had to see this 'terrible thing' for himself. Shaw commented to a friend
that the invitation was either a compliment or a design on his life.

There is something almost clinical in the way Shaw tried to probe one
Lance Corporal's response to the war situation:

Dear Mr Wells

How do you feel about it generally? Is your uprooting from the bank desk a calamity which you would undo if you could, or is it an enlargement of your experience & an intensification of your life which you would not have missed for anything, & which is worth the risks you have had to run? If it is at neither of these extremes, where does it come between the two? Are you married; & if so, how does that affect the situation (for the trench is sometimes happier than the home)? I take it for granted that you are fed up with it, and that the discomforts and fatigues of soldiering are often atrocious, like the discomforts and fatigues of travelling multiplied by 1000,000,000,000,000,000,000,000,000,000. Still, one travels and is glad afterwards one travelled, in spite of seasickness and all the contretemps of the road. All things considered, suppose you get through unscathed, or at any rate mended enough to enjoy life, will you say it was well worth while, or simple unmitigated hell? That is what I want to know. And what do the others say?

'I would join up without the slightest hesitation,' Shaw wrote to Miss May Broadley of Reading, 'if I thought the War Office would or could employ me better than I can employ myself. But I know very well that it cannot. It is my business to do some thinking about the war, and to tell salutary and unpopular truths about it – to you as well as to the Jingoes. War is a very horrible thing; but if people will do nothing until they are scourged into action by frightful calamities, why, the calamities must come: that is all.' Miss Broadley had written to Shaw criticizing his support for the war effort. 'Life,' he replied, 'is not so simple as you advocates of personal righteousness think. A conscience is a luxury that is sometimes beyond the means of all but the most unscrupulously selfish people. It may be very sound individual policy to go to Heaven alone when your neighbours are asking you to go to hell with them to save them from having their throats cut; but it is not really practicable.'

From time to time young men wrote to Shaw on the eve of going to war, as did sports enthusiast Norman Clark, a Shaw disciple. Clark later became a secretary and certified referee of the Boxing Board of Control and a judge at the National Sporting Club, as well as the author of a number of books on philosophy, aerial navigation and boxing. Shaw took an interest in the young man's career, over the years giving him literary and personal advice. When this letter was written G.B.S. was sixty-one.

'D' Company 5th (Res.) S. Staffs.
Bleak House Camp Mablethorpe Lincs.
8th June 1917

Dear Mr Shaw.

About a month ago you
would perhaps remember a young
subaltern impudently calling at 10,
Adelphi Terrace at his own invitation.

I am that young subaltern. I now
write to sincerely thank you for your
great kindness in wasting your time
with me. I can assure you I was fully
satisfied with you.

People had always told me you
would not see me; but I never had
doubts on the matter; for I pride myself
on being something of a judge of human
nature, and an artist's works reveal
more than his acquaintance. Perhaps
your time, too, was not entirely
wasted, for, in a measure, you have
given me inspiration, & that, after all
is the most valuable thing in this young
world of ours . . .

The all-woolen suit; the shirt; the
autumnal hair & beard; the tortoiseshell
glasses, the quality of everything, the total
absence in your face, clothes & furniture
of anything suggesting vice, extravagance
or vulgarity; all made one feel in
the presence of nature's aristocrat and
(excuse my vanity) quite at home. And
what politeness, & vitality for
so old a man! Remarkable! . . .

The reason I have not written you
before is because I have written you
once already, but destroyed the
letter. I wrote you a long letter all
about myself; not about my tragedies
(I dont have them now), but about my

farces, my interests, my various stages
of development, & the influence, in particular,
of your works (this last a tragedy of
course). I traced all the various stages
I have been through . . .

After I had written this long letter
telling you all about myself, I read it through
many times, & finally cooled myself down
to such a state of cold reason as to
lose confidence & decide I had no right to
send it to you . . .

I have to be off to France in
a week's time (due at Folkestone Thursday
morning), & I have a regimental boxing
tournament to organise before I go. I feel
rather shaky about the other side, as our
division is just within the area where
an advance is coming off – North West of
Sens – & we are, no doubt, in for a fair doing.

Everyman fears something, & I think I
have always feared war more than all else,
for to me (as a general rule) the thing
doesn't seem worth doing. Mind you,
I am all in favour of things that test
the metal of a man, say such sports as
boxing . . . However, our cause appears right
(so far as any 'cause' can be right);
it seems the only thing; so I suppose
my prejudice must be suppressed, &
I must do my best – though the man
who can do this easily is not a true
socialist I fancy. What say you?

If ever I write anything any good, I will
send it along & insist on your reading it.

Till then, adieu.

'I believe,' wrote a woman to Shaw in May 1916, seeking help for conscientious objectors, 'you have always had a warm corner in your heart for women and fanatics.' Indeed, where he could, Shaw tried to help those young men whose motives for avoiding active service he respected. He was willing to speak and write in their support, and, as was occasionally the case, testify at their trials. At one such trial he was unexpectedly successful:

> . . . because, although I told the exact truth and nothing but the truth, my evidence convinced and was meant to convince the court that the prisoner was an Evangelical fanatic, whereas he was a matter of fact a Freethinker. His case was quite genuine as a case of conscience; but a military court would not have held that a Freethinker could have a conscience; consequently it was necessary in the interests of justice to produce the evidence of fanaticism, of which there was plenty, and leave the court to infer that a fanatic must be a hyperpious Quaker.

As one of the most visible anti-war figures, Shaw received letters from many jailed conscientious objectors, and from those, who, like Private Owen Lewis, were jailed not for refusing to be drafted, but for refusing vaccination.

20th Batt'n
3rd Rhondda Welsh Rgt
Rhyl, North Wales
10th April 1916

Dear Sir:

I am writing you this from the Prison-room of the above Batt'n's Guard-room, hence the writing of it in pencil. I have been put in here since last Saturday under the charge of 'Improper Conduct'. I have refused to undergo vaccination. I have been in the army now over nine months, I have followed every parade drill and all marches, I have not shirked one duty. Of course I have refused Inoculation and vaccination, but nothing else. When joining on July 22nd 1915 I signed my attestation form without thinking as to Inoculation and vaccination. So when the matter was brought forward in Camp I objected to both treatments. I do not believe in them, and have decided not to undergo the same, even if it comes to the matter of being shot. I have told my officer that I am ready to go to the front to do what I can anytime they wish me to go. But that I shall never go there vaccinated . . . In the face of such a situation I thought of

you as one of the ablest men in the land to give me a help.
Even if my stupidity (as they call it) costs me my life I should
like some-one's help from anywhere. If you can kindly write
or do something for me I shall ever be thankful to you for
same . . .

In support of Pte Owen, Shaw publicly denounced the fact that a
conscript might be ordered to have his blood poisoned by 'the most
abominable inoculations . . .' He managed to get an M.P. to intercede on
Owen's behalf with the result that the private was released from detention
and returned to duty unvaccinated. In other cases Shaw was less successful.

Such requests for help didn't cease with the armistice. One young man
brought home from France suffering from Para-Typhoid B and dysentery
deserted after convalescence when he learned in July 1917 that he was
being returned to the Front. He deserted to Ireland and via Dublin went
north to Belfast, where, changing his name, he worked for two years until
the war ended. Returning to London in May 1919 he took a badly paid job
in Burlington Arcade, at which time he wrote to Bernard Shaw asking for
advice. What was he – a deserter – to do? Shaw's reply shook the young
man, who, forty-five years later in 1974, would recall that 'when I got
Shaw's letter I first learned that I had risked the death penalty. I had always
banked on revealing my tragic early life and couldn't believe they would
punish me.'

3rd June, 1919

Dear Sir,
    In the case you put to me, I suppose the man would be
technically a deserter, and liable to any penalty, from several
years penal servitude to death, which a court martial might
sentence him to.
    He cannot very well appeal for advice and assistance to
his friends, because if they do not denounce him to the
military authorities, they become themselves liable to severe
penalties as accessory to his desertion. Therefore the fact
that nothing has been heard of him need cause his friends
no uneasiness. He may take his chance of remaining

undiscovered where he is (wherever that may be), or move
to a safer place, by emigration or anything short of it.

I have no idea how energetic the pursuit is: apparently
men have braved it with impunity even when taking part in
anti-conscription agitation.

It is worth noticing that Quakers have been persecuted
with the utmost ferocity, whilst pugnacious objectors who
simply objected to this particular war and openly declared
that they would fight in a class war have been treated with
comparative indulgence.

Faithfully
G. Bernard Shaw

P.S. I hope I have your address
correctly. I destroyed your letter
before answering it.

The 'stay-at-homes' of both wars wrote to Shaw as well. These
letters were often rhetorical or semi-confessional in nature; not requiring
any response. Correspondents commented on what they saw – the everyday
occurrences in their lives – or, as was frequently the case during the war
years, aspects of wartime life; or perhaps current issues, whether social,
political, or economic; sometimes they wished only to reminisce or share a
memory with Shaw. A letter permitted the correspondent a sense of
intimacy with the great man.

Chelsea, London
21 July 1944

Dear Bernard Shaw,
    You never answer any of my letters or accord
the slightest recognition when I ask for an
interview, but I am not after an interview now,
I only wish to say I enjoyed your letter in the
Times 'Connemara and Berlin.' . . .
    When I was coming to Fleet Street on the
top of a bus this morning a fly-bomb nearly got
me – and Big Ben. The latter you may agree
would be regrettable. Do you think these
'miss-iles' as Hibbert calls them are an effective
or fair weapon of war? and do you think the
attempted bumping-off of Hitler was a frame-up?
These questions you will probably ignore. My
asking them is like the old Irishwoman who went
to confession and told the priest she had

slept with a man although she had never been married. 'You tell me that every week' he said. 'Have I not always given you absolution?' 'Oh yes yer riverence, but you know I likes talking about it.' My case is just as pathetic.

There were those with requests to make. Fearful that her children might have to wear gas masks, one worried mother from Ewell in Surrey made an audacious request of the 81-year-old Shaw in 1937 – that he join her in a protest.

Dear Mr. Bernard Shaw

I once read about you, 'he never despised genuine feeling'. With this in mind I am emboldened to write.

Firstly, do you not think that the task before the Government is to ensure that there will be no necessity for any child to wear a gas mask, not to manufacture them in readiness for such a horror, and with equanimity? After all, the children would be better dead than living under such conditions . . .

Do you not think that the only people who can effectually influence the Government are the mothers of the children? . . . I feel that something drastic & unorthodox should be done, and as you are the most unorthodox person I could think of, I thought you might help me. I want to rouse the mothers of this country out of their apathy . . .

My plan so far is this. To parade outside the Houses of Parliament one morning wearing a poster back & front, reading as follows. *'We dont want gas masks for our children, we demand, Sanity, Peace & Justice.' Please sign petition.* Also – *'mothers unite & save your children.' Sign now* . . . Then, if I am moved on, to take a walk round London, perhaps with my little boy of six year. Will you help me by coming with me, because after all you are what is known as front page news . . .

If you have a better plan than mine, I should be so glad to hear it. In the meantime I must purchase cardboard & paper, & my husband will paint the inscription. You are

entitled to know before you commit yourself that I am 34 &
my education was elementary, also that my husband is an
admirer of yours & a possessor of a fine intellect . . .

> P.S. On reading this over I feel
> that the zest has gone out
> of me. I am disheartened at the
> immensity of the task, & doubt
> whether I should send the
> letter after all, because my
> husband says you are used to
> receiving letters from cranks.
> Only the thought of my little
> boy in a gas mask spurs me on.

This same little boy, now nearing sixty, recalls that his mother,
Kathleen Mary Cole, never went ahead with her protest. 'I suppose,' he
writes, 'she thought that a lone voice, seemingly without massive support,
would be disregarded.'

However, requests did not cease with the war's end. From Hertford Heath,
Hertfordshire:

Dear Mr Shaw.

    Something is troubling
me so much that I cannot rest. I feel
I must <u>do</u> something, but don't know
what to do, or whom to ask. To-night,
in church, during the sermon (!!) suddenly
came the inspiration – 'Ask Mr. G.B.S. –
the very wisest man in the world.' (And
that not flattery, it's sober truth, and
you know it.)

    I am a very busy wife
of a very busy dairy-farmer, and
every day, while driving on my
round, I pass a load of German
prisoners. One of them is just like
my dear father, and he, and all
of them, look so forlorn and hopeless.
Mr. Shaw, I keep thinking of them
all the time, not knowing when they
will be sent home – but what can I,
and others like me, – <u>do</u> about it? . . .

    And <u>please</u> forgive my
presumption in writing to such
a great man, but you have always
been my literary hero, and I feel
as if I know you.

Your humble admirer
Clarice N. Pawsey

The late Mrs Pawsey's daughter believes that her mother wrote to G.B.S. in a moment of sadness. 'Feelings at that time were very high about the Germans, and one did not mention the relationship of my Grandfather being a German, so I think that if she did get a reply, she may have destroyed it.'

Shaw, however, did act on this issue, supporting an appeal in December 1946 for an amnesty for all prisoners of war and political prisoners. 'Until we have a genuine amnesty,' he predicted, 'we shall go on plundering and slaughtering and proclaiming peace where there is no peace.'

To Shaw war was the ultimate horror. 'A many good people have died of simple horror, mercifully without quite knowing it,' he wrote to fellow Fabian Henry Salt, February 25th, 1919, at the death of Salt's wife, Kate. 'It has been a frightful experience; and one knows now why Shakespear and Swift were so bitter . . . Four years of mud bath and blood bath, of intellectual and spiritual looting. If Kate had only died in the summer of 1914! We two have survived our wounds so far; but we shall always be revenging them . . .'

But other horrors were yet to come; the death camps of Germany and Hiroshima. When asked what World War II meant to him, G.B.S. was to reply, 'The war came to an end when the first atomic bomb was dropped. It is very doubtful if we have the right to drop another.'

'Grand Old Man':
G.B.S.
&
The Young

'Youth which is forgiven everything, forgives itself nothing: age, which forgives itself everything, is forgiven nothing.'

G.B.S.

A mother, when watching her children at play, remarked to Shaw 'What a wonderful thing is youth.'

'And what a sin it is to waste it on children,' Shaw replied.

G. Bernard Shaw.
at school

Whilst walking along the Volga during his 1931 Russian visit, Shaw got into conversation with a young girl. They strolled along the riverside, the child amusing Shaw immensely with her chatter and old-fashioned airs. After a while she announced that the time had come for her to go home. As they shook hands, G.B.S. said: 'Now, my dear, if any one should ask you what you have been doing you can tell them that you have been walking beside the Volga with George Bernard Shaw.'

Naturally, the famous name meant nothing to the child, but evidently something in Shaw's voice suggested the necessity for a courteous response, for she answered gravely: 'I will, indeed. And if any one asks you what you have been doing you can tell them you have been walking beside the Volga with Katerina Ivanova Fyodorovitch.'

Tributes from the young came indirectly. In 1926 a ten-year-old Colchester schoolgirl, whose father died before she was born, took part in a play at which G.B.S. was a spectator. Beforehand she was warned of the man's greatness and the necessity for observing and listening to him attentively. 'Dear mother,' she wrote after the event, 'I liked him ever so, and he is the only man I have ever seen I'd like to have for a father.'

In 1930 the conductor Albert Coates' five-year-old daughter looked up into Bernard Shaw's face and said, 'Uncle George, aren't you a writer?'

'I suppose so, my dear,' said G.B.S.

'But you've never written anything as good as *Alice in Wonderland*!' replied the little girl.

Shaw to a young man of Heckmondwike, Yorkshire, who had unwisely asked him for his views on press censorship:

> As you are only twenty, I may, as an old hand, give you a useful tip before you approach a well-known man. Take great care to find out what has made him well known; otherwise you may find yourself asking Einstein whether he believes in relativity, or Mr. Ramsay MacDonald what is his opinion of Socialism. One day perhaps you will read my work, for instance, the preface to 'Blanco Posnet'. You will then realise the unhappiness of the idea of asking me whether I approve of censorship.

Shaw's 1931 reply to a publisher's request for permission to include an extract from his work in an Indian schoolbook:

> . . . I have the strongest objection to the association in the infant mind of my name and work with school lessons. I have always refused to sanction the insertion of samples in school books. Why should I make my name loathed in India as Shakespeare's is loathed in secondarily-educated England? Please don't.

Shaw's reticence didn't stop the students of the Technical Institute, Dublin, from deciding by a large majority in a January debate the following year that 'George Bernard Shaw is a menace to society'. In 1933 a motion to that effect was defeated by twenty-one votes when debated at Armstrong College, Newcastle-on-Tyne, when 112 students declined to take him so seriously.

From '4 Indignant Matriculation boys' with a hobby:

> East London, South Africa
> 25 August 1946
>
> Dear Sir,
>   In one of your recent speeches you gave your opinion of the people of South Africa. We feel that it is incumbent upon us to inform you that you are under a misapprehension regarding the majority of us whom you accuse of being snobbish. We are sure that if you became better acquainted with us you would alter your option.
>   Our habits are similar to those of other normal Englishmen. We beg to bring to your notice that we bear no ill-feeling towards you, and greatly admire some of your works.
>   Wishing you the best of health,
>
>   We remain,
>   Yours sincerely,
>   4 Indignant Matriculation boys
> Derek Falkenberg
> John S. Godwin
> Robert Houston
> Norman Wagner
> *P.S. We are avid stamp-collectors.*

The following appeared in *Punch*, December 25th, 1935, referring to Shaw's Malvern Festival activities.

Another Apology Impending:

'Every year a Mormon festival is held especially for Bernard Shaw.'

School-girl's Essay

And, shortly afterwards from Burgess Hill, Sussex, came:

> Dear Mr Shaw,
>   Some body has sent
> what I wrote about you in
> my essay to 'Punch' it

must be our guverness   she
<u>is</u> a cat   she promised she
wouldn't tell any body.
    'Punch' says I ought
to apologise   I am awfully
sorry   I truly thought that
place was called Mormon.
English names are daft
and the English speak so
woollily.
    I have to write this from
a friends   if I wrote it
from home Miss Wade
wouldn't let it
go   she vets all
our letters.

With lots more apologies
I remain
yours sincerely
Mary Maclean

P.S.   I'm afraid this
      letter is rather mixed   I
      am sorry and I don't
      know where you live but
      I expect these publishers
      do.

Shaw offered to give a 'bad-conduct' prize to the worst behaved boy or girl at the Ayot St Lawrence village school. He suggested that the youngsters' careers should be monitored to find out who really turned out better – the rightly-conducted or the wrongly-conducted one.

From a young man 'lacking in stature':

26th November 1943

Dear Sir,
    I will try and state my reasons for writing this letter.
Before I do so I would like to say that previous to writing it I
asked myself how I should do it. Should it be in the nature
of a blunt enquiry or almost a dissertation. The latter would
be more courteous; the former would ask less of your time. I
chose the latter.
    I am sixteen years of age and write this now because I feel

it is probable that before I have made myself well known enough to be acquainted with a man such as yourself you will be out of my reach. Therefore I lose no time.

Whenever I read a letter, an answer to a critic, an article by the renowned G.B.S. I am consumed with an uncontrollable desire to speak with the figure that could have such self-assurance, such wit, such courage to tell the world to go and be damned . . .

Your reactions in reading this may take on many aspects; you may decide that it comes from a temperament that, for want of a better word, I will describe as of the schoolgirl type, and you may say 'I like this fellow's confounded cheek and I'll be interested to see what sort of an individual it emanates from . . .'

I have also been activated by living so near to you and as a last word would ask you, if ever I do meet you, not to be surprised at my lack of stature. I in no way regret this particular failing.

Advice to a young man wishing to live in a shepherd's hut:

Shaw to 23-year-old Thomas Tough Watson, a non-graduating student of Aberdeen University, 1890–93.

21st November 1893

Dear Sir

Obviously I can give you no advice at all. Your notion that living in a shepherd's hut without having any business there was a less artificial mode of living than going through with the Aberdeen curriculum, was quite the most artificial idea you could possibly have got into your head. The fact that you acted on it instead of merely thinking about it shews that you are an exceptional man, but whether you are exceptional by excess of qualities or by defect is more than the incident proves. To tell you the truth, I have rather a low opinion of you for taking to a shepherd's life and leaving out the sheep . . .

Advice to a young girl on what to do with her life:

To seventeen-year-old Edith Livia Beatty, second of the impecunious Pakenham Beatty's three children, whose education was partly funded by Mrs Bernard Shaw. G.B.S. similarly paid the school fees of Beatty's son, Mazzini.

7th January 1900

My dear Edith

I have just been studying your school report, and find it a most disheartening document . . . It is plain to me that this High School is teaching you nothing except how to become a High School mistress when you are too big to be a High School pupil. That is a miserable business unless you become a head mistress, and not a very delightful one even then . . .

You may ask me how you are to educate yourself. Well, chiefly by beginning to choose how and where you shall be taught what you want to know, instead of letting yourself be sent to school like a little lamb. You have at your disposal at present £100 a year (round numbers) to educate yourself with . . . The burden of absolute selfishness being thus laid on you, it behoves you to consider how to get the best value for that money . . .

Well, why dont you spend your hundred pounds on a visit to Greece to learn the language? I was once offered a trip to Athens with a party from Owen's College, Manchester, for £25, there and back, and a lot of other places thrown in. Call the two journeys £30, and you have £70 left, which would give you nearly three months at £1 a day, on which you could do yourself like a princess. Like a student, you could get six months easily . . .

You could have the next year in Russia, the next in Germany, the next in an American College or where you pleased. You would become governess to a Russian Grand Duke and marry his son clandestinely, and starve with him when his father found it out, and finally succeed to millions on the father's death . . .

Think it over: keep always thinking it over. The High School teacher business is only Irish snobbery . . . Remember that all the advice given by grown up people to young people has interested motives, and that the world belongs to the rebellious.

yours sincerely – *really*
G. Bernard Shaw

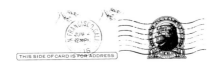

THIS SIDE OF CARD IS FOR ADDRESS

The young wrote to Shaw for advice and to share experiences:

> National Bank
> Portarlington
> Eire

Saturday, July 22nd 44.
My dear Mr Shaw.
    This is to wish you Very Many Happy Returns
of the Day – that is, of next Friday.
I wrote to you once before. I wasted a lot of
eloquence, and also enclosed English stamps
– I expect the whole outfit didn't get beyond
your secretary; for I got no reply! This
time I hope to fool him by putting 'Personal'
on the envelope!

PLEASE. *send me your autograph, again* I
enclose English stamps (which are very hard
to get over here). I'll be awfully disappointed
if I don't get your signature this time. (It's
cost me eleven pence so far!)
    St Joan is my favorite of your plays –
& Michael Dolan of the Abbey Theatre says
I'd suit the part – I hope you can read this
(someone has bust my pen.)
    Do you think the War in the Far East
will be very much longer? My boyfriend is
in Chungking –
If you are still in London I think you
should get out – My great-aunt was bombed
out (Maida Hill W9) by a 'doodle-bug' –
a ghastly experience, hearing the
vile thing getting nearer & nearer
& then the engine switching off – then
everything crashed around her. Fortunately
she was not injured – Aren't you scared of
those raids?
An Allied plane crashed on the bog here
a couple of days ago.
Once again with Best Wishes for a Happy
Birthday

> Yours Sincerely Pamela Scott.

Shaw to Edward Ralph Cheney, an American university student, on the
social value of university education, December 1913:

Dear Sir
    ... There is one character in which you will be welcomed
nowhere, useful nowhere, and a nuisance everywhere; and
that is in the character of an erratic half-educated youth
excited with revolutionary ideas, at odds with his family and
his school and all the other institutions within his reach
because he is really at odds with his own unstable nerves.
Your letter fills me with horrible suspicions of you in this
direction. If they are justified, I have no use for you; the
Socialist movement has no use for you; the world has no use
for you; and I pity your family. So you just drop it; and see
what you can do under the easy circumstances of convention
before you ask to be trusted in the difficult circumstances of
revolution ...
    Please remark that I do not advise you to strain after
academic honors, or to aim at a University career. However,
you will probably not be in any very great danger in this
direction ...

Advice to seventeen-year-old Victor Jeffery Richards Dalrymple Prendergast on being a Winchester College prefect:

25th June 1919

Dear Sir,
    Of course become a prefect if you get the chance. If you
stay at Winchester you must play the Winchester game and
be reasonably loyal to the school. I happen to think that the
capitalist system is 'fundamentally vicious'; but I am a
capitalist and have to accept and even work the system until
I can persuade the community to adopt a better one.
    If you feel that Winchester is intolerable, do not in the
name of common sense stay there and make futile attempts
to convert it to some other sort of school by mere wrecking.
Even if there were the slightest chance of such a policy
succeeding it would be unsocial and unjustifiable, as
Winchester is a very good school for people who like that
sort of school ... It is clear that you are at the wrong school
... Even Rugby, which is at least partly modernized, would
be better than either Winchester or Harrow which are quite

the worst schools for your temperament . . .

You cant smash the system. I cant. If I could it would have been smashed before this. And while it lasts we must make the best of it . . . But even then those who are destined to live as Conservative country gentlemen until such people are abolished will need a school to fit them for that life; and Winchester, Harrow and Eton will still do that job better than it can be done elsewhere.

(Young Prendergast took Shaw's advice, remaining another year at Winchester before attending Balliol College, Oxford, 1920–24. He travelled and did literary work, and after World War II worked for the United Nations and the International Refugee Organisation. He died after a long illness in July 1979.)

The young came to him with Life's 'great questions':

> East Molesey, Surrey
> 29th July 1946

Dear Sir,

When you receive this letter, I sincerely hope you will spare a moment to read it. It's hard for me to contrive an approach of expressing my thoughts in words – but I'll write conversationally and personally. Forgive my audacity – but the following are the circumstances.

To-day, – the 26th of July – is your 90th-Birthday and as a coincidence, my 20th. By deduction you are 70 years my senior. I'm not particularly well educated, – as I left school as a kid – but continued at night-school. Education is something I have always strived for, having had a vague introduction at an elementary school. I have been working for some time now – and reached the position of a 'chief tool draughtsman' . . .

As a boy, I used to continually travel in my mind with childish curiosity as to know how people lived, worked and died. Many incidents can easily be recalled to mind, but to make an intelligent remark, I realise how weak human nature really is and how much one needs a faith. I'm taking this audacious and intrepid opportunity to ask you a few questions – because I feel in want for some first class information. I deeply and emotionally hope that you will consider my 'intellectual requests'.

(1) Do you think Christianity is effete in this chaotic Cobden-Croce world?

(2) As I'm in my 21st year now – with a niger's niger knowledge of the performances in this world – its vacillations-vodoo-hypocrasy-science and materialism and vegetation, – I want to practise a correct and logical attitude towards life with a religion, a political outlook and mainly an understanding relationship toward my fellow beings. Do you believe in the Darwinian Theory of the evolution of man or in the religious belief of the divine creation of mankind and the universe by the omnipotent creator – 'Our Lord.'?

(3) As politics, economics, sciences and morals seem so incompatible to a Christian code, do you think perfection and real human welfare will ever be accomplished?

(4) What does it really feel like to be 90, and to still see the follies, and the repetitious 'trials and errors' of ideals, morals and universal social 'egotism' and unrest in the world.

Well, sir, if you can spare a moment, I should appreciate a reply – as an insight of your views to help me temper my own.

May God bless you and keep you always,

Yours Hopefully,
Patrick J. O'Higgins.

From a would-be biographer wanting a 'communication' from Shaw:

Washington, D.C.
22nd September 1946

Dear Mr. Shaw;

Having just finished Archibald Henderson's 'Bernard Shaw, Playboy and Prophet', I thought of writing you a letter . . .

I have merely wished at some time to have communication from the great man. I do not mean to presume on your time or anything of the sort; but I expect someday to write plays, and to write a definitive work on you; and I would like the encouragement of a post card or a letter. I have just finished a paper on Shelley; and I realize now how difficult and uninspired the work is because of not having a conviction as to the personal existence of the man. Can you understand this? Wouldn't you have liked to have a post card or a letter from Ibsen? . . .

So as to make this letter a bit more conspicuous, I am

enclosing a snapshot. (Henderson inadvertently indicates that as the infallible method of getting to you.) . . . Not to burden you, I end this hoping that you can read this without laughing, if you do.

Most sincerely,
Thomas P. O'Keefe.

HOW TO BECOME A MODEL PARENT

By BERNARD SHAW

 MY parents took no moral responsibility for me. I was just something that had happened to them inevitably and had to be put up with and supported. They did not worry themselves uselessly about my character and my future. I suffered nothing from the intolerable meddlesomeness of the conscientious parents who are so busy with their children's characters that they have no time to look after their own. I cannot remember having ever heard a single sentence uttered by my mother in the nature of moral or religious instruction. My father made an effort or two. When he caught me imitating him by pretending to smoke a toy pipe he advised me very earnestly never to follow his example in any way ; and his sincerity so impressed me that to this day I have never smoked, never shaved, and never used alcoholic stimulants. He taught me to regard him as an unsuccessful man with many undesirable habits, as a warning and not as a model. In fact he did himself less than justice lest I should grow up like him ; and I now perceive that this anxiety on his part was altogether admirable and lovable, and that he was really just what he so carefully strove not to be : that is, a model father. Many of us who are parents go through agonies of hypocrisy to win a respect from our children which we do not deserve. In our virtuous resolution to do our duty as parents we become humbugs ; and when our children are old enough to find us out, as they do at a very early age, they become cynical and lose the affectionate respect which we have destroyed ourselves morally to gain. Be advised by me : do as my parents did : live your lives frankly in the face of your children according to your own real natures and give your sons a fair chance of becoming Bernard Shaws.

Life & Death

'. . . So I do not appeal to you as a kind soft hearted and soft headed man – but as a fellow human, who is eminently sane knowledgeable and clever. But my appeal comes from the very depths of my soul – Will you consider the case and advise me? Will you be the one man out of about forty seven million to help me . . .'

a would-be suicide and murderer

Most correspondents wanted something. 'When one summons up courage at last to speak to the household oracle,' one correspondent wrote, 'it is not about the weather.' More often than not, it was to ask a favour. He was asked to be marriage counsellor, careers advisor, court of last resort, counselling attorney, charities organizer, banker, loan agent, pawnbroker, psychiatrist, matchmaker, literary advisor, father confessor, dietician . . . Daily he was faced with a multitude of professional and personal demands: for copies of his books; for help with getting a pension, with getting a Jewish professor and his wife to Palestine from Germany in 1939, with getting radio apparatus for an Antarctic whaling expedition, with introducing the Russian frost resistant tuber potato in England, with finding a job, accommodation, publishers, a wife; for advice on diet, on how to sell a Caruso caricature, become a journalist, make friends, make Henry Ford President of the U.S.A., get started as an artist, educate oneself, keep (or get!) out of jail; and what to do about marital despair and the desire to commit suicide.

One man attempted to justify his criminal activities by claiming to be a Shaw disciple. And another, an American, wanted Shaw's help to keep him out of jail, having 'borrowed' $800 from the cash drawer of his office. When young people asked for advice he had one reply only: 'Never take advice. If I had taken the advice given to me when I was young I would now have been a decrepit unemployed clerk.'

And yet he certainly did give advice on a great variety of subjects, for 'I couldn't throw off the schoolma'am in me, the don't do this and do that . . .' Whenever a young man asked G.B.S. for advice as to promising careers, there was always one suggestion and one only: he should take up statistics if he had the brains, and if he hadn't, he should consider politics or the stage. Old age was the beginning, not the end of life, he told one seventy-year-old, who had asked him to map out a course of reading in 'happy, optimistic literature' and 'an itinerary where all the scenes were beautiful'. Take up a course of study in a subject needing 'hard grind', he advised.

He told a man who thought his talents were wasted in the Army that:

> You must find a woman willing and able to keep you as a
> household pet on the chance of your proving a genius. It is a
> rash speculation for the woman, but not an unhappy one
> compared to the average woman's lot, provided she is clear
> in her mind as to you being no use as a breadwinner or
> anything else that is normal, useful and sensible.

Shaw's broadcast talks could have unfortunate effects. Once, when he advised listeners always to be honest and tell their families the truth about themselves, a listener complained that, taking him at his word, he had confessed an earlier infidelity to his wife, at which she had broken down; his daughter had almost gone out of her mind; and his son had rushed at him with such violence that he had given him a double rupture.

'THE BRITISH CHURCHGOER PREFERS A SEVERE PREACHER, BECAUSE HE THINKS A FEW MORE HOME TRUTHS WILL DO HIS NEIGHBOURS NO HARM'

There were many who wrote to 'G.B.S.' – the public Bernard Shaw – out of desperation, asking him the most intimate questions, and confessing their darkest secrets. He would later complain, 'I have become the father-confessor of the whole world. Because I have managed to amuse one or two people they now insist on making this thin stick of a body into a Nelson column of Agony. They never try to amuse me . . .'

Elsewhere in conversation Shaw referred to himself as 'the grandfather-confessor.'

From South Africa in June 1946, a troubled youth appealed:

Dear Mr Shaw
   I am a young boy of 15 years old
and I am seeking advice.
   Due to circumstances beyond my
control I am rather stout and ugly
and thus I am not desired in anybody's
company. The worst is that I am not
told so directly but they just ignore
me. Consequently I buried myself in my
books and succeeded in coming first
every year in class, now I find myself
in a even worse predicament than before.
What should I do about this, how should
I go about getting friends.
   I would be grateful for your advice.

Thank You,
Yours Faithfully,
Julian Salomon

This was not young Julian's first letter to Shaw. As he recalled in 1985 when traced to his present home in England: '. . . I had a sort of correspondence with G.B.S. for several months in 1946. I was interested in getting his autograph. My first letter just asked for this and the (typewritten) reply was that he did not give autographs. I then sent a food parcel for which I received a typewritten thank you but "as he is a vegetarian" most of the food (tinned ham, etc.) was given away. Later I wrote the request for advice which elicited a handwritten signed reply telling me in effect to devote more time to my studies and leave an old man alone . . .

   You are very young and things seem worse than they
probably really are. Be yourself and do not try to imitate
others and you will be surprised at the result.
   Get on with your life and allow an old man to get on
with his.

JULIAN SALOMON (LEFT) IN 1946

On getting a wife:

A 'noble youthful poet' asked for 'a very modest favour'. Addressing G.B.S. as 'most respectable Mr. Poet, this young man explained that his own works were masterpieces, and wondered whether he might marry into the Shaw family.

> . . . Oh! Would it not be wonderful, if Mr. Poet could indicate me a young lady of his family or relationship? Up to date I have not yet entered into relations with a lady in order that I can confer my undivided sentiments to that lady whom I should marry . . .

On 'finding a man':

To Mary Hamilton, November 23rd, 1910

> You need not marry a drunkard or an epileptic or a man

like the hero of Brieux's *Les Avariés*, because you wouldnt enjoy the company of such a person; but short of that you can just go out into the street and marry the first reasonably decent fellow with an adequate income ($30 a week will be enough) that you find there. Then <u>you</u> will have done your best, anyhow. Surely, though you have played the fool with your chances so long, you can still lift your finger and get a husband as easily as call a cab.

This is the common sense of the case. But of course no case is quite a common case; and each individual must make the necessary adjustment to their idiosyncrasy. There is such a thing as a virginity that must wait for the right man even if it waits forever; but that is not the same thing as waiting for an impossible man under the spell of inhuman ideals. And beware of exaggerating the value of your present body. It will wear out . . .

To May Broadley of Reading he wrote:

30th May 1919

Dear Madam

Of course marry your man and go to Canada or wherever else he belongs. Is there no clergyman with a bible in his hand to give your mother a good talking to? I cannot imagine how any woman of sense or character could hesitate for a moment. You say you are fond of your mother. Pray how long do you suppose you would remain fond of her if you allowed her to ruin your life?

Has not some philosopher [Bernard Shaw in *Man and Superman*] said 'If you begin by sacrificing yourself to those whom you love, you will end by hating those to whom you have sacrificed yourself.' Besides, your turn will come when your own children leave you and cleave to their husbands and wives.

To Rosemary Frost of London, who, influenced by Shavian ideas, left her husband: (The letter was either not posted or else returned to Shaw as undeliverable.)

1st July 1919

Dear Madam

On attempting to clear up my desk before going to Ireland for the rest of the summer I find a letter of yours from which I gather that you wrote to me before, and on receiving no reply revenged yourself by leaving your husband on the responsibility of my ideas. You then came upon a play of mine in which you found that the lady did *not* leave her husband, but very deliberately and wisely stayed where she was most wanted . . .

If you had been 'brave enough to go to your poet,' he would certainly have been embarrassed; and he might have taken to his heels . . . However, that is a question which people must settle for themselves. It cannot be settled on principle, or in fits of enthusiasm. Any reasonable woman ought to be able to live with any reasonable man; for they are all much alike when the glamor wears off; and the sober, honest, and industrious ones are the best to live with; but sometimes there are inscrutable antipathies and incompatibilities that cannot be overcome.

You are kind enough to say that I am brave. Why should I not be? I have an independent income . . .

Over the years many people asked Shaw for help getting jobs or for career advice. Offers of service included one from a 'trustworthy Private Detective for Confidential Enquiries or business of a private nature.' When, in August 1944, the 88-year-old Shaw wrote a lengthy piece in *The Irish Times* indicating his intention of devoting the income of his residuary estate for twenty years for the furtherance of his new alphabet proposals, the response from one Belfast man was immediate.

Dear Sir,

In reply to your 2 column advertisement in the 'Irish Times' August 9th, I wish to apply for the post of alphabet-maker. At 36 years of age I find it almost impossible to survive, due to a life-long addiction to the literature of visionaries like yourself. As a result of this weakness I am almost unemployable in a capitalist society. Now however you, a Communist, have a job and I a communist need it, and I am prepared to tackle it with the enthusiasm born of the knowledge that I'll make more out of it than my employer will . . .

It is only the tiresome biological necessity of eating and drinking that prevents me from producing the nimble-witted dissertations on the various 'Isms', that have made yourself famous and wealthy. Who knows what great masterpiece I might filch from the National Library if I once got on to the Shaw pay-roll. This of course is a risk you may not be prepared to allow, in which case we can come to the usual restrictive arrangement whereby the employer demands the total use or abuse of the wretched worker's body & soul . . .

For many years after Shaw's death would-be alphabet-makers, like Dubliner Patrick Hourihane, would lay claim to the Shavian inheritance. When arrested by New York police in January 1955 for illegally entering the United States, Hourihane informed them that – having 'fulfilled' Shaw's alphabet requirements – he had lodged a million-dollar (£375,000) claim on the playwright's estate.

In 1929 came a request from Dr Josef Strasser of Vienna regarding Shaw's career decisions. Strasser was engaged in 'psychological research work on the growth of the far reaching decisions in the careers of leading personalities of modern civilization'. He posed three questions to Shaw:

> *(1) Which resolution reached by you seems to you the most*
> *telling and most decisive in your career?*
> *(2) Did you come to this resolution spontaneously without a*
> *long inner struggle and without consulting others and*
> *without being influenced by them?*
> *(3) Were you influenced in coming to the resolution by the*
> *prospect of a decisive success, or exclusively by a moral*
> *principle, without regard to the issue of the resolution*
> *taken?*

Before returning Strasser's letter, Shaw penned on the bottom of it:

> My case is one of many which you will have to deal with.
> I never made a resolution in my life.
> I never struggled nor consulted other people.
> I took all occasions as they came, and dealt with them according to my nature.
> My need for expression was not a desire for success.

Like Hamlet – 'I lack ambition'. I strive automatically to bring the world into harmony with my nature; but I tell you this because I have observed it, just as I have observed the color of my hair in a mirror, not because I am always conscious of it.

Shaw's advice to a troubled clergyman, the Rev. Andrew Fish of Sleaford, Lincolnshire, on whether he should give up 'the Church':

Dear Sir,
. . . I have not the remotest idea of what you can do if you give up your present occupation. To be the secretary of an individual is an appallingly hazardous position . . .

At the same time, if you are really going to give up your job, you can hardly give it up too soon. The older you are, the more impossible it becomes. The real question is, need you change it? . . . If you are a born preacher, stick to your pulpit: it is a delusion to imagine that any pulpit or platform in the world is any freer than the man in it has strength of mind to make it. If not, then you may be right to change; but you must do it on your own responsibility: no sane man can take on himself the responsibility of advising you to do such a thing . . .

Yours faithfully,
G.B.S.

From a man wishing to be a World-Betterer:

[Handwritten annotation across the top:] I get about a hundred letters a month to the same effect in the same words. Go ahead with your world bettering, and leave me alone. You will soon realize that if you cannot work with other people you cannot work politically at all. Probably you do not know enough to manage a baked potato stall, much less the world. Anyhow KEEP OFF, and read my books. I have nothing to add to them.

[Typed:]
KIN.3890.

49 Derwent Avenue.
Kingston Vale.
S.W.15.
30th May 1947.

G.B.Shaw Esq.

[Handwritten:] 31/5/1947

Dear Sir,

As I had not received an acknowledgment of my two recent letters to you I took the liberty of telephoning your Secretary at Whitehall Court today.

I only took this course because the matter on which it is my desire to speak to you has assumed such an importance I felt justified in proceeding further with my request for an interview.

Your secretary suggested I could write direct to you at Ayot St.Lawrence and gave me your address.

I will come to the point as briefly as possible.

About three months ago I decided to go into action in an effort to make the World a better place to live in. I have always wanted it so, but due to a multitude of circumstances have lived my life until now largely as any other ordinary man would.

The first thing was to co-ordinate my casual thinking of the past twenty years and it very soon led me to a quick visit to the coal face.

I have tried hard but am not so far making sufficient progress to do the trick. In fact, due to the conclusion that I must enter the arena completely free from established organisations of any kind, it could fairly truthfully be said that I have hardly moved at all.

I wanted to start right, low down, with very ordinary people but, of course, I got nowhere. But at least I have established proof that my efforts were made in that direction.

Now I have decided to take the 'By-pass' and so I have swung right across to the other end of the scale. There might be greater thinkers in the country than your goodself, but they are not known to me. So I approached you.

Basic conclusions I reached, by using my feeble instruments, I have since found you are teaching. I feel I am on the right track.

Exactly what I require of you I am not quite certain, but I feel that if you could talk to me for a very brief while you might feel disposed to talk still more and let me benefit by listening.

And even if you have'nt the slightest inclination to see me, do please instruct your secretary to acknowledge my letter, even if it is on plain paper and without a signature. This would at least spare me the misery of concluding that all our learning merely brings us to being discourteous to, or frightened of, our inferiors.

Yours very sincerely,

[Signature:] E. A. Sheppard

E.A.Sheppard.

[Handwritten:] Enclosure.

355

'Getting patronage is the whole art of life. A man cannot have a career without it.' – Bernard Shaw

Over the years Shaw was asked to give patronage to many different things including public houses, brass bands, a means of creating crystals out of circulating water, and F. S. Freestone's Smoke Burner & Coal Econo- miser, guaranteed to cut down smoke by 75%! There was, for example, the woman who wanted him to sponsor a very special scheme of family allowance; one which coincidentally suited her own domestic situation.

> Dear Mr Shaw
>   Im not an Irish
> beauty seeking your
> influence to secure a
> part in one of your plays.
> I'm just a faded married
> woman of 35 with a family
> of nine children whose
> ages range from 6 months
> to 14½ years.
>   I neither drink,
> smoke nor go to the
> pictures. The first two
> I dont care for & the
> last I cant afford.
> My only extravagance
> is 1½d per day for the
> 'Irish press' & its just
> a bit annoying that
> almost every time I
> open the paper I see
> something about
> famous Irishmen
> abroad & of famous
> foreigners coming
> here & it all makes me
> mad, for I think I'm
> doing just as good a
> job of work as the next . . .
> Please dont say if
> I'm silly enough to have
> a big family its my own
> funeral for if there
> werent any fools like

me there wouldn't
be any famous men
like yourself to receive
the freedom of the City.
I'm just wondering if
you would be game
enough to sponsor a
scheme whereby poor
mothers with families
of nine & over whose
eldest is still at school
could benefit. There must
be a few intrepid souls
who would contribute
& the suggestion from
you would carry much
weight.

I am if you come
to this part
yours hopefully.
(Mrs) Elizabeth Kellegher

'Never use an introduction. At best it is an annoyance: at worst it creates a violent prejudice against the introducee . . .'   Shaw.

12th June 1919

Sir Thomas Barclay, the Friend of Man and of Ententes, has introduced to me Mr Liang-Chi-Chao, former Minister of Finance and Justice to the Chinese Republic, and, I learn, regarded in China as a Man of Letters in the most Celestial sense. As he is staying at Claridge's, I fully accept this assurance of his importance.

To me Liang-Chi-Chao sends V. K. Ting, Director of the Geological service of Pekin (probably a young necromancer); and Mr Ting informs me that the Celestial purview of English literature includes, in alphabetical order, only five illustrious names, Ah-Bennet, Ji Kai Chesterton, Jan Galsworthy, myself, and Aytch-Ji-Wells. I am held to be the patriarch of the group; and the rules of Chinese politeness oblige me to introduce Mr Liang-Chi-Chao (only one letter between him and chaos) before he can present himself or entertain us all at Claridge's.

Accordingly I do now solemnly present the gentleman to

357

you, and ask you as a man and a brother to back me up, and receive with distinguished consideration the approaches of Mr Ting, a Celestial Knut of modest and affable manners, much better dressed than any of you. The next move is with him.

I am sending this letter in quadruplicate to the whole galaxy. Dont bother to answer me. I presume you will have to answer Mr Ting when he approaches you.

Forgive me; but what can I do?

Ever

Shaw on the proprieties of an introduction –

As to Anatole France, I am on speaking terms with him, having met him on two rather exceptional occasions, once in the Sistine Chapel, and once when he convulsed a British audience at a big reception by kissing the chairman, who happened to be me. But as I have never entered his house, nor he mine, I do not feel quite entitled to give you an intimate introduction, which is the only sort of introduction that is better than a frank petition from yourself as a devotee. All I can do is to wish you success in your designs on him. You can give me as a reference if you like . . .

According to the *News Chronicle*, 23 November, 1936:

Nazi authorities in the Free City of Danzig have condemned Henry Toshke, a bookseller, to three years' imprisonment for selling the works of Bernard Shaw.

When the 'News Chronicle' told Mr. Shaw of the prosecution, his first reaction was one of sympathy. The soft Dublin voice came over the wire, 'I'm sorry for the bookseller. But why? Was it anything specific in my work?'

'The Socialistic philosophy you advocate, Mr. Shaw.'

'Well, why don't they put Mr. Hitler in prison? All the most valuable work he has done is Socialistic work. He's probably read my books himself and got his ideas from them.

Good-bye.'

And Mr. Shaw rang off.

Similarly, four years later in February 1940 Shaw received a letter from Poland asking him to intercede for the release – from Warsaw's Pawiak Prison – of Polish actor and director, Josef Wegrzyn, who before the war had staged G.B.S.'s comedy, *Geneva*, at the Polski Theatre, playing Battler, a role which heavily caricatured Hitler.

> As Wegrzyn may be condemned to death, I beg you to do all
> to deliver this innocent and eminent Polish artist from that
> danger and to raise the world's opinion against that new
> proof of German 'culture and humanity' in Poland.

Shaw passed the Wegrzyn appeal to the British Press Association, noting on the back:

> If Herr Hitler is responsible for this I am shocked at his
> ingratitude. I have handed him down to history in the play
> with gifts of eloquence, debating power and readiness in
> repartee which no mortal fuehrer ever possessed or ever will
> possess, and this is how he requites me. If he had an atom of
> common sense he would decorate the great Polish actor and
> order a thousand performances.

(Although Wegrzyn was released several months later, his tragic circumstances during the war – his arrest and the Auschwitz death of his son – led to alcoholism, depression, and, in 1952, at sixty-eight, his death in a mental hospital.)

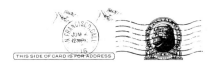

There were those who, like Miss A. Louise Shaw, a Department of Agriculture librarian in Ottawa, dreamt of establishing a genealogical link with Shaw. A lot of use it would have done her, as G.B.S. had in fact informed one first cousin once removed, 'I cannot acknowledge removed cousins.'

> Dear Madam
>   My pedigree, as far as I know anything about it, is to be
> found in Lodge's Peerage, in the genealogy attached to
> Professor Archibald Henderson's biography of me, and in a
> history of the Shaw family, compiled for or by Sir Robert
> Shaw of Terenure, which traces us back to the
> Shakespearean Macduff . . .

It seems, then, that for a common origin we (you and I) should have to go back to the 17th century. I forget exactly how many centuries you have to go back to reach a period at which every living person was an ancestor of every person now living; but the number is surprisingly small. We must be content with the bond of our common humanity.

Eula Shaw Hereford from Lometa, Texas, was more blatant about her desire to prove Shaw kinship:

> . . . It would give me great pleasure, if I could, by some good streak of fortune, just hear from you and let me know if you think there is the possibility of us being kin – (I am not a fortune hunter – I do not want nor would I have any of, your wealth) . . . My husband's people are so haughtily proud of their ancestry (There is a Lord Hereford in England, too) that they make me feel inferior even tho' I know my people have a cultural background even tho' not wealthy or highly educated . . .

C. George Engert, 'Age 84½ next month', tried in 1941 to establish a link with Shaw through a non-existent brother. This was one of the most inaccurate and convoluted letters Shaw received.

26.7.1941
AGE 84½ next month
C. GEORGE ENGERT,
CLIFTONVILLE,
WHITE PIT,
SHILLINGSTONE,
NR. BLANDFORD,
DORSETSHIRE.

'Dear famous gentleman'
Your brother and I were
schoolchums at Ramsgate.
He told me of your hopes of the DUBLIN family often.
I was only a 7 months quart-pot babe, 9.3.1862 and have
had weak arms since. I liked Shaw as he taught me a
lot in 1872–74, and much of that City's surroundings as
I'm fond of HISTORY & GEOGRAPHY, since reading an
interesting book on Ireland by a gentleman-pedestrian.
I did not get on as an engineer's draughtsman at 21,
because of weak eyes, but I now manage to do
2 CROSSWORDS on Weekdays, each week, to keep a clear

mind, & post 1/. to the Wireless's 'Good Cause' fortnightly
out of my Old-Age Pension 22/6. My favorite
sentence is GLADSTONE's 'The Impregnable Rock of Holy
Scripture. Teetotaler & widower 39 years. I
boarded 10 years at jolly Ringwood 24 miles east
but for LUMBAGO Doctor Kitchen approved transfer
and I hope to end my years by Our Lord's Mercy, there,
for maybe some lady or gentleman may forward
from New Zealand, S Africa, or Canada something
to aid me, as examined – written to Colonial Papers
by Colonel Torkington, who administers a famous
High class Young Ladies Boarding School here upon this
hilly healthy Shillingstone. He was in the Camerons
in last war, & is an old WINCHESTER COLLEGE boy. By hook
& crook during 42 years I wrote hundreds of readable
letters to elderly HIGH SCHOOL girls & boys who wrote short &
long jolly interesting letters on the Maple Leaf page of the
great MONTREAL Herald from English-speaking Dominions
in all quarters of God's beautiful Earth about school & home.
Few thought I was only a small-annuitant, but I have
even occasionally lived in London near the Zoo at 71-for . . .

Your jolly brother would do any Service for me, &
I for him 73 years ago . . .

There were those who wanted to know what to do with their retirement and
old age. From the Golfers Club, Whitehall, came the following request in
1939 from a 61-year-old to the 83-year-old Shaw.

> Dear Sir,
> At the age of 61 I am retiring from Gov.t Service on a
> pension of £450 a year and a capital sum of £1,200. My
> other assets are 1) a small house at Harrow Weald and, 2)
> an extremely lively mother age 86 who, incidentally, has
> been writing to you about me at intervals during the last
> 30 years. Your kind replies on post cards are carefully
> preserved by her.
> I have always relied upon you to tell me what to think.
> Now, can you tell me what to DO with a Desert of 20
> years in front of me and no work to Do?
> As an architect the prospects, I think you will agree, are
> as Dismall as they could be – In spite of the address on
> this sheet I take no interest in golf. Frankly I am in a
> quandary in addition to being a bachelor –
> What would you do?

And where to live?

> Perhaps you remember on Sunday affernoon you came to
> Hyde Park and I have been the first one to reconize you and
> I always wanted to speak to you, & did had the Pluck to
> speak to you. I told you my Husband done once a drawing of
> you. . . . I do not want anythink for it – if you could help me
> to go away from her [Camberwell]. I have enough for life
> anywhere, but as my husband always keept me for himself I
> have not one soul her where I can go. I do like to write hence
> my long letter to you. I wish you would write a story the
> artist and his mate. I could tell you a lot as I never have been
> separet from my Husband for 23 years. he has been 77 years
> old when he did Christmas tree years ago. Please forgive me
> writing to you expressing my heart. but Lonliness is a terble
> thing

Now and again Shaw would take a quite disproportionate interest in letters
from people who wrote to him at great length about their domestic affairs.

> PO Box 157
> Oradell, New Jersey
> U.S.A.
> December 5th, 1925

Dear Sir:

I wonder if you will help me in my dilemma? Omitting at
once all the ups and downs of my thirty-nine years of
existence, I set before you my problem as it is today.

I am a night watchman employed by a dye works located
in New Jersey. I live at home with my Mother, and a family
circle composed of two uncles, one aunt, three cousins, and
a younger brother and sister. All the family, with the
exception of my Mother, commute to New York daily,
where they are engaged at clerical work in various offices.
Now here's the rub: Whenever I express an opinion the
entire family always shouts in unison, 'Oh, of course, you
think that way – that's why you are a night watchman.' I used
to laugh at this, but at last they have gotten my goat for fair. I
am all on edge and as nervous as a March hare. The other
day I ventured the opinion that Harvard would defeat
Princeton in their annual football encounter. My kid
brother, who is a bookkeeper, said, 'Get a bet down on
Princeton folks; the night watchman says that Harvard will
win.'

All this may seem trivial and absurd to you, but after putting up with this kind of treatment for more than three years I have decided to make a change. Of the 160 books that are in our home I bought 158. The other two, 'Swiss Family Robinson' and a book on animal husbandry issued by the State, were found in the attic of this house when we moved into it nearly four years ago. I mention this to prove that if there is a spark of culture in this family I am the one who has fostered it. My sister did bring home, 'The American Hoyle, or Gentleman's Handbook of Games,' but as this was presented to her as the booby prize at a bridge party held in Hackensack last winter, it is only further proof with what regard literature is looked upon in our home. Needless to say your plays are lost on every person in this house except the night watchman. The funny part of the whole business is that my weekly wage exceeds by $5.00 the salary of any other member of the family.

If you were in my position, would you quit the family or would you quit the job?

Respectfully yours,
Henry T. Bellew

To which Shaw replied by scribbling on – and returning – the disgruntled correspondent's own letter:

Quit the family, of course, unless the house belongs to you, in which case your remedy is eviction. A family without good manners is impossible. This one is so large – it is not really a family but a group of relatives – can only be kept intact if all the parties behave with the most scrupulous consideration for one another. Possibly you are too sensitive: in that case you are the difficulty, and had better quit. Why not marry?

G.B.S.

And then there was the woman for whom marriage was no solution. The dramatist's Ayot neighbour, Stephen Winsten, later recalled being shown a letter from a stranger who thought Shaw had a kind face and would not mind answering. The letter in a round schoolgirl hand informed him that she had been married for ten years and for the last year had not been on speaking terms with her husband but had had to concede his conjugal rights. She had always remained completely passive but it was driving her mad. She wanted Shaw's advice on what to do. 'Shall I throw it in the wastepaper basket?' Shaw asked Winsten:

. . . I have thought out an answer but it occurred to me that it
might be a trap to get me in correspondence. I get three
such letters a day. When my face was demoniacal I received
ten such letters every day. I am advising her to put common
sense before passion. A silent man is worth his weight in
gold, women have worshipped worse deities in their time. I
must write something to make her laugh . . .

The following is an example of a woman bearing her heart and soul to
Shaw, whom she had not seen for fourteen years until a recent chance
encounter. In a lengthy letter she told Shaw of her childhood, the long
illness, death and funeral of her beloved mother, and her developing love
for her mother's doctor – twenty years younger than herself. Troubled by
the disparity in their ages, she wrote to G.B.S., less for advice than
reassurance:

12th December 1937

. . . when you can spare the time, I would be
eternally grateful to you, if you would – just
in pencil, at odd moments, perhaps, jot down
any instances you can think of, where couples
you have known, or heard of, have been happy
and devoted – in spite of the fact that the woman
may have been older, or much older, than her
mate – and, if possible, stating (about) what the
difference in their ages may have been . . . You
won't tell anyone, will you? About my love, I
mean? If you can 'think up' all the couples you
can, that have been happy – in spite of the
woman being older – it might just make the
scale turn in my favour . . .
PPS.
   Leaving out of the question what you
think I really am – will you tell me
the age you would take me to be, had you
never seen me before, and knew nothing
of my people's age? – I have asked
various people whom I've met on trains or
waiting rooms – the last was a young and
ultra modern girl, of about 18, in an office –
and she replied at once, that I couldn't
be more than in my thirties! – None of
them have, in fact, guessed more than
the thirties – strangers I mean.

When I saw you on Friday, I was not
looking right at all – the germs were to
blame – and I'd been in bed two days, earlier
in the week – so in your judgement, please
try to allow for that!

By the way, I want to make it quite clear
that I <u>never tried to mislead my 'Peter Pan'</u>, as to
this – and told him my exact age – <u>long</u>
ago – I would never try to win him by a
trick! . . .

To more than one, Shaw was, as one correspondent described him, 'a doctor of the human soul.' Most agonizing of all were the pleas from suicidal men and women. 'I believe you will help me,' wrote one. 'You have always had a warm corner in your heart for women and fanatics.' There was the letter signed 'a despairing woman', from a lady with four daughters aged seven to twenty married to a paranoiac drunkard:

> . . . I am living a life of mental torture and hell. I have tried
> to help myself but find it impossible. I am only an ordinary
> working woman, but intelligent nevertheless; should my
> children and I subjugate ourselves and live like pigs without
> thought or refinement for the sake of a drunken moron.
> Surely there is a way out without publicity or disgrace . . .

And, from a 'drowning' man:

New York, N.Y., USA
16th October 1937

Mr. George Bernard Shaw
London, England.

Dear Mr Shaw.

I'm a drowning man clutching at a
straw. Hence I write to you.

I am physically 23 years old, mentally
much older, and emotionally a child. I was born
with a tissue paper skin and have always been
too ashamed to admit it. My family could not
see through my pose and hence I never received

the warmth of understanding that a sensitive
child needs. My soul has been chilled so long
by lack of understanding, fear and self-distaste
that is now well nigh frozen. My mother
has an undeveloped intelligence, is sensitive
and emotionally starved. My home has always
been an unhappy one.

I was nurtured on neuroticism. I saw
through my religion at the age of fourteen and
have had nothing to cling to in the interim. I
have suffered from conscience and an almost
constant feeling of weariness. I sought con-
solation from liquor and cigarettes. They at first
gave me temporary easement but now merely
sicken me and I have had to give them up.

I worked for somewhat over a year as
a stenographic-clerk in a law firm. I had to
resign – it nearly drove me crazy.

Of late I have acquired a little hope as
a result of reading *The Way of All Flesh* and of
meeting a sympathetic young girl. I yearn for the
freshness and strength that I find in your writings.

My ambition is to act. I have the ability
but lack control of my nerves – fear saps my
will. I fear myself and I fear the lack of money.
Yet I know I have spirit for it bubbles
through occasionally in spite of all.
To know you can but can't
for fear is maddening.

This is jumbled but then so am I.

Sincerely,
Frank Finnerty

Then there was the American who, having 'borrowed' $800 from the cash
drawer of his office, wanted Shaw's help to keep him out of jail.

Philadelphia, Penn.
8th May 1946

Dear Mr. Shaw,
I am writing this letter to you
in the anxious hope that perhaps you
can help me. I've tried every well known
financier, and big figure in the

sports and entertainment world to
aid me in my desperate plight,
but you know the old saying 'the
rich get richer and the poor get
poorer', and they wouldnt know or
understand or want to help any one
but their own selfish motives . . .

I am a respectable young man
who manages a large store here in
Philadelphia. I started very heavily
to gamble and lost quite a large sum
of money in a month, namely $3,000.
In order to cover myself up I made loans
from different banks, took some savings
my wife and I had put away for
emergencies and to top it all I
borrowed $800 from the cash drawer.

I had to go into our N.Y. office
yesterday and confess this breach. They
had me sign a confession and I will
know to-day the outcome. I stand to
lose my family, relatives, friends I
know, and my position and then be put
in jail. I dont know where or whom
to turn to. When I saw your smiling
countenance in a newsreel yesterday
then I knew here is the man who
can understand the trouble I have
gotten into and perhaps help me . . .

Shaw on how not to waste your suicide:

When I was a young man doing what is called beginning
life I took two precautions.

First, I went to a friend of mine, a chemist, and asked him
how I should proceed in the event of my deciding to commit
suicide. I stipulated that his method should kill me like a
thunderbolt. He gave me a very simple prescription which I
still prefer to all the poisons since discovered.

My second precaution was dictated by a strong feeling
that I was much more likely to commit murder than suicide.
Therefore, as I had another friend who was an Alienist: that
is, a specialist in lunacy (he was on the medical staff of a
famous asylum) I asked him how I should simulate madness

in the event of my having to plead to an indictment on a
capital charge . . .

Genuine suicides never say they are tired of life. Death
fascinates them; they have a real taste for it; and I have
found the most effective means of baffling them to be a
reminder that as something amusing may turn up in the
course of the afternoon they may as well wait till to-morrow.

To-morrow is the day that never comes.

In one case, as the patient was an ardent social reformer,
I pointed out that if he was going to kill himself, and thereby
place himself beyond the reach of the law, he might as well
begin by assassinating the six most disastrously obstructive
statesmen within his reach.

That was many years ago; and he is still trying to make up
his mind which are the six.

At least one youth, a 23-year-old Canadian, Wallace Baker, failed to heed
Shaw's advice. Baker's body was found in October 1913 off Manhattan
Beach, New York, with directions for finding a diary which revealed that
reading Shaw, Ibsen and Strindberg had 'driven' the youth to suicide.
Baker urged in a note that the 35,000-word diary be published as an
example of self-analysis. 'Reading Bernard Shaw,' he wrote,

> showed me that much that I had thought to be artistic
> temperament, ideals, sentiment, was plain romantic illusion,
> and I did not feel I was called upon to sacrifice myself for
> humanity without the aesthetic pleasure my illusions had
> given me. Before this I had unwittingly cloaked my own
> desires and passions under the guise of doing something
> worthwhile, of uplifting, and what not. Curiously enough, all
> my ambitions, ideas, etc. returned on further reading of
> Shaw in Chicago. I took them back with the idea that now I
> was through with romantic illusion and prepared to face
> reality.

From a man who came out of World War II a nervous wreck:

> Dear Sir
> You may have written the words yourself at some
> time, certainly you will have come across them   'a soul in
> torment –' but have you ever been just that yourself?
> No: Then you cannot realise just what it can
> mean. I am a soul not only in torment but so angry and
> desperate that it is using every ounce of energy in me to fight

off the urge to kill my children and myself. I did not decide
that that was the best way to deal with the situation in a
moment of unbridled anger   Not by any means. I have
given the whole matter all the calm thought possible long
enough ago and all the time struggling desperately to go the
other way to find a satisfactory way out.

But the whole thing is beating me. I never did care for
sloppy sentiment and useless pity   it is sense I
want   wisdom

That is why I write to you. I do not think there is a
saner man in the country than you   Nay There cannot be
anywhere.

So I do not appeal to you as a kind soft hearted and soft
headed man – but as a fellow human who is eminently sane
knowledgeable and clever. But my appeal comes from the
very depths of my soul – a mere figure of speech   but you
will know what I mean.

I am inclined to think that mine is a very strange case or
is it that I am a very strange man.

Be that as it may

Will you consider the case and advise me? Will you
be the one man out of about forty seven million to help me
to avoid committing a terrible crime as the vast majority
would call it?

If your answer is in the affirmative   Then I will give
you all the details or answer any questions.

Hoping

Yours Very Respectfully
WmRowbottom

5th January 1946

Dear Sir

Killing yourself is a matter for your own judgment.
Nobody can prevent you; and if you are convinced that you
are not worth your salt, and an intolerable nuisance to
yourself and everyone else, it is a solution to be considered.
But you can always put it off to tomorrow on the chance of
something interesting turning up that evening.

As to killing the children, it would be the act of a madman
or a murderer. They may have the happiest disposition.
They may be born to greatness: the children of
good-for-nothings (Beethoven and Isaac Newton for
instance) have grown up to be geniuses. My father was a
failure: only his latest years (he was longlived) could be

called happy. I am conceited enough to believe that it is just as well that he did not kill me in a fit of low spirits. Instead, he relieved himself by drinking occasionally, though it only made him worse.

Have you consulted a psychologist? Soul torment is not a philosophy: it is a disease, and usually cures itself after a time. A quick medicine for it may be discovered tomorrow. Read the autobiography of John Stuart Mill, who gives a graphic description of a long fit of depression which passed away completely and was the prelude to an illustrious future.

Life, happy or unhappy, successful or unsuccesful, is extraordinarily interesting; and children left destitute by their parents do not die of starvation but are taken care of in Barnardo homes or public institutions or adopted. These are sometimes more wisely and kindly treated than they too would have been at home, especially if their parents are morbid patients who think it would be kind to kill them.

In short, dear sir, dont be a damned fool. Get interested in something.

faithfully
G.B.S.

On Illness and Death:

'I cannot tell you the exact date of my death,' Shaw informed critic Hannen Swaffer in 1938, 'It has not yet been settled.'

Owing to a message received in London in January 1909 announcing that Shaw was seriously ill, the Press Association sent him the following telegram:

> YOUR SERIOUS ILLNESS REPORTED. KINDLY
> OBLIGE WITH AN ANNOUNCEMENT FOR
> PUBLICATION.

To which Shaw replied:

> KINDLY INFORM THE PUBLIC THAT I AM DEAD. IT
> WILL SAVE ME A GREAT DEAL OF TROUBLE.

A March 1946 report from New York that George Bernard Shaw was gravelly ill at his Ayot St Lawrence home led to a news agency telephoning late at night for confirmation. Coming to the telephone, G.B.S. snapped: 'Do I sound as if I were gravelly ill?'

After reading his obituary in a Lagos newspaper, the *West African Pilot*, shortly before his ninety-second birthday, Shaw immediately cabled the editor:

> YOUR NOTE IS PREMATURE. I AM ONLY
> HALF-DEAD. PLEASE CONTRADICT.

Shaw turned down an American offer to issue a filmed fifteen-minute farewell message to mankind on the day he died. His postcard refusal was sent to Michael Mindler who had made the offer.

> Quite impossible now. The Bernard Shaw you contemplate
> is dead, and cannot be resuscitated by an ancient spectre
> exactly like every other old dotard with a beard, piping and
> croaking into a microphone.

Persistent, Mindler wrote, denying that the Shaw he contemplated was dead. 'More fool you,' replied G.B.S. on Mindler's own letter, 'when I say no, I mean no, and there is nothing more to be said. Now go back home, and when you have any other proposal to make, put it on a postcard which will cost you only a few cents.'

Shaw on canine afterlife:

> To the Editor of *The Dog World* (October 3rd, 1924)
>
> I have never had a dog stupid enough to want to live for
> ever. And I have never hated a dog enough to wish him such
> a horrible fate.
>
> G. Bernard Shaw.

Doctor Johnson noted that we shall receive no letters in the grave; Shaw, however, received messages from beyond.

Kew, Surrey
August 15th 1946

Dear Mr Shaw, –
   I think that it is my duty to write to you
as follows, –
   For some little while I have dabbled in
esoteric Buddhism. I wish to heaven I hadn't.
It is a frightful business. For a few days
I have not been well, and it seemed to
me that some kind of message was being
confided by your great contemporary
H. G. Wells.
   He said, George Bernard Shaw and I have
been almost equal upon the level of
our doctrine, the doctrine of socialism.
Sometimes he has gained the upper hand
and sometimes I have. George Bernard
Shaw has said in his essay 'The
Adventures of the Black Girl in Her Search
for God,' Myna's sex is the key to the
riddle of the universe. I say (H. G. Wells)
that envy is the key to the riddle of the
universe.
   If I, the writer, can claim a single thought
as my own. – I don't think now that I have,
or ever did have, a single original thought
in my head. I got them all from other people; –
that envy is the key to the riddle of the
universe.
   I pondered over Mr Well's statement, and
finally I agreed with him, after a long and reasonable
conversation. Then last night in bed,
a strange thing happened to me. I was completely unsexed.
Frantically, I tried all sorts of
frantic lures to get back the sex function. I was
not successful. Finally, I went to sleep and
this morning I was happy to find that my
sex instinct had returned.
   The writer has to agree with you sir, that
sex is the key to the riddle of the universe.

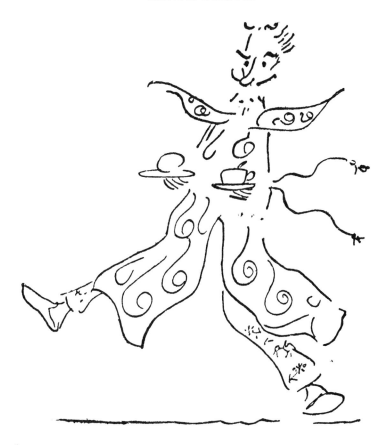

'MR BERNARD SHAW DECLARES THAT THIS CARICATURE OF HIM DELIVERING
BREAKFAST TO MRS SHAW ON BOARD TRAIN BY MR H. G. WELLS "SURPASSES ALL
PROFESSIONAL CARICATURISTS THAT HAVE HAD A GO AT ME."'

At a Plymouth shop in 1933, a woman who had obtained Shaw's controversial *The Adventures of the Black Girl in Her Search for God*, tore the book to pieces before the assistant could intervene. After flinging the pages and empty binding to the floor, she produced her purse and paid for the book, explaining that she had been directed in a dream to destroy Shaw's book in that manner.

There was the case of 27-year-old Frederick Dousbery from Southsea, who, when taking part in a seance had been directed to visit Shaw's Adelphi Terrace flat. While there, he had displayed his partiality for Shaw's doormat, by stealing it!

This incident elicited a letter – from Brixton Prison's Senior Medical Officer, S. R. Dyer, M.D. – regarding the remanded prisoner's mental condition. Dyer thanked Shaw for supplying information which, he claimed, 'has helped me in dealing with the mental aspect of the case,' and to the conclusion that whatever the man's previous mental condition, he was now 'insane & a fit case for asylum care & treatment.'

> . . . The secret of his unwelcome attention to your doormat was that he wanted 'bold advertisement' & he thus explains that erratic episode. 'I took Mr Shaw's mat as I think some benefit might accrue to me as Mr Shaw might go with my case & say, this man is highly intellectual, & this might lead to my getting a job' & he also elaborates this idea by saying 'If all the unemployed would simultaneously commit some technical offence the state would recognise their position & give them work'
> Now for his less sane productions – He believes he is a genius, & obtains knowledge without knowing how, that he is under the magnetic influence of some spirit power & this strong influence dominates his every movement & life generally. That at a Seance in Southsea he saw a spirit who directed him to go to see Mr Shaw. He has 'impressions when any magnetic influence is near', & can see peoples faces clearly & distinctly when his eyes are shut. Says he saw Mr Shaw's address in the paper first by accident 'but directed by the magnetic influence' etc etc etc. I feel sure the poor chap wants a long mental rest . . .

One woman's 'message from beyond' took a more tangible form. In 1962 it cost £13,000 to turn a fourteen-room Cotswold farmhouse into a luxurious shrine befitting the new 'Messiah' that Mrs Patricia Steele announced would be born to her. The birth of her fourth child, she said, would be the result of an immaculate conception arranged from the spirit world by George Bernard Shaw. Forty-year-old Mrs Steele claimed that she spiritually divorced her Canadian-born husband John and 'married' Shaw (twelve years after his death) in a hotel in Killarney, Ireland. Mrs Steele, who later called herself 'Mrs Shaw', claimed that between May 1961 and September the following year, she had produced forty-five major works by translating spirit messages from such authors as Shakespeare, Tolstoy, Barrie and Shaw.

These secondhand 'great works' found no market and months after the arrival of the new 'Messiah' – who, ironically, was a girl – the 'shrine' builders remained unpaid and ice-cream salesman Mr Steele appeared at Cheltenham bankruptcy court with admitted debts of £23,235. He said that the new Messiah – given the name Felicity Mary Shaw – was to be the founder of a new religion entitled 'Complete Christianity'. Its headquarters was to be the Steeles' Withington farmhouse 'Shornhill'. The conversion, which included a chapel, was on credit. Steele claimed that his bankruptcy was the result of a 'tax from the powers of darkness', who didn't want the news of his wife's 'spiritually-transmitted' plays to be revealed.

The cradle is ready for the child Patricia believes she is expecting. She says that John Steele (left) is not the baby's father.

After his death, a number of Shaw's former associates, including actress Frances Day and critic Hannen Swaffer, claimed to have been 'haunted' by Shaw. Swaffer's Shaw spectre berated the quality of Frances Day's ghost, commenting, 'I remembered reading how Frances Day, who acted in *The Millionairess*, his last-produced play, had told a reporter that G.B.S. had been "haunting" her, tapping her on the shoulder and continually tearing a flap of wallpaper in her room. "Surely, Shaw," queried Swaffer's spectre, 'if he wanted to do any hauntings, would do better than that.'

'AND *THEY* ARE ASKING WHETHER *I* SHALL SURVIVE . . . ?'